thinking was basically empirical and exploratory, not subject to the frequently applied labels "neoclassicist," "authoritarian," or "didacticist." The author's fresh view of his subject appears everywhere in the analysis, from the study of Johnson's theory of the mind to the definition of Nature, that most important of all eighteenth-century literary terms.

Jean H. Hagstrum is professor of English at Northwestern University. He is the author of *The Sister Arts: The Tradition of Literary Pictorialism and English Poetry from Dryden to Gray* and *William Blake, Poet and Painter: An Introduction to the Illuminated Verse*, both published by The University of Chicago Press.

SAMUEL JOHNSON'S LITERARY CRITICISM

Samuel Johnson's Literary Criticism

by

JEAN H. HAGSTRUM

The University of Chicago Press

CHICAGO & LONDON

Library of Congress Catalog Card Number: 52-12060

THE UNIVERSITY OF CHICAGO PRESS, CHICAGO 60637

The University of Chicago Press, Ltd., London W.C. 1

To

CHAUNCEY BREWSTER TINKER

Preface, 1967

I REPUBLISH *Samuel Johnson's Literary Criticism* convinced that its topical approach remains an important means of mastering the diverse, practical, often occasional, but always principled thought of one of the greatest English critics. The hard bones of what Johnson called "naked criticism" — but also of his minor and passing judgments — become apparent only if one sees clearly the structure of the great topics: nature, pleasure, wit, and the other subjects of my chapters.

I am fully aware that my book is not the definitive or final one on the subject; and I fervently hope that it will not deter further investigation but will instead stimulate the research and thought necessary to a major scholarly enterprise. If I may presume to make a blueprint for a house I may myself never build, I should like to suggest that we need a book rigorously and imaginatively historical — historical, that is, in two important senses. (1) Johnson's ideas must be traced within the body of his own criticism, from the very early commentary on Crousaz to the last critical judgment of the last of the *Lives of the Poets*. (2) The sources of Johnson's ideas and methods must be carefully established, as must a broad but precise context in all Western thought. The future student of Johnson's criticism should study not only other critical essays in English or other lives of poets but also the whole range of critical speculation classical and modern, English and Continental. And almost more important than purely critical sources, occasions, and analogues is the relation of Johnson's thought to logic, law, epistemology, rhetoric, and scholarship in Latin and English. Not until such an investigation has been thoroughly made will we be in a position to know whether Johnson fulfilled the neoclassical tradition or subverted it, whether he was a man of the Renaissance or of the Enlightenment, whether he was essentially an empiricist or a rationalist or both, whether his general laws were neo-Platonic or Lockean, or, indeed, whether these are the appropriate terms of analysis.

Ways in which my work can and ought to be extended appear clearly and promisingly in scholarship on Johnson's criticism that has appeared since 1952 and that I record in a list appended to this preface. My topical approach has been supplemented by studies of Johnson on particular poems, particular authors, or particular schools. Robert E. Moore* analyzes Johnson's criticism of Fielding and Richardson; David Perkins concentrates on Johnson's admiration of the lively and original thinking of the metaphysical poets and relates that admiration to his theory of the imagination; and Warren Fleischauer demonstrates that Johnson's often condemned judgment of *Lycidas* arises logically from his critical assumptions. The critic's and biographer's sources for the *Life of Pope* have been investigated by Benjamin Boyce and his methods of research and composition by Frederick W. Hilles — in meticulous and interesting studies that show by what means one can determine Johnson's originality and the matrix out of which his insights came. It is gratifying to see that the importance of epistemology to Johnson's criticism (the subject of my first chapter) is conceded and made the basis of further consideration. Robert Voitle, whose book is about Johnson's moral criticism, provides nevertheless a basic context for literary speculation in his chapter on the mind,

---

* In this preface I refer to articles and books by the name of the author only. A full reference appears in the list that follows. Moore's article appeared in 1951, before the publication but after the writing of my book. I therefore include it here.

in which he discriminates Lockean and Peripatetic reason, provides a precise definition of intuition, and places Johnson's view of the mind in a historical context. Rodman D. Rhodes's analysis of *Idler* No. 24 shows how Johnson reshaped the assumptions of Locke — a process which, in my view, did not lead Johnson to abandon his basic affiliation. Mr. Rhodes stresses the importance to Johnson of active thought — of what Johnson himself once called the "stream of mind"; and the discussion is extended from epistemology to literary criticism and even to the conversations. Arthur Sherbo — in what has already appeared and in what at this writing has been announced as volumes VII and VIII of the Yale edition of the *Works* — tells the full story of the genesis and progress of Johnson's criticism of Shakespeare, provides a guide to Johnson's reading, illuminates the relation of the *Dictionary* to the edition, evaluates Johnson's debt to others,* discusses later editions of the work and its reception, and gives us what we have not had in modern form, the complete and revised notes to that poet Johnson so substantially helped to establish as the classic of our tongue.

Four authorities on literary criticism have made important statements on Johnson since the publication of my book. Two of them, William K. Wimsatt and René Wellek, may disagree with some of my assumptions; at the very least these scholars provide important differences of emphasis. Before accepting the essentially empirical approach of my study, which invokes for Johnson psychological, educational, and rhetorical norms and which denies neo-Platonic content to his notion of generality, the student will wish to read Professor Wimsatt's brief but stimulating analysis of Johnson's thought as a "massive summary of the neo-Platonic drive in literary theory and of its difficulties"** and to study the ninefold definition of what neoclassical theorists meant by universality. And before agreeing with me that for Johnson the enjoyment of literature rested on the mind's lively commerce with experience and

---

* But see Arthur Eastman's answer to what he regards as Sherbo's implication of plagiarism.

** Wimsatt, p. 331; but see my pp. 83–85 and esp. pp. 190–91, n. 18.

that that intercourse could lead to "turbulence of pleasure," the reader should consider Professor Wellek's analysis, which finds that Johnson has lost faith in art and tends to dissolve the differences between literature and life. Professor Wellek regards Johnson as a great critic, who can even be called "liberal" in his reinterpretations of neoclassical tenets; but in this essay the historian of modern criticism stresses the "realism," "moralism," and "abstractionism" of the critic's philosophy, looking at Johnson, as it were, from later epochs when there had been developed a radically new view of the artistic imagination.

I am of course happy that the essays of Walter Jackson Bate and William R. Keast enforce some of the central theses of my study. Professor Bate sees Johnson as a critic unintimidated by arid systems, independent of the rules and pomp of the critical tradition; in fact, his dynamic originality is said to alter the chemistry of traditional beliefs. Professor Bate eloquently expresses what I continue to find absolutely central — that Johnson's criticism springs from the experience of life and that he views literature as something the mind generates in the "interplay of familiarity with novelty" (Bate, p. 181). President Keast derives from Johnson's scattered critical dicta a tightly coherent conceptual framework, which is, however, faithful to the force and form of the critic's essential positions. The attentive reader will find important differences between President Keast's analysis of nature and the one that constitutes my fourth chapter. But we are in firm agreement about the intellectual dignity and integrity of Johnson's philosophy and have both tried (in different and fully independent ways) to base a topical analysis on the essential coherence of the critic's system. Those who feel that any systematization of Johnson's thought represents a betrayal of its practical and empirical nature should contemplate Johnson's sentence that "it is the task of criticism to establish principles." They should also contemplate President Keast's highly successful attempt to work out of the practicing critic the guiding premises.

It is clear that Johnson has, though in complex and often underground ways, exerted considerable influence on twentieth-century criticism. As Edward Emley has pointed out, I. A. Richards and William Empson have, in their preoccupation with Coleridge and other critics, never fully realized their own affinity with the psychology and semantics of Johnson. But the so-called New Critics have more than once had to test their strength against Johnson, especially in their rehabilitation of the metaphysicals, and have more than once come out of the fray admiring their adversary. T. S. Eliot and Mr. Leavis may owe some of their deepest insights to the force of Johnson's authority and the subtlety of his analyses.

The Johnson circle of the twentieth century is large and includes radically diverse points of view. There are of course those who come to Johnson for the rightness and relevance of his views. Thus Eliot has found his example highly important to our own needs and problems and has therefore rated him very high indeed: "I consider Johnson one of the three greatest critics of poetry in English literature; the other two being Dryden and Coleridge." Professor Donner finds Johnson great because he still possesses great authority: "after two hundred years his judgments stand, and I doubt whether any critic after Aristotle has carried more weight." But others ought not be excluded from the modern circle because they find not guidance so much as charm and stimulation — those who read Johnson not for his doctrine but, as it were, for his music — for the eloquence and vivacity of his language. Lytton Strachey, after all, said of Johnson's judgments that "they are never right," but that view — perverse, in my judgment — did not deter him from seeing those critical statements as also being "subtle, or solid, or bold."* Subtlety, solidity, boldness and — to add qualities F. L. Lucas finds in the criticism — "style and personality" are not found growing on every tree. And the reader who remains intellectually unpersuaded by Johnson's ideas is invited to gather such fruits and flowers as these.

* Donner, p. 107.

STUDIES OF JOHNSON'S LITERARY CRITICISM
SINCE 1952

ABRAMS, M. H. "Dr. Johnson's Spectacles," in *New Light on Dr. Johnson*. Edited by Frederick W. Hilles. New Haven, Conn.: Yale University Press, 1959. Pp.177–87.

ADLER, JACOB H. "Johnson's 'He That Imagines This,'" *Shakespeare Quarterly*, 11 (Spring, 1960):225–28.

BATE, WALTER JACKSON. *The Achievement of Samuel Johnson*. New York: Oxford University Press, 1955. Chap. 5, "Johnson as a Critic: The Form and Function of Literature." Pp.177–233.

BLOOM, EDWARD A. *Samuel Johnson in Grub Street*. Providence, R. I.: Brown University Press, 1957.

BOYCE, BENJAMIN. "Samuel Johnson's Criticism of Pope in the *Life of Pope*," *The Review of English Studies*, New Series, 5 (January, 1954):37–46.

DONNER, H. W. "Dr. Johnson as a Literary Critic" in *Samuel Johnson A Collection of Critical Essays*. ("Twentieth Century Views.") Edited by Donald J. Greene. Englewood Cliffs, N. J.: Prentice-Hall, Inc. 1965. Pp.102–13.

EASTMAN, ARTHUR M. "In Defense of Dr. Johnson," *Shakespeare Quarterly*, 8 (Autumn, 1957):493–500.

ELIOT, T. S. "Johnson as Critic and Poet" (1944), in *On Poetry and Poets*. London: Faber & Faber, 1957. Pp.162–92.

EMLEY, EDWARD. "Dr. Johnson and Modern Criticism," *West Virginia University Bulletin Philological Papers*, 8 (October, 1951): 66–82.

FABIAN, BERNARD. "Samuel Johnson Ein Forschungsbericht," *Die Neueren Sprachen*, September, 1959, pp.393–407; October, 1959, pp.441–54.

FLEISCHAUER, WARREN. "Johnson, *Lycidas*, and the Norms of Criticism" in *Johnsonian Studies*. Edited by Magdi Wahba, Cairo, 1962. Distributed outside the United Arab Republic by the Oxford University Press. Pp.235–56.

GREENE, DONALD J. "Was Johnson Theatrical Critic of the *Gentleman's Magazine?*" *The Review of English Studies*, New Series, 3 (April, 1952):158–61.

HILLES, FREDERICK W. "The Making of *The Life of Pope*," in *New Light on Dr. Johnson*. Edited by Frederick W. Hilles. New Haven, Conn.: Yale University Press, 1959. Pp.257–84.

JONES, W. POWELL. "Johnson and Gray: A Study in Literary Antagonism," *Modern Philology*, 56 (May, 1959):243–53.

KALLICH, MARTIN. "The Association of Ideas in Samuel Johnson's Criticism," *Modern Language Notes*, 69 (March, 1954):170–76.

KEAST, WILLIAM R. "Johnson and 'Cibber's' *Lives of the Poets*, 1753," in *Restoration and Eighteenth-Century Literature*. Edited by Carroll Camden. Chicago: University of Chicago Press, 1963. Pp.89–101.

———. "The Theoretical Foundations of Johnson's Criticism," in *Critics and Criticism: Ancient and Modern*. Edited by Ronald S. Crane. Chicago: University of Chicago Press, 1952. Pp.389–407.

LUCAS, F. L. *The Search for Good Sense*. London: Cassell & Co. Ltd., 1958. Pp.25–128.

MOORE, ROBERT E. "Dr. Johnson on Fielding and Richardson," *Publications Modern Language Association*, 66 (March, 1951):162–81.

PERKINS, DAVID. "Johnson on Wit and Metaphysical Poetry," *ELH, A Journal of English Literary History*, 20 (September, 1953):200–17.

RHODES, RODMAN D. "*Idler* No. 24 and Johnson's Epistemology," *Modern Philology*, 64 (August, 1966):10–21.

SCHOLES, ROBERT E. "Dr. Johnson and the Bibliographical Criticism of Shakespeare," *Shakespeare Quarterly*, 11 (Spring, 1960):163–71.

SHERBO, ARTHUR. *Samuel Johnson, Editor of Shakespeare. With an Essay on the Adventurer*. ("Illinois Studies in Language and Literature," vol. 42.) Urbana: University of Illinois Press, 1956.

———— (ed.). *Samuel Johnson's Notes to Shakespeare*. ("The Augustan Reprint Society.") Los Angeles: William Andrews Clark Memorial Library, University of California. Vol. 1, Comedies, Nos. 59 and 60 (1956); vol. 2, Histories, Nos. 65 and 66 (1957); vol. 3, Tragedies, Nos. 71, 72, and 73 (1958).

———— (ed.). *Johnson on Shakespeare* ("The Yale Edition of the Works of Samuel Johnson," vols. 7 and 8.) New Haven, Conn.: Yale University Press, 1966.

VOITLE, ROBERT. *Samuel Johnson the Moralist*. Cambridge, Mass.: Harvard University Press, 1961. Chap. 1, "Reason and Empiricism." Pp.1–21.

WATSON, TOMMY G. "Johnson and Hazlitt on the Imagination in Milton," *Southern Quarterly*, 2 (January, 1964):123–33.

WELLEK, RENÉ. *A History of Modern Criticism: 1750–1950*. Vol. 1: *The Later Eighteenth Century*. New Haven, Conn.: Yale University Press, 1955. Chap. 5, "Dr. Johnson." Pp.79–104.

WIMSATT, WILLIAM K., JR., and CLEANTH BROOKS. *Literary Criticism: A Short History*. New York: Alfred A. Knopf, 1957. Chap. 15, "The Neo-Classic Universal: Samuel Johnson." Pp.313–36.

Preface

SOME years ago, in *Homage to John Dryden*, Mr. T. S. Eliot said that "we must not reject the criticism of Johnson (a dangerous person to disagree with) without having mastered it, without having assimilated the Johnsonian canons of taste." It is the purpose of this study to provide assistance to any one interested in achieving some understanding of the thought of one of the greatest English critics. One obstacle is that few writers have been so often quoted out of context as has Dr. Johnson, with the result that many students, acquainted with only a limited amount of evidence but nevertheless unable to refrain from forming a theory, have constructed a framework upon isolated passages and have imagined that they have understood the critic's system. Even the careful student of Johnson is handicapped by the fact that, in literary criticism as well as in all areas of human concernment about which he spoke and wrote, he was not a theorist: he pursued no lengthy systematic analyses; he wrote no "Enquiry into ——." This of course does not prove that he was unsystematic or inconsistent, but it does mean that the inquirer must labor to make explicit what is implicit and to deduce theory from practice. My purpose, then, is to attempt to do somewhat more systematically and thoroughly what every reader tends to do for himself, often inadequately and impatiently: to get behind the particular critical occasion to the underlying principle. In so doing I have tried not to oversimplify what is complicated but to be faithful to the complex richness and variety of the critic's mind.

Although grateful for the revision of opinion about Johnson that has been and is now being made, I am nevertheless not fully satisfied that his criticism has been described with accuracy or that the depths of his insights have been sounded. Most of the nineteenth-century ghosts about Johnson the critic have fortunately been laid, and it would now be work of the sheerest supererogation to demonstrate that he was no arid neoclassicist. But in the process of historical revision many of the shibboleths of the last century have been retained only to be reversed in their application. If Johnson was not in actuality the insensitive rationalist and literalist that Wordsworth and Coleridge felt him to be, perhaps he was the opposite. Thus some have been impressed with the "romanticism" of the Great Cham: he did actually love outside nature; he was capable of wonder and even terror; he was a friend of the Wartons and praised Chatterton. But to attempt to determine the ingredients in the Johnsonian mixture of the classical and the romantic is, it seems to me, an impossible task, chiefly because the terms have not been and perhaps can never be satisfactorily defined and because no great writer of the Age of Reason can be pressed into those molds.

For the same reasons, attempts to affirm or deny that Johnson was predominantly a humanist, an authoritarian, a traditionalist, a skeptic are necessarily obfuscating. The terms used are either too vague or too intimately a part of our own intellectual battles. Johnson was all of these or none depending on the particular meanings attached to these indeterminate expressions. I have therefore attempted to confine myself to the language of exposition and to avoid the language of persuasion.

I hold no brief for the order of topics followed in this study. There is some repetition and I have been forced to make some cross references. But that is, I think, unavoidable in any outline which must separate for purposes of expository analysis what is not separated in the data being considered. It has seemed to me that a chronological plan was out of the question for the kind of thing that I have attempted. All that needs to be said by way of introduction and defense of the plan followed is that I have taken up first what is general and fundamental and also the farthest removed from practical criticism in order to provide some kind of theoretical foundation for the more specific aesthetic considerations that follow. I have done this at the risk of driving away those readers who may wish to study Johnson on metaphors before, and perhaps even without, studying Johnson on the mind.

Perhaps no period in English literature, not even the eighteenth century, has pursued "critic learning" more assiduously than our own. Samuel Johnson himself cannot therefore fail to be of interest. Although many will surely feel that his example is not one to be followed in our day, few, I think, will be disposed to deny that his was one of the most powerful and experienced minds ever to operate upon literary data. Nevertheless, it may be an act of temerity to produce a book about a critic at a time when professional criticism is most active — especially a book that for better or for worse adheres to no particular system and neither praises nor censures its subject from the vantage point of any contemporary critical movement.

> Prophete rechts, Prophete links,
> Das Weltkind in der Mitten.

Each of the following has read the entire manuscript and has made valuable suggestions: Dr. R. W. Chapman, Dr. Paul Elmen, Professor W. R. Keast, Dr. Karl Olsson, Dean Moody Prior. The following have provided skillful assistance: Mrs. Ann Durham and Mrs. Pauline Mayo, who typed out materials to be used; Mrs. Ruth Peterson, who assisted in like manner and also typed the manuscript; Miss Zelma Leonhard, who helped prepare the manuscript for publication, read the proof, and prepared the index. The Graduate School of Northwestern University has provided research grants, which have facilitated the preparation of this study. The staff of the Minnesota Press has been courteous and efficient; the editorial labors of Mrs. Doris Franklin were as thorough as her suggestions were acute. To all of these I am most deeply grateful. The editors of *ELH* and of *PMLA* have graciously consented to the republication of materials in Chapters I and VII which first appeared in those journals.

My profoundest debt is owing to that distinguished teacher, scholar, and essayist to whom this book is dedicated.

Contents

SAMUEL JOHNSON'S LITERARY CRITICISM

CHAPTER I

Experience and Reason

THE author of the leading article in the London *Times Literary Supplement* for March 17, 1950, said that "it is practically impossible, even for an Englishman, to make any judgment about politics or morals which does not appeal to three distinct authorities, reason, experience and revelation." Whatever the truth for all Englishmen, one of them at least, the subject of this study, everywhere acknowledged the claims of all three authorities, not only in his political and moral discussions but in his literary criticism as well. Two of them, experience and reason, and the relations between them will be discussed in this chapter.

I

An exact understanding of the psychological terms which Samuel Johnson used is complicated at the very outset by the fact that he was in no way a professional psychologist or philosopher and was perhaps at no time interested in becoming one. Moreover, Johnson found that those who were thus inclined had provided no satisfactory definition of the mind and no careful discrimination of its functions. The result is that here, as elsewhere in matters abstrusely speculative, we are left without clear guides and fundamental certainties. Johnson once rejected a currently popular definition of the soul on the grounds that "it supposes what cannot be proved, that the nature of mind is properly defined"; he also said that no accurate answer can be given to the question of the way in which reason differs from instinct because "we do not know in what either reason or instinct consists . . ." [1]

Johnson was fortunately not one who ate his heart out while waiting for the determinations of the speculatists. The exigencies of life and the practical needs of criticism made decision necessary, and he soon found that it was impossible to proceed very far as a critic of morals, manners, and literature without a working conception of the mind and its faculties. This he provided in an essay that appeared only a few months after his complaint that no one had as yet clarified the nature of mind.

"Memory is, among the faculties of the human mind, that of which we make the most frequent use, or rather that of which the agency is incessant, or perpetual. Memory is the primary and fundamental power, without which there could be no other intellectual operation. Judgment and ratiocination suppose something already known, and draw their decisions only from experience. Imagination selects ideas from the treasures of remembrance, and produces novelty only by varied combinations. We do not even form conjectures of distant, or anticipations of future events, but by concluding what is possible from what is past." [2]

This passage offers neither complete nor satisfactory definitions of any of the mental powers mentioned — memory, reason, imagination — but it does order their relations in such a way as to illuminate Johnson's conception of how the mind works, a conception that is the very foundation of what will be referred to in this study as his empiricism. That operation of the mind which is "the primary and fundamental power, without which there could be no other intellectual operation," is the memory. The memory is linked with "experience," with "something already known," and with "what is past" — not indeed with a fixed, traditional, or authoritarian past but with the individual's own "treasures of remembrance." Moreover, those other faculties of the mind, judgment and imagination, are not only secondary in time of operation but are completely helpless without the antecedent operation of experiential memory; they draw their decisions and select their ideas "only from experience." [3]

I have applied the word *empiricism* to the process described in this passage because it suggests a more philosophical and rigorous reliance upon observation and experience than does the word *experience*, but I am fully aware that Johnson himself would have disapproved of using the term in connection with any of his ideas. He defined *empiricism* in his Dictionary as "Dependence on experience without knowledge or art; quackery." An *empiric* he defined by a quotation from John Quincy, the medical writer, which reads: "A trier or experimenter; such persons as have no true education in, or knowledge of physical practice, but venture upon hearsay and observation only." [4] The emphasis here should be placed upon the word *only*, since that may give a clue to Johnson's frequently opprobrious use of the term. The word did not convey to him what it conveys to us: knowledge *based upon* observation and experiment. To him it seemed to mean practice (perhaps usually medical practice) based not upon careful study but only upon casual observation and experience.

But experience for Johnson did remain the foundation of all knowledge. He would have objected only to mistaking the foundation for the whole structure. And his objection to relying upon experience alone is nowhere so clear or so forcible as his objection to relying upon the reason or the imagination alone. "Judgment," he said in the *Life of Pope*, "is forced upon us by experience." In the Dictionary he defined a *rationalist* as "One who proceeds in his disquisitions and practice wholly upon reason." And the similes from Bacon, which Johnson quoted to illustrate the word, express most felicitously his own position: ". . . the empirical philosophers are like to pismires; they only lay up and use their store: the *rationalists* are like to spiders; they spin all out of their own bowels: but give me a philosopher, who, like the bee, hath a middle faculty, gathering from abroad, but digesting that which is gathered by his own virtue."

Bacon's little fable of the bee (perhaps an anticipation of Swift's) leaves room for the rational faculty, since the mind must, by its own power, digest at home the materials gathered abroad. But before everything else it must collect its materials through empirical observation and search. Johnson accepted this Baconian conception not only as the proper explanation of the relations between observation and reason but as a fundamental epistemological truth applicable to the relations between experience and any kind of mental operation. This is also true of the imaginative faculty: "Imagination is useless without knowledge: nature gives in vain the power of combination, unless study and observation supply materials to be combined." On his tour of the Hebrides with Boswell, Johnson expressed the opinion that the poetry of St. Kilda must be very poor because the locality was barren of images and therefore starved the poet's fancy. To Boswell's objection that even what material there was could be combined into poetry by "a poetical genius," Johnson replied: "But, sir, a man cannot make fire but in proportion as he has wood. He cannot coin guineas but in proportion as he has gold." *Nil est in intellectu, quod non prius fuit in sensu.*[5]

Although I am not prepared to argue for a direct or exclusive philosophical influence, I think it is true to say that Johnson's conception of the mind as necessarily anchored in experience is reminiscent of the main emphasis in Locke's epistemology. Locke, in one of the most famous sentences in his *Essay*, had said: "All those sublime thoughts which tower above the clouds, and reach as high as heaven itself, take their rise and footing here: in all that great extent wherein the mind wanders, in those remote speculations it may seem to be elevated with, it stirs not one jot beyond those ideas which *sense* or *reflection* have offered for its contemplation."[6] To Coleridge, on the other hand, Aristotle (and he might have added Locke and Johnson) "never could raise himself into that higher state, which was natural to Plato, and has been so to others, in which the understanding is distinctly contemplated, and, as it were, looked down upon from the throne of actual ideas, or living, inborn, essential truths."[7]

To attain that eminence Coleridge had to postulate (and he did so under influences from Plato, the Neoplatonists, and the Germans) powers of the mind more subjective and more innately powerful in both destruction and creation than Johnson or Locke ever dreamed of. To most eighteenth-century thinkers judgment, understanding, and reason were virtually synonymous, as were fancy and imagination — all of them faculties which, in a sane mind at least, could never be free of antecedent experience. In and of themselves they could create nothing. But in Coleridge's conception, the higher powers of reason and the primary imagination were constitutive of everything. "Thus, God, the soul, eternal truth, &c. . . . are themselves reason . . . [Reason] has the power of acquainting itself with invisible realities or spiritual objects." [8] The common notion that Johnson was rational and Coleridge imaginative is therefore a false and misleading one. A truer distinction is this: for Johnson all mental action, whether rational or imaginative, is always secondary to the direct experience of reality and is, apart from experience, seriously suspect; for Coleridge all mental action, whether rational or imaginative, is primary; it does not depend upon experience but constitutes experience.

The results for literary criticism should be obvious. For Johnson experienced reality can be an objective test of art because the mind — even though it may combine, divide, and order that reality — never gets very far away from it. But for Coleridge objective reality can never be a satisfactory test of art, for the mind destroys it and then creates it in new fusions; the only valid tests are either the organic principles within the work itself or the type of mental operation that was concerned in creating it. It would be wrong, I think, to say that for Coleridge reality was entirely enclosed within the mind of man and within the inclusive mind of God in which the human mind partakes, even though he at times seems to come very close to such an idealistic view. But for Johnson, it is clear, the mind at both ends is open to reality. "It is reasonable to believe," he said, "that thought, like every thing else, has its causes and effects; that it must proceed from something known, done, or suffered; and must produce some action or event." [9]

II

If Johnson's theory of knowledge is rooted in experience, it will be well to determine as exactly as we can the full significance of that term. His Dictionary persistently defines it as *practice* or *trial,* and his own use of *experience* points to at least the following meanings and associations: (1) sensation and firsthand observation, (2) scientific experiment and research, (3) the general processes of learning and of scholarship.

1. Johnson as a moralist was often inimical to the senses because they diverted the attention from the moral and rational ends of life. "Thus it appears . . . that, supposing the mind, at any certain time, in an equipoise between the pleasures of this life, and the hopes of futurity, present objects, falling more frequently in to the scale, would in time preponderate, and that our regard for an invisible state would grow every moment weaker . . ." [10] To prevent such an issue, man must attempt assiduously "to transfer the weight" to the side of virtue and distant reward. When the senses tended to make the visible present preponderate over the invisible future, they were of course mischievous. Equally mischievous was any philosophical attempt to sensualize the mind and soul of man. Johnson vigorously opposed the *école sensualiste.* He disagreed strongly with Locke's and Bolingbroke's argument that the immateriality of the soul is not essential to its immortality. "Immateriality," said Imlac, "seems to imply a natural power of perpetual duration, as a consequence of exemption from all causes of decay . . ." For Johnson the mind is as completely spiritual as matter is completely "inert, senseless, and lifeless." As Imlac said, "All the conclusions of reason enforce the immateriality of the mind, and all the notices of sense and investigations of science concur to prove the unconsciousness of matter." [11]

Such were Johnson's reactions to the hesitations of Locke on the subject and to the outright mechanical and materialistic views of the soul of many of those who marched under his banners. But this view in no way, I think, weakens what I have called the basic empiricism of Johnson's conception of mental action, which was never intended to imply anything at all about the *nature* of mind-stuff itself or about matter itself, but merely to state the *relations* between mind and outside experience. The two can be entirely distinct entities and yet be forced to cooperate indissolubly in the creation of knowledge.

But when such moral and metaphysical considerations as these were not relevant, Johnson was firm in his admiration of the senses. The many occasions on which he recommended firsthand sense-observation need not be instanced here; one example will suffice. "Trust as little as you can to report," he advised George Staunton, who was about to go to America; "examine all you can by your own senses." Nor is it necessary to discuss here what will be discussed later in other connections, the firm belief that accurate and full observations of nature are requisite to the preparation of the poet. But it may be informative to remind ourselves of his unhesitating solution of the much debated problem of whether the visual descriptions and imagery of the blind poet Blacklock could in any way have been a mental creation. Johnson said that "we may be absolutely sure that such passages are combinations of what he has remembered of the works of other writers who could see. That foolish fellow, Spence, has laboured to explain philosophically how Blacklock may have done, by means of his own faculties, what it is impossible he should do." For an empiricist no other position would have been possible.[12]

Recently Johnson's famous kicking of the stone in refutation of Berkeley has been reinterpreted and found by H. F. Hallett to be not "the mere humorous exemplification of vulgar misunderstanding" that it is often considered, but an occasion "radiant with a philosophical acuity transcending [Johnson's] power of general analysis."[13] Professor Hallett feels that for Johnson the object of perception "has a being of its own, *i.e.*, an activity of its own distinct from all mental activity, finite or creative." If this is true, the stone is more than a passive idea; it is an agency. Boswell has made it clear that Johnson struck his foot "with mighty force against a large stone till he rebounded from it" — language which Hallett interprets to mean that the stone showed itself "capable of *doing* something to establish its reality independent of being observed."

One can understand the philosopher's caution in crediting Johnson with the full insight expressed in this analysis. Johnson's comment, quoted above, that matter is "inert, senseless, and lifeless" would seem to belie any notion that he might have looked upon it as an active agency. But Johnson's staunch and repeated insistence upon the need of contact with the outside world makes it plausible to believe that he looked upon reality, even material reality, as something compulsive — in Santayana's phrase, "a collateral power, pressing and alien." [14] What John Dewey has said about Locke's conception of experience may, I think, with full justice be applied to Johnson's: "What characterizes sensation and observation, and hence experience, is, in Locke's thought, their coerciveness. . . . This coercion of will and of opinion is the essential guarantee of their validity. . . . Compulsion is the safeguard against vagaries of fancy and accidents of conventional beliefs." [15]

2. Experience for Johnson not only meant firsthand observation of life, but observation organized into experiment. In his Dictionary he defined *experience* as (a) "practice; frequent trial" and (b) "knowledge gained by trial and practice." It is unnecessary to develop at length what is now well known: that Johnson distrusted speculation and purely discursive reasoning; that he preferred experiments to theorizing, and observation to metaphysics; that he himself was addicted to amateur experimentation; that he was well informed, if not about all sciences, at least about a respectable number of them, and also about many of the industrial arts and processes; and that his very style reflects his absorbing interest in natural phenomena and in the language used by the scientists to describe them. But there is a statement from the *Life of Boerhaave*, written when Johnson was thirty years of age, which shows theoretical comprehension and approval of the scientific method. It deserves more attention than it has received, for it justifies placing Johnson, at a fairly early age, "among th' asserters of free reason's claim."

"When he [Boerhaave] laid down his office of governour of the university, in 1715, he made an oration upon the subject of 'attaining to certainty in natural philosophy'; in which he declares, in the strongest terms, in favour of experimental knowledge; and reflects, with just severity, upon those arrogant philosophers, who are too easily disgusted with the slow methods of obtaining true notions by frequent experiments; and who, possessed with too high an opinion of their own abilities, rather choose to consult their own imaginations, than inquire into nature, and are better pleased with the charming amusement of forming hypotheses, than the toilsome drudgery of making observations.

"The emptiness and uncertainty of all those systems, whether venerable for their antiquity, or agreeable for their novelty, he has evidently shown; and not only declared, but proved, that we are entirely ignorant of the principle of things, and that all the knowledge we have, is of such qualities alone as are discoverable by experience, or such as may be deduced from them by mathematical demonstration." [16]

Johnson also expressed a principle of Locke which has been of crucial importance in all scientific advance and which Bertrand Russell in our own time has made basic to what he calls logical atomism — further evidence that Johnson understood the implications of the scientific revolution of the preceding century: "The chief art of learning, as Locke has observed, is to attempt but little at a time. The widest excursions of the mind are made by short flights frequently repeated; the most lofty fabricks of science are formed by the continued accumulation of single propositions." [17]

Johnson, of course, seriously censured too great a preoccupation with physical science, just as he censured any kind of obsession. The scientist becomes contemptible when he neglects moral duty or when his researches are insignificant and useless. But to those temptations all students, whether their subjects were human or natural, have at times succumbed. Johnson's Polyphilus, the dabbling pedant, preoccupied with the Chinese language, English law, and ancient Corinthian brass as well as with anatomy, botany, and chemistry, is fully as contemptible as his more exclusively scientific pedants like Gelidus and Gelasimus. So great, in fact, was Johnson's admiration for natural experiment that he wished to conciliate mankind to that "species of projectors . . . who are searching out new powers of nature," and expressed the wish that royal and military "projectors," like Caesar, Catiline, Xerxes, Alexander, Charles of Sweden, and Peter of Russia, had been "huddled together in obscurity and detestation." Morality and divinity come first in Johnson's hierarchy of values, but he regularly prefers the natural scientist to the metaphysician and places medicine next to divinity as the pursuit most beneficial to mankind.[18]

3. In addition to being used to describe firsthand observation and organized scientific experiment, the term *experience* was also intimately associated with learning and scholarship in general. One of the earliest extended remarks Johnson made to Boswell was the following:

"Human experience, which is constantly contradicting theory, is the great test of truth. A system, built upon the discovery of a great many minds, is always of more strength, than what is produced by the mere workings of any one mind, which, of itself, can do little. There is not so poor a book in the world that would not be a prodigious effort were it wrought out entirely by a single mind, without the aid of prior investigators. The French writers are superficial; because they are not scholars, and so proceed upon the mere power of their own minds; and we see how very little power they have."

Most of Johnson's comments on human learning are couched in such empirical terms as these. Anyone who wishes to become eminent in any field of knowledge, said Johnson, "must first possess himself of the intellectual treasures which the diligence of former ages has accumulated, and then endeavour to increase them by his own collections." In so doing, he will escape the "mental disease" of those who "rely wholly upon unassisted genius and natural sagacity" and who hope to "solve difficulties by sudden irradiations of intelligence, and comprehend long processes of argument by immediate intuition." [19]

Of these three important constituents of experience, the first (the direct observation of nature and life) and the third (the mastery of an intellectual tradition) are the most relevant to a consideration of literary criticism and the preparation of the writer for his task. Johnson, although always aware of the importance of both, seems now to have considered one the more important and now the other. He once said that "the first task is to search books, the next to contemplate nature," and in conversation with Boswell he opposed the notion that enough knowledge may be acquired in conversation. "The foundation must be laid by reading. General principles must be had from books, which, however, must be brought to the test of real life. In conversation you never get a system." On the other hand, in literature — at least in its descriptive portions — Johnson seems to have preferred the direct observation of the scene, for he blames Milton for not always having "copied from original form" and being therefore deficient in "the freshness, raciness, and energy of immediate observation," while he praises Shakespeare for demonstrating "plainly, that he has seen with his own eyes" and for being "an exact surveyor of the inanimate world," whose "descriptions have always some peculiarities, gathered by contemplating things as they really exist."[20]

Of the overwhelming importance for Johnson of experience in the attainment of intellectual certainty and literary excellence there can be little doubt. This emphasis may have been derived ultimately from the empiricism of John Locke. But it may well have been Isaac Watts's repeated insistence upon the identical intellectual methods that commended them to Samuel Johnson, for Watts, more than any other single person, was Johnson's mentor and guide in matters relating to logic and the human mind. In his *Improvement of the Mind,* a Lockean treatise, of which Johnson once said that "few books have been perused by me with greater pleasure,"[21] Watts distinguishes five methods of improving the mind: observation, reading, instruction by lectures, conversation, and meditation. The following description of the mental operation called *observation* may well serve as a summary statement of that basically Lockean point of view that underlay everything that Johnson said of experience:

"Observation is the notice, that we take of all occurrences in human life, whether they are sensible or intellectual, whether relating to persons or things, to ourselves or others . . .

"When this observation relates to any thing, that immediately concerns ourselves, it may be called experience . . .

"Observation therefore includes all that Mr. Locke means by sensation and reflection . . .

"It is owing to observation, that our mind is furnished with the first, simple and complex ideas. It is this, lays the foundation of all knowledge; and makes us capable of using the other methods for improving the mind. [Without the ideas introduced by observation] it would be impossible either for men or books to teach us any thing." [22]

III

We have already discussed what is perhaps the most fundamental characteristic of Johnsonian reason — that it is a faculty of mind which is helpless without materials provided by sense and reflection, that is, by the experience and contemplation of objective life and nature. But human insight only begins in empirical observation and investigation; it does not end there. It is therefore important to determine the specific meanings Johnson attached to that protean and ever changing term, *reason*. There are two large classes of meaning in which most of Johnson's uses of *reason* may be placed. (1) Reason is associated with universal, immutable truth. When Johnson says that "truth indeed is always truth, and reason is always reason; they have an intrinsick and unalterable value, and constitute that intellectual gold which defies destruction," [23] he refers generally and metaphorically to the following universals which the mind of man perceives as constituting the very structure of the natural and moral world: (a) moral and religious truth, (b) the immutable and uniform order of nature, and (c) the unalterable mind of man. Reason, in these senses, becomes virtually a synonym for general nature — a subject which will be discussed in a subsequent chapter. (2) Reason is also considered to be a faculty of the mind, which operates in the following five separate but closely related functions.

(a) As that quality in man which understands and appropriates general truth and reality, reason watches scrupulously the data of the senses and the combinations of the imagination to make certain that they resemble the facts of life and the order of reality. It is thus distinguished from the imagination or fancy, which creates fictions, adorns nature, and paints reality. It continually forces the mind back upon nature and life.

(b) The reason is a dividing, partitioning faculty, and may be expected to "disentangle complications and investigate causes," "to divide the object into its parts, or mark the intermediate gradations from the first agent to the last consequence." As such, it is again distinguished from the imagination, which unites disparate data into new images; it is also distinguished from that species of imaginative wonder which Johnson calls "a pause of reason, a sudden cessation of the mental progress."

(c) But the reason is also a concatenating and synthesizing faculty, which establishes order, provides transitions, and properly arranges the disposition of materials — a kind of mental architect which in speculation constructs systems and in poetry creates form and structure.

(d) Reason, as one would expect, is a moderating force, the enemy of all manner of excess and ecstasy, always perceiving both the ethical and the aesthetic mean and always resisting any tendency toward disproportion, lack of symmetry, or inappropriateness of language and ornament.

(e) Reason is an abstracting and generalizing power, of moral importance in detaching the mind from the insistent claims of sense and habit, and of aesthetic importance in guiding the writer to select general and therefore more permanent reality for literary imitation. Here one may see not only the intuitive perception of general truth and nature but also the slower inductive process of generalizing and making abstract those data which were originally concrete.[24]

The ideas that appear in this schematization of the functions of reason have their roots in the traditions of classical logic, criticism, and morality, and indeed in the whole intellectual legacy of Western Europe. No attempt will therefore be made to assign specific sources to conceptions that have for generations passed current in the Republic of Letters. The five functions just outlined, however, should never be regarded as autonomous functions of the mind or as any kind of evidence of what is commonly called rationalism. They all point to an antecedent operation of the mind — the appropriation of nature and life through the senses and through an empirical collection of materials. The mind obviously cannot watch, divide, combine, moderate or generalize *in vacuo*. Reason (as understood in these five functions) and experience are not contradictory but complementary.

And yet the eighteenth century was fully aware that the claims of experience and the claims of reason were not always fully compatible. The intellectual battles between Cartesian rationalists and the empiricists, between the adherents of natural light and David Hume, had made men highly conscious of the need of determining to which of those two great authorities, the empirical or the rational, they owed their chief allegiance. Edward Gibbon credited the Swiss Lockean, Jean Pierre de Crousaz, with having formed his mind to a habit of reasoning that moved inductively "from our simple ideas to the most complex operations of the human understanding" and with having thus given him a "free command of a universal instrument." Such empirical logic, however, Locke himself had ignored in his political writings: "Locke's *Treatise of Government*," said Gibbon, "instructed me in the knowledge of Whig principles, which are rather founded in reason than experience" — an obvious flick at the political Locke and at the Whigs.[25]

Crousaz, whom Johnson, like Gibbon, admired and whose work on logic Johnson had recommended in his *Preceptor* preface as being of the empirical and not the peripatetic school,[26] criticized Montaigne for preferring reason to experience and for making the latter secondary to the former: "*When Reason fails us, we have Recourse to Experience, which is a Method much more feeble and inferior*, says *Montaigne*. It is quite the contrary: when we cannot find out any thing by Experience, then we have Recourse to Conjectures." Crousaz then says that he decided to submit to experiential test his attitude toward the opera, which he had previously disliked on purely rational and *a priori* grounds. The result was a complete change of opinion, and what he had formerly condemned on rational grounds he now praised on the basis of experience gained at first hand.[27] Consider also the grounds on which Bishop Warburton defends the national religious establishment and supports a test-law administered by the state:

"Our theory is an explanation of an *artificial*, not a *natural* system: in which measures very different are to be followed. For truth being the end of all kinds of theories, a right theory of *nature* is to be obtained only by pursuing fact; for God is the author of that system: but in a theory of *politics*, which is an *artificial* system, to follow fact is no certain way to truth, because man is the author of that system. . . . As therefore the method to be pursued is different, so should the judgment be, which is passed upon it: the goodness of this theory being estimated, not according to its agreement with *fact*, but *right reason*. In the former case, the theory should be regulated by the fact: in the latter, the fact by the theory." [28]

Although Johnson accepted Warburton's belief in established religion, he would never have defended it on the blandly self-assured grounds that in some cases fact and experience can be ignored and artificial theory imposed as a necessary rational alternative. For the most part Johnson found that reason and experience, although separate routes, ended at the same destination. The following sentence is typical: "That every man should regulate his actions by his own conscience, without any regard to the opinions of the rest of the world, is one of the first precepts of moral prudence; justified not only by *the suffrage of reason* . . . but by *the voice* likewise *of experience.*" When (as was the case in that old and perplexing dilemma of man's freedom and God's foreknowledge) Johnson found logic in conflict with experience, he boldly and unhesitatingly decided in favor of experience. "You are surer that you are free, than you are of prescience; you are surer that you can lift up your finger or not as you please, than you are of any conclusion from a deduction of reasoning. . .

All theory is against the freedom of the will; all experience for it." [29]

Nevertheless, Johnson, like everyone else, was compelled sooner or later to make assumptions. One cannot always reason inductively; one cannot always rely upon experimental certainties or even upon experience which is as broadly conceived as Johnson's. When evidence from direct experience is not available, what does one do? If one resembles Johnson, one invokes what Isaac Watts called "intelligence" — the perception of self-evident propositions, "those first Principles of Truth which are (as it were) wrought into the very Nature and Make of our Minds." [30] Johnson was often forced to seek what he called the "principal and axiomatical truth that regulates subordinate positions." [31] In defining terms for the Dictionary, he found it necessary to use a principle which, as he says, is closely analogous to the making of common-sense assumptions: "To explain, requires the use of terms less abstruse than that which is to be explained, and such terms cannot always be found; for *as nothing can be proved but by supposing something intuitively known, and evident without proof,* so nothing can be defined but by the use of words too plain to admit a definition." [32]

The principle is at least as old as Aristotle — a fact obscured during the centuries in which that philosopher was unnaturally mated with the Scholastics and even during those years in which the Baconians revolted against syllogistic reasoning. "All instruction given or received by way of argument," said the Stagirite, "proceeds from pre-existent knowledge." This is true for both syllogism and induction, "for each of these latter makes use of old knowledge to impart new, the syllogism assuming an audience that accepts its premises, induction exhibiting the universal as implicit in the clearly known particular." [33]

Johnson occasionally used the word *intuition*, which he defined in the Dictionary as (1) "Sight of anything. Used commonly of mental view; immediate knowledge" and (2) "Knowledge not obtained by deduction of reason, but instantaneously accompanying the ideas which are its object." "To know" he defined in part as "To perceive with certainty, whether intuitive or discursive." But intuition was not for him what it was for Descartes, "the undoubting conception of an unclouded and attentive mind" which *"springs from the light of reason alone,"* which is "more certain than deduction itself" and the "fluctuating testimony of the senses." [34] It is rather the plainer and less exalted intuition which Locke considered inferior to discursive reason and which he explained in the following sentence (cited by Johnson to illustrate the definition of *intuition* given above): "The truth of these propositions we know by a bare simple *intuition* of the ideas, and such propositions are called self-evident."

Such intuition Johnson had to admit as a practical necessity. Decision is impossible without an appeal to common sense and self-evident, axiomatic propositions. But such intuitions are always radically simple, plain, and fundamental; and they are close to experience — if not always the experience of the individual, certainly of the race. Consent to basic moral and natural truth is never far removed in Johnson from the *consensus gentium.* It is a kind of inevitable and necessary assent to the *communes loci* of centuries of human thought and experience. Without such acquiescence in moral certainty, reason itself would "prove a burden to us, rather than a privilege, by keeping us in a continual suspense, and thereby rendering our conditions perpetually restless and unquiet." [35]

Virtually everything that Samuel Johnson said about the mind indicates firm adherence to the principle that most human knowledge arises from the closest possible contact with objective, inescapable, coercive experience. His realism may seem naive, his reliance upon experience unsophisticated, to an age that is becoming increasingly aware that rational and imaginative hypothesis is present in all perception and has an important directive function to perform even in scientific research. But the fact that Johnson had learned well the lessons of Locke gave firmness and sanity to his determinations. One feels that Johnson's feet are always firmly planted on the ground. It is inevitable, in view of his basic empiricism, that he should have found the "world-makers" intolerable — Spinoza, Leibniz, and Descartes — and that he should have been a formidable foe of the intuitive rationalists, the exponents of fitness, the Deistic believers in unaided reason and natural light, and indeed any and all who relied upon the mind alone or any of its faculties alone to the neglect of primary experience. Samuel Johnson's basic intellectual loyalties lay with what David Mallet called "the Baconian succession" — Boyle, Locke, Newton, and all others who acknowledge Bacon as "the father of the only valuable philosophy, that of fact and observation" [36] — always provided, of course, that they did not allow empirical investigation to take the place of divinely revealed truth and morality.

CHAPTER II

The Theory of Criticism

SAMUEL JOHNSON practiced most of the forms of literary criticism known to his own day. He emended corrupt passages and explained obscure and difficult ones. He traced the development of an author's genius — that "chymical process," in the words of a contemporary review of his criticism, by which the earliest yield is "transmuted into a substance of a more valuable kind" while "still preserving some analogy to its pristine form." He occasionally studied "the gradual progress and improvement of our taste," and he comprehended "as it were in one view the whole circle of the arts and sciences, to see their mutual connections and dependencies." But above all he sat on the judicial bench of criticism, inquiring into the beauties and faults of literary works and pronouncing "with great accuracy on the merits of literary productions."[1]

His own learned labors resulted in an edition of Shakespeare which a contemporary scholar has characterized as "the best which had yet appeared" and "still one of the few editions which are indispensable." Johnson himself held the task of a scholarly editor in the highest possible regard. "Conjectural criticism demands more than humanity possesses. . . . Let us now be told no more," he said, glancing at Pope, "of the dull duty of an editor."[2]

His achievement in literary scholarship, however distinguished and important, does not directly concern us here. Our subject is Johnson as judge of literature. Nevertheless, it is important to be fully aware of the extent to which one who was primarily a judicial critic accepted the soundest insights of the eighteenth-century school of literary historians. His criticism must be viewed — as he himself apparently viewed all previous literature — against a background of factual knowledge rescued from the elusive past by assiduous scholars. He has, of course, been looked upon as a traditionalist and a belated neoclassicist. But as one would expect from the intellectual affiliations discussed in the first chapter, one of the most important respects in which he differed from his predecessors, the great literary Augustans of the earlier part of the century, lay in his staunch allegiance to modern learning and investigative technique. In commenting on the quarrels between the Ancients and the Moderns, he revealed that he was in the camp of the Moderns, on the side of editor and scholar against Swift. "The digressions relating to Wotton and Bentley," he said in discussing *A Tale of a Tub*, "must be confessed to discover want of knowledge or want of integrity; he [Swift] did not understand the two controversies, or he willingly misrepresented them. But Wit can stand its ground against Truth only a little while. The honours due to learning have been justly distributed by the decision of posterity." [3]

Johnson was as aware as any student of the literary past in his own day of the importance of historical insight for critical evaluation. "To judge rightly of an author we must transport ourselves to his time, and examine what were the wants of his contemporaries, and what were his means of supplying them." [4] Moreover, although he was not qualified in all areas to be a professional literary historian, yet both his literary biographies and his criticism contain many examples of the genetic method, which Professor Wellek has described as "little exercises in literary history." [5]

It was only when history became metaphysical and only when the historian presented his facts less as facts and rather as illustrations of a speculative theory (and that happened all too frequently) that Johnson divorced himself from the historical school. He opposed all such theories as the dependence of genius upon climate; the theory of progressive, regressive, or cyclical development; the association of belles-lettres and political liberty, of poetry and politeness, of sublimity and republicanism, of wit and aristocracy, of "luxury and laughter." [6] He also disagreed with many of the particular judgments and the special pleadings of some of the historical scholars, who not only resurrected, but also recommended as guides out of the contemporary literary desert, medieval ballads and romances; Ossian, Tasso, Dante; Norse, Erse, and Saxon antiquities. Johnson was also undeniably opposed to many other points of view associated with historical investigation: the emphasis upon the flux and "differentness" of history and the consequent relativism of aesthetic standards; the attempt to introduce and commend the individual and the eccentric in taste, the particular and idiosyncratic, the mysterious and the "romantic." But his strictures upon such theories as these should never be interpreted as a lack of appreciation of history itself but only as the opposition of a man of fact to speculations about history. Johnson was himself extremely chary of expressing in his own works any philosophy of literary history. The only philosophy of that kind that emerges in the *Lives of the Poets* is that there had been something like progressive development in the art of regularizing prosody, a process which reached its culmination in the verses of Pope.

For Johnson, history did not carry its own interpretation along with it; and that meant that history ought never to be identified with criticism. Nevertheless, he believed that history can be of great service to criticism and that proper literary judgment can often be made only after the historian has recovered the facts upon which such judgment can be based:

"How much the mutilation of ancient history has taken away from the beauty of poetical performances, may be conjectured from the light which a lucky commentator sometimes effuses, by the recovery of an incident that had been long forgotten: thus, in the third book of Horace, Juno's denunciations against those that should presume to raise again the walls of Troy, could for many ages please only by splendid images and swelling language, of which no man discovered the use or propriety, till Le Fevre, by showing on what occasion the Ode was written, changed wonder to rational delight." [7]

But after the duties of the historian have been completed, the problem of judgment still remains. And that brings us to the topic of this chapter, judicial criticism, the type of criticism most characteristic of Johnson and the eighteenth century.

I

In his Dictionary Johnson defines a *critick* as "A man skilled in the art of judging literature; a man able to distinguish the faults and beauties of writing." The first definition of *criticism* consists of a quotation from Dryden: "*Criticism*, as it was first instituted by Aristotle, was meant a standard of judging well." This definition brings together the names of Aristotle, Dryden, and Johnson — a circumstance which in the Dictionary may well have been fortuitous but which actually points to a legitimate critical filiation. In calling Aristotle the "father of criticism," Johnson was following Dryden, whom, in turn, he denominated "the father of English criticism." These three were basically alike, not so much in their conceptions of art nor in the subjects to which they devoted themselves, as in their belief that criticism was essentially an exploratory intellectual process based upon the actual practice of writers and capable of being dialectically reduced to basic principles. Although Johnson found Dryden to be "sometimes interested, sometimes negligent, and sometimes capricious," he distinguished such "occasional" or "defensive" criticism, appearing often in fulsome dedications or hastily written prefaces, from his "general" or "didactick" criticism, which depended "upon the nature of things and the structure of the human mind." In such criticism Dryden "first taught us to determine upon principles the merit of composition." [8]

In reading what Johnson has to say about criticism as an art, one receives an impression that may at first seem somewhat paradoxical. Ideally, criticism bore in her right hand an amaranthine scepter, which touched the true work of art and "consigned it over to immortality"; and in her left hand "an unextinguishable torch," which showed everything "in its true form," which "darted through the labyrinths of sophistry," and which "pierced through the robes, which Rhetoric often sold to Falsehood." But in actual practice, "criticism is a study by which men grow important and formidable at very small expense . . . and he whom nature has made weak, and idleness keeps ignorant, may yet support his vanity by the name of Critick. . . . Criticism is a goddess easy of access and forward of advance, who will meet the slow, and encourage the timorous; the want of meaning she supplies with words, and the want of spirit she recompenses with malignity." [9] There is ample precedent for both points of view in the eighteenth century. Pope had exalted the critic almost to the level of the poet:

> Both must alike from Heav'n derive their light,
> These born to judge, as well as those to write.

But Swift had described the critic as an ass with horns, whose flesh was full of gall and bitterness, who had descended in a direct line from Momus and Hybris.[10]

Johnson was aware that the good estate of criticism had often fallen into the hands of the weak-witted and the malevolent; that one critic saw nothing but petty faults through a microscope and missed the general excellence, while another saw only chimeras and cloudy phantoms through a telescope; that original simplicity had been encrusted with the unfounded and accidental prescriptions of authority. But he never lost sight of what criticism ought to be and what it had approached being in the hands of practitioners like Aristotle and Dryden — a rigorous intellectual discipline, based upon wide experience and hard thinking. "It is . . . the task of criticism to establish principles; to improve opinion into knowledge; and to distinguish those means of pleasing which depend upon known causes and rational deduction, from the nameless and inexplicable elegancies which appeal wholly to the fancy. . . . Criticism reduces those regions of literature under the dominion of science, which have hitherto known only the anarchy of ignorance, the caprices of fancy, and the tyranny of prescription." [11]

Such a comment as this gives to criticism, in theory at least, the autonomy of an independent and recognized discipline. Johnson's point of view does not, of course, intend to exalt the critical above the creative faculty. Quite the contrary. "Next to the excursions of fancy are the disquisitions of criticism, which, in my opinion, is only to be ranked among the subordinate and instrumental arts." But it does clearly and unmistakably intend to separate literature and criticism to the benefit of each. The mischief is that criticism has often been dyed in the color of its subject matter. "Criticism has sometimes permitted fancy to dictate the laws by which fancy ought to be restrained, and fallacy to perplex the principles by which fallacy is to be detected; her superintendence of others has betrayed her to negligence of herself; and, like the ancient Scythians, by extending her conquests over distant regions, she has left her throne vacant to her slaves." Such an opinion should be sufficient to distinguish Johnson from all "appreciators" who dwell upon the experiences of their own palates, from all who wish to recreate the original creation, and from that object of Mr. Eliot's scorn, the "impressionistic critic," whose "suppressed creative wish" is often "apt to interfere fatally" with his judgment.[12]

More specifically, Johnson's opinion separated him from one important "school" of taste in his own day just as certainly as it affiliated him with another. Two definitions of *taste* in the Dictionary are relevant here, because they epitomize two conceptions of taste prominent in seventeenth-century France and eighteenth-century England: "Sensibility; perception" and "Intellectual relish or discernment." One group, represented by the Chevalier de Méré, Bouhours in part, Shaftesbury, Hutcheson, Temple, and others, who judged literature somewhat in the spirit of the *Précieuses*, tended to identify taste with sentiment and instinct and to divorce it from reason, knowledge, and authority. The other group, consisting of Hédelin, Rapin, Dacier, Bossu, and La Bruyère in France, and of Rymer, Dryden, Dennis, and others in England, held that "Taste in writing," to quote the words of Dennis, "is nothing but a fine Discernment of Truth," or, in the words of Gerard, that "good sense is an indispensable ingredient in true taste, which always implies a quick and accurate perception of things as they really are." [13]

There is little doubt that Johnson's sympathies lay with the latter group, even though he may have conceded that there is in art a *je ne sais quoi* not fully amenable to the determinations of reason. He found difference of taste to be difference of skill, and he defended Addison, a critic whose affiliations in these matters have to some readers seemed ambiguous, from the charge that he decided "by taste rather than by principles." Perhaps remembering the essays on wit, especially *Spectators* no. 58 and no. 61, in which Addison based a taste for polite writing upon reason, reflection, and good sense, Johnson chose to consider him a kind of popular Dryden, whose "purpose was to infuse literary curiosity by gentle and unsuspected conveyance into the gay, the idle, and the wealthy" without departing from the austere view that taste was intellectual discernment.[14]

So much for those types of criticism — impressionistic, "creative," "romantic," sentimental, intuitive — from which Johnson's conception of criticism as a learned discipline clearly separates him.

II

Even if one confines consideration only to those critics who are in some positive and important way related to Samuel Johnson, one soon discovers that the critical methods followed are bewilderingly diverse. Nevertheless, it is possible to discern, within the tradition of rational and "scientific" criticism, at least two related but divergent groups. One is the school of nature represented by Rapin and Bossu, which tended to be rationalistic. The other is the more empirically oriented school represented, to select only one example, by David Hume.

Bossu had said that "*Arts*, as well as *Sciences*, are founded upon

Reason, and in both we are to be guided by the *Light of Nature.*
But in *Sciences* [and this includes criticism but not of course
poetry itself] neither the *Inventers,* nor the *Improvers* of them,
are to make use of any other Guides but this *Light of Nature*
. . ." [15] The title page of Rymer's translation in 1694 of Rapin's
Reflections on Aristotle's Treatise asserted that it contained the
"Necessary, Rational, and Universal Rules for *Epick, Dramatick,*
and the other sorts of Poetry." Hume, on the other hand, although
he admitted "certain general principles of approbation or blame"
and conceded that there is much less variety and flux of general
opinion in aesthetics than in other philosophical speculation, considered it "evident that none of the rules of composition are fixed
by reasonings *a priori,* or can be esteemed abstract conclusions of
the understanding. . . . Their foundation is the same with that
of all the practical sciences, experience; nor are they any thing
but general observations, concerning what has been universally
found to please in all countries and in all ages."

Hume bases critical validity upon experience and not upon
"the abstract conclusions of the understanding," and that in itself
should be sufficient to distinguish him from the French school of
literary "deists," who talked of the fitness of things in art and
of the light of nature in criticism. There are universals in Hume,
but they arise, not *a priori,* but from a consideration of what has
been "found to please in all countries and in all ages." If such
are Hume's assumptions, it is quite inevitable that he should be
found to rely heavily upon that most empirical of all critical
techniques, comparison. He said that "it is impossible to continue
in the practice of contemplating any order of beauty, without
being frequently obliged to form *comparisons.* . . . By comparison alone we fix the epithets of praise or blame, and learn how
to assign the due degree to each." Comparison arises from a
broadening experience with all kinds of literature, and, as the
earlier passage from Hume suggested, leads to certainty in matters
of taste when it is universal and collective rather than individual
and local. [16]

Both the assumptions and the technique of Hume are eminently

Johnsonian — a fact which need not be obscured by Johnson's unrelenting opposition to the philosopher's skepticism about religion and about moral absolutes or even by the resentment that he almost certainly would have felt had he known that his name was to be linked with Hume's in any connection, even that of literary criticism. Johnson, as we observed in the first chapter, relied whenever he could upon experience and empirical investigation; he therefore relegated reason to an inferior role and considered the memory (the organ of treasuring experience) to be the primary faculty which distinguished human nature. Hume's emphasis upon experience, upon comparison, and upon what is found to please universally is the emphasis of Johnson, who was always skeptical about Rapin's "Necessary, Rational, and Universal Rules." The technique of literary comparison was especially congenial to Johnson, who frequently wielded this critical weapon and who made it the only satisfactory means of determining whether a work of art had attained the stature of a classic. That famous passage on the *consensus gentium*, which introduces the *Preface to Shakespeare*, is an empirical affirmation. Comparison is conceived of as a kind of trial and error conducted over a long period of time by all sorts and conditions of men.

"To works, however, of which the excellence is not absolute and definite, but *gradual* and *comparative*; to works not raised upon principles demonstrative and scientifick, but appealing wholly to *observation* and *experience*, no other test can be applied than length of duration and continuance of esteem. What mankind have long possessed they have often *examined and compared*; and if they persist to value the possession, it is because frequent *comparisons* have confirmed opinion in its favour. As among the works of nature no man can properly call a river deep, or a mountain high, without the knowledge of many mountains, and many rivers; so in the productions of genius, nothing can be stiled excellent till it has been compared with other works of the same kind. Demonstration immediately displays its power, and has nothing to hope or fear from the flux of years; but works *tentative* and *experimental* must be estimated by their proportion to the general and collective ability of man, as it is discovered in a *long succession of endeavours*." [17]

The critic, however, cannot always await the determinations of long-run experience. The mind must sometimes "find the nearest way from truth to truth, or from purpose to effect." [18] But when it is forced to move in the more rapid manner of deduction rather than in the slower manner of induction, it will do so by making only those assumptions that are self-evident and fully acceptable to common sense. The application of this fundamental principle to literary criticism appears nowhere more clearly than in Johnson's discussion of the dramatic unities. In his first extended analysis of the unities, in *Rambler* no. 156, he invokes the law of nature and reason and decides to accept only those rules that conform to "the laws of nature" or to the "order of nature and operations of the intellect." From the language used, one might perhaps expect to find here a full-blown statement of a rational literary ideal or some absolute canon of criticism revealed by Rapin's light of nature. But what one actually encounters is common-sense reasoning based upon what a play actually is and upon what playgoers are really like — determinations self-evident to anyone with any experience at all of dramatic art.

Johnson finds the unity of action to be "more fixed and obligatory" than the unities of time and place. Why? Simply because "it is necessary that of every play the chief action should be single; for since a play represents some transaction, through its regular maturation to its final event, two actions equally important must evidently constitute two plays." [19] The key words are *necessary* and *evidently*. The somewhat grandiose appeal to universal nature, which is prominent in the earlier discussion of the unities just cited but which has disappeared from the closely parallel discussion of the same topic fourteen years later in the *Preface to Shakespeare*, is in reality only an invitation to use a rather plain and unsophisticated variety of common sense.

In such manner as this Johnson usually admitted the claims of reason in literary criticism. It would of course be impossible and fruitless to attempt to measure for each critical decision the proportions of reason and experience that went into making it. "To these meditations," he might well have said, in words that he once applied to the hapless Soame Jenyns's cosmology, "humanity is unequal." [20] In our own day there is little agreement about the exact nature of the mental operation present in a much more objective field, that of scientific research. In spite of the amount of rigorous thought devoted to the philosophy of such investigation during the last three centuries — to the roles of observed fact and of mathematical hypothesis — Alfred North Whitehead was forced to conclude that "the theory of induction is the despair of philosophy." [21] Nevertheless, the fact remains that there are unmistakable differences between a rationally and an empirically centered criticism. In Johnson, if the analysis presented thus far has been sound, it is the latter that predominates.

III

Let us now consider those obviously related but distinct orientations which have always been present in criticism and which were especially prominent in the eighteenth century, even though few writers may have been fully conscious of them. I refer to the consequences that arise from giving attention primarily to one of the following: (1) the art itself considered either abstractly and generally or in one of its several genres; (2) the specific work of art; (3) the writer; and (4) the audience. One can detect all these focuses of critical attention in Johnson, sometimes within the compass of a single paragraph. This is no more than one would expect, since for him the art of poetry was not very far removed from the art of persuasion, and since it was Aristotle's *Rhetoric* [22] which made clear to Western thought that the character of the speaker, the emotions of the hearer, and the logic of the speech itself were all modes of persuasion.

With these categories in mind, let us examine the three paragraphs that Johnson devoted to a criticism of Congreve's *The Old Bachelor*. In the first he is concerned with the requirements of a literary genre, "the lighter species of dramatick poetry." In the second he examines the work itself but soon shifts his attention to the writer and his qualifications — a shift anticipated in the first paragraph. In the third he makes his final evaluation, not on the basis of the generic requirements with which the analysis began but on the basis of communication between author and audience.

"Such a comedy written at such an age requires some consideration. As the lighter species of dramatick poetry professes the imitation of common life, of real manners, and daily incidents, it apparently presupposes a familiar knowledge of many characters and exact observation of the passing world; the difficulty therefore is to conceive how this knowledge can be obtained by a boy.

"But if *The Old Batchelor* be more nearly examined, it will be found to be one of those comedies which may be made by a mind vigorous and acute, and furnished with comick characters by the perusal of other poets, without much actual commerce with mankind. The dialogue is one constant reciprocation of conceits, or clash of wit, in which nothing flows necessarily from the occasion, or is dictated by nature. The characters, both of men and women, are either fictitious and artificial, as those of Heartwell and the Ladies; or easy and common, as Wittol a tame idiot, Bluff a swaggering coward, and Fondlewife a jealous puritan; and the catastrophe arises from a mistake not very probably produced, by marrying a woman in a mask.

"Yet this gay comedy, when all these deductions are made, will still remain the work of very powerful and fertile faculties; the dialogue is quick and sparkling, the incidents such as seize the attention, and the wit so exuberant that it 'o'er-informs its tenement'." [23]

Although in this passage Johnson sets out to examine a play, how very little is said about *The Old Bachelor* itself that is not related in some way to a frame of reference outside the play — to the author's faculties, to what he knew of real life and of other dramas, to what is "dictated by nature" or outside reality, and to what "seizes the attention" of the reader. All this is most typical and may be illuminated by considering more closely (1) Johnson's generic criticism (somewhat apparent in the first paragraph on Congreve's play), the criticism that studies the work as an illustration of a general literary type or kind; and (2) his psychological criticism (apparent in the last paragraph), the criticism which has shifted the emphasis from the work itself and from the tradition it seeks to embody to its psychological effects upon the reader. The work of art in relation to its author and in relation to truth and reality will be discussed in subsequent chapters.

Traces of the generic method appear everywhere in Johnson's criticism. He is careful to draw the Aristotelian distinction between the epic, which comprises "narration, not acted, but rehearsed," and the drama, "in which the action is not related but represented; and in which therefore such rules are to be observed as make the representation probable." He carefully distinguishes comedy from farce, in the manner of Congreve, Fielding, and Hogarth. He is also concerned that "proper satire [be] distinguished, by the generality of the reflections, from a *lampoon*, which is aimed against a particular person." He devoted some attention to defining and to determining exactly what rules are applicable to each of the following: local descriptive poetry, macaronic verse, fables, easy poetry, the exordial verses of epics. He once attempted to state the rules for expressing sentiments in verse. He devoted one essay to letters and the epistolary style and devoted two to a discussion of pastorals. In his early "Essay on Epitaphs" he set himself "to examine . . . in what the perfection of epitaphs consists." Although he is best known in his rejection of the unities of time and place, he sometimes censured Shakespeare for having violated them. Unlike Aristotle but like most of the critics of the Italian Renaissance and of the French Enlightenment, he found the epic to be the loftiest literary expression of human genius. He often divided even his important essays into a consideration first of beauties and then of faults, and *Paradise Lost* he examined under the traditional heads of fable, sentiments, manners, and language — an outline used with wearisome iteration by almost every critic of the period, including Parson Abraham Adams.[24]

But if anything is clear about these attempts at generic criticism, it is that Johnson's heart was not in them. Anyone who examines fully the passages just referred to cannot, I think, escape the feeling that he was seldom making more than a conventional gesture. In the *Essay on Epitaphs*, for example, he says: "To examine, therefore, in what the perfection of epitaphs consists, and what rules are to be observed in composing them, will be, at least, of as much use as other critical inquiries; and for assigning a few hours to such disquisitions, great examples, at least, if not strong reasons, may be pleaded." He dismissed as purely conventional and academic Dryden's opinion that Adam was unheroic because he met an unfortunate end: "There is no reason why the hero should not be unfortunate except established practice, since success and virtue do not go necessarily together." But then Johnson salutes the convention: "However, if success be necessary, Adam's deceiver was at last crushed; Adam was restored to his Maker's favour, and therefore may securely resume his human rank." This is surely to treat venerable matters with the utmost casualness.[25]

IV

The reason for Johnson's dissatisfaction with generic criticism, which appears everywhere, not least when he is employing its methods, lies deep and is not to be sought in a pettish refusal to accept critical authority or in weariness with the sheer weight of the tradition. It lies rather in his deep-seated skepticism (somewhat surprising in a dictionary-maker) about the validity of literary definition, the very heart and core of generic criticism. In the statements which follow he cuts the ground from under the type of criticism that rests its claim on its ability to define, to isolate, to locate, and to distinguish aesthetic genres. To Boswell's demand, "Then, Sir, what is poetry?" Johnson replied, "Why, Sir, it is much easier to say what it is not. We all *know* what light is; but it is not easy to *tell* what it is." Some twenty-five years before this comment, which Johnson uttered in April 1776, he had said:

"Definition is, indeed, not the province of man; every thing is set above or below our faculties. The works and operations of nature are too great in their extent, or too much diffused in their relations, and the performances of art too inconstant and uncertain, to be reduced to any determinate idea. . . . Definitions have been no less difficult or uncertain in criticisms than in law. Imagination . . . has always endeavoured to baffle the logician, to perplex the confines of distinction, and burst the inclosures of regularity. There is therefore scarcely any species of writing, of which we can tell what is its essence, and what are its constituents; every new genius produces some innovation, which, when invented and approved, subverts the rules which the practice of foregoing authors had established." [26]

This points, I think, to the very heart of Johnson's dilemma as a generic critic and accounts for the conventional, half-hearted, and undistinguished way in which he practiced what he referred to as "mechanical" criticism. Its sterility, in his hands at least, forced him to turn to other areas of investigation in which the principle that criticism was an intellectual discipline that should "improve opinion into knowledge" could remain intact. "Comedy has been particularly unpropitious to definers. . . . If the two kinds of dramatick poetry had been defined only by their effects upon the mind, some absurdities might have been prevented, with which the compositions of our greatest poets are disgraced . . ." [27]

The suggestion made here, that literary forms be defined "by their effects upon the mind," points to a critical approach which Hobbes had adumbrated and which I. A. Richards has made central to his system. But Johnson surely found criticism of this sort congenial for reasons that may well seem completely unscientific and unpsychological to members of this school. For him to turn to the mind of man and its responses was in no way to abandon himself to individualism or to relativism, both of which he regarded as mischievous. The constitution of the mind was for Johnson as immutable and universal as nature itself, with which it was often associated. Books that have endured have proved themselves "adequate to our *faculties*, and agreeable to *nature*"; "the province of poetry is to describe *nature* and *passion*, which are always the same"; Dryden's general precepts depend upon "the *nature of things* and the *structure of the human mind*"; some literary rules are to be retained because of their conformity to the "order of *nature* and operations of the *intellect.*" [28] In such phrases as these Johnson lays a foundation for psychological criticism in the unchanging order of nature and provides for criticism materials that are almost as amenable to investigation as the natural laws of physical science.

In what is perhaps the most revealing passage in Boswell's *Life* about the theory of criticism, Johnson praises Du Bos and Bouhours for having shown that all beauty depends upon truth. He then makes it clear that the truth he had in mind was not at all the "sixth sense" of Du Bos or the aesthetic "truth" of Plotinus and Keats, but was merely psychological truth about man's response to art. "There is no great merit in telling how many plays have ghosts in them, and how this ghost is better than that. You must shew how terrour is impressed on the human heart." [29] In the same context he praised Burke's essay on the sublime and the beautiful as "an example of true criticism" — a work which, as its very title suggests, inquires into "the origin of our ideas" of these qualities and which, as Burke himself says, is built upon "a more extensive and perfect induction" and upon that type of investigation which, "not content with serving up a few barren and lifeless truths," leads "to the stock on which they grew." [30] Burke's method is to study, not the qualities resident in a work of art per se, but the emotional responses that they evoke.

Johnson persistently demanded a scientific and dialectical criticism, which would reduce the flux and change of literature to principles upon which sound judgment could be based. And yet he found unsatisfactory the tradition of codified rules which he had inherited, which within limits he drew upon, but which never brought him the certainty and success that he was seeking. He was too much aware that literature, produced in part by that "licentious and vagrant faculty," the imagination, was material too intractable for the codified rules of the rationalists. He would never have subscribed to James Beattie's comment that "poetry is a thing perfectly rational and regular; and nothing can be more strictly philosophical, than that part of criticism may and ought to be, which unfolds the general characters that distinguish it from other kinds of composition." [31] Beattie is here recommending that generic criticism which Johnson found to be ineffectual. But he did not turn, as did many of his contemporaries, from the intellect to the subrational powers of the mind or to any kind of capricious dilettantism. If investigation of literary art and its genres and of the work itself as an embodiment of literary type proved nugatory, there still remained other areas: the outside truth and reality which the work attempted to represent and by which it could be tested, the mind of the author that produced it, and the emotions that it evoked. And in each case Johnson was able to subsume such data under those empirical-rational realities about which he felt the highest degree of certainty.

It was perhaps inevitable that Johnson's attention should have turned away from the work of art itself and from the general aesthetic laws which it was supposed to illustrate. A poem seemed to him to possess no independent, autonomous existence. It was in no sense a Neoplatonic thing, a particular that occupied a place in an ever ascending hierarchy of spiritual reality. Nor was it an Aristotelian thing with a genus and an assortment of differentiae. It was for Johnson a moral and psychological instrument of communication that pointed outside itself to the empirical reality which it "imitated," to the mind that had created it, or to the mind that was to enjoy it and be instructed by it. It is perhaps for this reason (and not for the reason that he was following the Horatian tradition of the *dulce* and the *utile*) that most of Johnson's definitions of poetry are couched in the language of psychology, of education, and of communication: the business of the poet is to "move . . . with delight or terrour"; "the end of writing is to instruct; the end of poetry is to instruct by pleasing"; every author undertakes either "to instruct or please, or to mingle pleasure with instruction"; "poetry is the art of uniting pleasure with truth, by calling imagination to the help of reason." [32]

CHAPTER III

Literature and the Author

THERE is no occasion on which Dr. Johnson praised another's criticism more enthusiastically than he did in commenting on Dryden's "character" of Shakespeare, which appears in *An Essay of Dramatic Poesy*. He found all the portraits of the English dramatists in that opulent and lively treatise to have been "wrought with great spirit and diligence," but it is that of Shakespeare, only one short paragraph in length, which evoked his highest praise.

"The account of Shakespeare may stand as a perpetual model of encomiastick criticism; exact without minuteness, and lofty without exaggeration. The praise lavished by Longinus, on the attestation of the heroes of Marathon by Demosthenes, fades away before it. In a few lines is exhibited a character, so extensive in its comprehension and so curious in its limitations, that nothing can be added, diminished, or reformed; nor can the editors and admirers of Shakespeare, in all their emulation of reverence, boast of much more than of having diffused and paraphrased this epitome of excellence, of having changed Dryden's gold for baser metal, of lower value though of greater bulk." [1]

Johnson's praise is not only eloquent. It is also a brief general description of this type of criticism, known in the period as the "character" of an author.

Johnson himself practiced extensively and skillfully what he praised Dryden for doing. Brief literary characters appear everywhere in his criticism: Imlac's character of the poet in the tenth chapter of *Rasselas*; the description of Pope's intellectual character in a long section of the life of that poet which divides the purely biographical from the purely critical portions; the antithetically presented evaluations of Dryden and Pope; and that lofty and dignified account of Milton's genius which possesses, if anything of Johnson's does, the "grandeur of generality."

Such literary characters as these are to be distinguished carefully from biography itself, to which they are of course related. They are, one would suppose, a manifestation of the desire, prominent in Johnson and in the biographical age in which he lived, to follow the ancient Egyptian custom of solemnly canvassing the characters of the dead in order to "regulate what was due to their memory." [2] But a literary character of the kind with which we are here concerned is not a factual account of the life and deeds of the author. It is a summary of subjective qualities of mind and heart, but only of those relevant to the literary qualifications of the author. William Lisle Bowles wrote what he entitled "General Observations on the Character of Pope," which summarized and evaluated the poet's personal and moral qualities; but Bowles clearly separated and distinguished that "moral character" from the "poetical character" of Pope. [3]

In Johnson the two must also be distinguished. He wrote both kinds, but they are not actually coterminous. Although he was perhaps morally the sternest of all great English critics and although ethical values are consulted always, yet he does not confound them with aesthetic considerations. Nor is he often found to express — perhaps because he did not always find it to be actually true, however much he may have wanted it to be — that favorite idea of Renaissance criticism, the "impossibility," in Ben Jonson's language, "of any mans being the good *Poët*, without first being a good *Man*." [4] Boswell notes that Johnson "allowed high praise to Thomson as a poet; but when one of the company said he was also a very good man, our moralist contested this with great warmth, accusing him of gross sensuality and licentiousness of manners." Johnson usually avoided praising what seemed to him a morally unacceptable piece of literature, but he did manage pretty well to separate strictly aesthetic from strictly moral and religious considerations. "With the philosophical or religious tenets of the author I have nothing to do; my business is with his poetry." [5] Neither Johnson nor his contemporaries confused the moral with the literary personality of the author, however dependent one may have seemed to be upon the other.

The character of the author in criticism is genetically related to those portraits that appear everywhere in the pages of both ancient and seventeenth-century historians. But classical portraits, like Pausanias's character of Hesiod or Lucretius's Empedocles, and seventeenth-century portraits, like Arthur Wilson's Bacon, Clarendon's Waller, and even Cowley's Cowley, are, however brief, usually intended to be portraits of the whole man, not solely of those characteristics most relevant to aesthetic evaluation. The specifically literary characters of Dryden and Johnson are adaptations to the purposes of critical evaluation of the earlier and more comprehensive characters of Theophrastus, Overbury, and Earle and those of Tacitus, Clarendon, and Burnet. [6] Both the Theophrastian character, the description of a general type, and the portrait of a particular individual appear in Johnson's criticism. Imlac's character of the poet in *Rasselas* is general – a statement of the ideal qualifications of the *poeta*. There are also the characters of particular poets, among which one of the fullest and best is that of Pope. In one case at least, that of Milton, a particular character is laid alongside and presented as the achieved embodiment of an ideal portrait.

When Eugenius in Dryden's *Essay of Dramatic Poesy* said, "I beseech you, Neander, gratify the company, and me in particular, so far, as before you speak of the play [*The Silent Woman*], to give us a character of the author," he knew, as any literate person of the seventeenth century would have known, exactly what to expect. He would have been dismayed had his friend assumed the worshipful and reverential posture of a romantic contemplating Shakespeare; and he would have been bored had Neander, in the manner of countless critics of the Renaissance, merely praised poets as "the first raysors of cities, prescribers of good lawes, mayntayners of religion, disturbors of the wicked, aduancers of the wel disposed, inuentors of laws, and lastly the very fot-paths to knowledge and vnderstanding." [7] But he was fully gratified when his companion presented a series of brilliantly expressed but coolly judicious summaries of the distinguishing characteristics of each of these dramatists — considered not in any one of his works but in the distinctive totality of his entire achievement. The author thus displayed was in no sense the historical man. "Shakespeare" refers not to the man of Stratford at all but to those qualities of mind and of literary excellence that appear prominently and consistently in his works and that distinguish him from others. The portrait is a general summary, intended to fulfill the aim of all summaries and to facilitate the evaluation of the author and the determination of his position in the literary hierarchy. The purpose is thus a fairly comprehensive one. The character of the author might either be encomiastic or censorious and might conceivably be concerned with everything that ought to be said about the poet's work and about his characteristic excellence.

> Know well each ancient's proper character;
> His fable, subject, scope in every page;
> Religion, country, genius of his age:
> Without all these at once before your eyes,
> Cavil you may, but never criticise. [8]

In drawing characters in his criticism Johnson likewise aimed to achieve judicious summary, useful in literary comparison and evaluation. His character of the poet is not unlike his "character" of a particular Shakespearean play or his "character" of a particular Shakespearean personage. There is this significant difference, however: the character of the poet does tend to look away from the literary work to the author, to his mind and his endowment. It therefore suggests important implications, which we shall now explore, about the relations between an author and his work and about the nature of genius.

The surprisingly frequent occasions upon which Johnson throws the critical emphasis back upon the author seem to imply that the canons of formal criticism are not adequate to account for literary effects and that it is the genius of the author, and not his work or the genre within which he has written, that ought to be applauded and set up as bearing the force and validity of instructive example. Some years before he wrote the *Preface to Shakespeare*, Johnson in *Rambler* no. 156 had accepted tragicomedy on the familiar and characteristic grounds of experience. "Is it not certain that the tragick and comick affections have been moved alternately with equal force and that no plays have oftener filled the eye with tears, and the breast with palpitation, than those which are variegated with interludes of mirth?" But Johnson does not wish approval of tragicomedy to establish the genre for all time to come. As he was fully aware, that had happened all too often. One successful play or type of play could establish a norm, and, by the very veneration which it aroused and by the prescriptive authority which its example seemed to justify, could easily discourage originality and experimentation. In order to obviate, if possible, the stifling tyrannies of generic criticism, Johnson preferred to credit the mind of the author and not the genre with the power of evoking response:

"I do not however think it safe to judge of works of genius merely by the event [emotional responses to one play or to one particular kind of play, like the tragicomedy he has been discussing]. The resistless vicissitudes of the heart, this alternate prevalence of merriment and solemnity, may sometimes be more properly ascribed to the vigour of the writer than the justness of the design: and, instead of vindicating tragicomedy by the success of Shakespeare, we ought, perhaps, to pay new honours to that transcendent and unbounded genius that could preside over the passions in sport; who . . . could fill the heart with instantaneous jollity or sorrow, and vary our disposition as he changed his scenes." [9]

But such considerations are practical and arise in part from the critic's sense of obligation toward the Republic of Letters. Contemplation of the author is in and of itself as praiseworthy as it is inevitable and natural: "There is always a silent reference of human works to human abilities, and . . . the enquiry, how far man may extend his designs, or how high he may rate his native force, is of far greater dignity than in what rank we shall place any particular performance . . ." This highly revealing comment is subordinate in the paragraph from which it was drawn to a plea for historical criticism. "Every man's performances, to be rightly estimated, must be compared with the state of the age in which he lived, and with his own particular opportunities; . . . curiosity is always busy to discover the instruments, as well as to survey the workmanship, to know how much is to be ascribed to original powers, and how much to casual and adventitious help." [10] Thus literary research is often based upon a desire to determine the extent of an author's originality. If "the highest praise of genius is original invention" [11] — and no dictum of Johnson is more characteristic than this — it follows that criticism must be silent until it is determined just how original the author was; and that can be discovered only by means of scholarly tools. The *apparatus criticus*, which displays what the author knew, quoted, copied, and echoed, has never been justified on better grounds than these. At least when he wrote his most important critical document, the *Preface to Shakespeare*, from which the sentences quoted in this paragraph have been taken, Johnson considered historical investigation of literature to be "of far greater dignity" than determining the rank of any particular performance.

Johnson firmly believed that a work of art should be viewed as a revelation of the powers of the author. That was by no means his only perspective upon literary performance. He also considered the work as an expression of the reality and nature that the poet had observed and contemplated, and he was profoundly concerned with the psychological effects of the work upon its reader. But the consideration of the performance as evidence of personal endowment is at least of cognate importance with the others.

It fully explains Johnson's stand on two historically important and long-agitated problems of critical evaluation. One of them, the question of which represented the greatest of all literary achievements, the tragedy or the epic, had been widely discussed both in antiquity and in post-Renaissance Europe. In the *Poetics* Aristotle had given the palm to tragedy for several reasons, chief among which were these: that it required less space to achieve its ends and hence produced a less diluted and more highly concentrated form of pleasure, and that it possessed a higher degree of organic unity than did the epic. Johnson decided otherwise, basing his judgment on grounds that were not in the least Aristotelian. "By the general consent of criticks the first praise of genius is due to the writer of an epick poem, as it requires an assemblage of all the powers which are singly sufficient for other compositions."

The debate over the comparative positions of Vergil and Homer had also been an important one of long standing, not least because of the literary values that seemed to be involved. Johnson's preference of Homer to Vergil is significant not so much because it breaks with a powerful neoclassical tradition stemming from the formidable Julius Caesar Scaliger's championship of Vergil as very Nature of very Nature, but because it attempts to shift the grounds of the dispute from comparisons of the epics themselves to a consideration of the authors who produced them. According to Boswell, Johnson said that "the dispute as to the comparative excellence of Homer or Virgil was inaccurate. 'We must consider (said he) whether Homer was not the greatest poet, though Virgil may have produced the finest poem. Virgil was indebted to Homer for the whole invention of the structure of an epick poem, and for many of his beauties.' " [12]

One of the most important consequences of this emphasis in Johnson's criticism is the determined and at times naive way in which he applied the canon of sincerity. He insisted that the artist must feel the emotion that he expressed and that there must be as little as possible in the work itself to interfere with the direct and effectual communication of that emotion. His famous strictures upon pastoral poetry, especially the pastoral elegy, upon much love poetry, and upon lyrical verse in general, should be ascribed less to a dissatisfaction with these as genres and less to a constitutional hostility to all forms of cant than to a critic's desire to maintain intact the literary ideal of emotional communication.

He was inimical to the tradition of Petrarch, who had "filled Europe with love and poetry," because "he that professes love ought to feel its power." The doctrine of simplicity and sincerity, which Johnson always invoked in connection with shorter poems of emotion, forbade artifice and elaboration of any kind. The "Amourous Effusions" of Prior are "the dull exercises of a skilful versifier resolved at all adventures to write something about Chloe, and trying to be amorous by dint of study." *Lycidas*, said Johnson in what is usually regarded as his greatest critical *faux pas*, "is not to be considered as the effusion of real passion; for passion runs not after remote allusions and obscure opinions." "He that courts his mistress with Roman imagery deserves to lose her; for she may with good reason suspect his sincerity." So committed was Johnson to this principle that he consulted the author's biography to determine whether he had actually suffered the pangs he sings about. "Of Cowley we are told by Barnes, who had means enough of information, that, whatever he may talk of his own inflammability and the variety of characters by which his heart was divided, he in reality was in love but once, and then never had resolution to tell his passion. This consideration cannot but abate, in some measure, the reader's esteem for the work and the author." [13]

Nowhere has Johnson more dismayed his nineteenth-century successors and even many in our own day than in his relentless, literal-minded, and unsophisticated application of the doctrine of sincerity. But nowhere was he more the child of his own age. Fielding had done no more than utter a contemporary critical commonplace when he wrote: "The author who will make me weep, says Horace, must first weep himself. In reality, no man can paint a distress well, which he doth not feel while he is painting it; nor do I doubt, but that the most pathetic and affecting scenes have been writ with tears." Dennis, the aesthetician of the passions, had drawn a most typical conclusion about the implications for language when he said that similes are not natural in the language of grief, since the mind, in producing them and other similar adornments, must exercise faculties "utterly inconsistent" with grief, a state in which the soul is confined and the imagination straitened. For similar psychological reasons, Hume had found wit and passion "entirely incompatible." [14]

However much one may be outraged by Johnson's particular application of this principle or even by his original adherence to it, one cannot justly accuse him of inconsistency. For the doctrine of sincerity is, after all, a natural outcome of a psychological theory of poetry which wishes to emphasize and facilitate the communication between the man who creates the poem and the man who reacts to it. It was quite as inevitable that Johnson, Tolstoy, and I. A. Richards, each in his own way, should use the test of sincerity as that T. S. Eliot should reject it. [15]

But Johnson usually applied the theory negatively rather than positively; that is, he used it as an instrument of attack upon Petrarchism, pastoral conventionality, affected archaism of diction and form, and anything that he considered coldly artificial and merely embroidered, but he did not use it to demand an unmodified and unrefined transcription of raw emotion or anything resembling what we think of as self-expression. He said of Pope's *Elegy* that "poetry has not often been worse employed than in dignifying the amorous fury of a raving girl"—a censure that would in no way have been mitigated had the "amorous fury" been Pope's rather than the Unfortunate Lady's. [16] Nor was Johnson guilty of what has been called the personal heresy. He did not expect a poet to hold a mirror up to the events of his own life or to the variegations of his own taste, nor did he examine poetry in order to reconstruct the poet's biography or to psychoanalyze his personality. Anticipations of such modern doctrine were not unknown in Johnson's day, an age that liked to preserve and to contemplate itself in diaries and letters, novels and memoirs. But Johnson himself remained incredulous about the validity of reading a man's life and personal character or habits out of his poems:

"The biographer of Thomson has remarked that an author's life is best read in his works: his observation was not well-timed. Savage, who lived much with Thomson, once told me how he heard a lady remarking that she could gather from his works three parts of his character, that he was 'a great lover, a great swimmer, and rigorously abstinent'; but, said Savage, he knows not any love but that of the sex; he was perhaps never in cold water in his life; and he indulges himself in all the luxury that comes within his reach." [17]

Is Johnson inconsistent in believing that art is communication and ought to be sincere, and at the same time opposing the interpretation of art as self-revelation or self-expression? I think that he is not. The difference between Johnson and any exponent of literature as self-expression lies not in the fact that one accepts and the other does not accept the view that literature is communication. It lies rather in the nature of the thing communicated and in the nature of the act of communicative expression itself. For Johnson the thing to be communicated was not emotion in all the flux and flurry of its original presence in the human soul. It is never a stream of consciousness. It is emotion selected and generalized into the simple universals that move all men everywhere. To generalize an emotion was not, as the romantics tended to believe, to evaporate it but rather to make it available. To fictionalize it excessively, however, to complicate it into "metaphysical" analysis, or to overlay it with classical allusions and an outmoded mythology was, in Johnson's view, effectually and irremediably to smother it.

II

In Boswell's record of his journey to the Hebrides with Johnson there is an entry for August 15, 1773, that may well serve to introduce Johnson's conception of genius. Upon the arrival of Dr. William Robertson after dinner the conversation, which then turned to the mental powers of Edmund Burke, became animated. Johnson said "he could not understand how a man could apply to one thing, and not to another. Robertson said one man had more judgment, another more imagination. JOHNSON. 'No, sir; it is only one man has more mind than another. He may direct it differently; he may by accident see the success of one kind of study and take a desire to excel in it. I am persuaded that had Sir Isaac Newton applied to poetry, he would have made a very fine epic poem. I could as easily apply to law as to tragic poetry.' BOSWELL. 'Yet, sir, you *did* apply to tragic poetry, not to law.' JOHNSON. 'Because, sir, I had not money to study law. Sir, the man who has vigour, may walk to the east just as well as to the west, if he happens to turn his head that way.' " [18]

In this lively interchange of opinion Johnson denies any special position to literature and removes from it the mystification that has often surrounded it. He relates it to the law, to mathematics, and to other coordinate disciplines. The assumption is that literature, like the other fields, is an austere and rigorous mental pursuit. But the passage also expresses a kind of dynamism. Excellence depends upon vigor of mind, and upon the total cooperation of all the faculties of the mind—a conception that transcends the conventional distinctions Robertson had introduced between the imagination and the judgment; and the particular expression of genius depends upon a kind of accidentally determined application to one type of study rather than to another.

The last idea seems almost to have been an obsession with Johnson. "The true Genius is a mind of large general powers, *accidentally determined to some particular direction.*" Cowley became "irrecoverably a poet" by reading Spenser's *Faerie Queene*, which lay, quite by accident, in the window of his mother's room, and Reynolds's love of art was first excited by reading Jonathan Richardson's treatise on painting. "Such are the accidents which, sometimes remembered, and perhaps sometimes forgotten, produce that particular designation of mind and propensity for some certain science or employment, which is commonly called Genius." [19]

What was Johnson getting at in his frequent reiteration of this notion? He apparently meant to emphasize this point, that the particular expression of genius is never in any way a description of its nature and essence. One cannot conclude from achievement in mathematics that the mind that produces such achievement is a mathematical genius. "No, sir; it is only one man has more mind than another." "The true Genius is a mind of large *general powers* . . ." In such comments as these and in others which will be cited presently Johnson seems seriously to qualify the traditional faculty psychology and the kind of criticism that had depended upon it. Such psychology and such criticism had tended to separate rigidly the mental faculties, partly in order to understand them better and partly in order to give sanction to the judgment which would moderate the excesses to which other faculties were all too prone.

Although Johnson often drew the conventional distinctions between invention, wit, natural genius, and imagination on the one hand, and judgment, reason, restraint, and artifice on the other, he more often tends to unite them in the larger conception of genius, in which all the mental powers work together to produce excellence. He therefore found it "ridiculous to oppose judgment to imagination; for it does not appear that men have necessarily less of one as they have more of the other." He pours scorn upon Dick Minim's cant that "a perfect writer is not to be expected, because genius decays as judgment increases." Pope is a great poet because he "had, in proportions very nicely adjusted to each other, all the qualities that constitute genius" — invention, imagination, judgment, and powers of language.[20]

These are but a few examples of what was a prominent and always a vigorously expressed idea in Johnson's criticism. It attacks any attempt to effect an artificial separation of the faculties, whether to exalt the judgment at the expense of the imagination, as in the older neoclassical school, or to exalt the inventive imagination at the expense of reason, as in the newer school of Young, Hurd, the Wartons, and of Blake. Johnson believed in the integrity of the mind and in the idea that excellence was achieved only by a dynamic and vigorous cooperation of all the faculties.[21]

Johnson once described poetical genius as "that energy which collects, combines, amplifies, and animates."[22] The word *energy* and its synonyms — *force*, *vigour*, *life*, and *spirit* — he regularly used to express that operation of the whole mind and all its faculties which we have been describing. In the Dictionary Johnson defines *spirit* as "Genius; vigour of mind," and *vigour* as "Mental force; intellectual ability." These are, of course, not the only definitions given, but they are the ones relevant to our present consideration. Johnson used the words thus defined again and again, not usually of any one faculty but of several faculties indiscriminately and, more typically, of the mind as a whole. He implied once that the impulse of genius is being "invigorated with stronger comprehension." Addison, who thinks justly but faintly, writes poetry that is "the product of a mind too judicious to commit faults, but not sufficiently vigourous to attain excellence." Pope's judgment "often makes the representation more powerful than the reality." Scientific projects are often the product of minds "heated with the intenseness of thought." [23]

The terms of criticism which we have been discussing may become clearer if we look more closely at one of them, the word *energy*. The only meaning of that word relevant to literary criticism Johnson expresses as follows in his Dictionary: "Strength of expression; force of signification; spirit; life." That definition indicates that he not only stood in a long critical tradition stemming from classical times, but also felt it necessary to extend the use of the term beyond the limits imposed upon it by ancient and Renaissance critics and rhetoricians. The first phrase of the definition, "strength of expression," conveys the meaning of *energy* most common in ancient thought. Liddell and Scott define ἐνέργεια in its rhetorical signification as meaning no more than "vigour of style." Aristotle uses the word to refer to the ability to convey actuality in language, or, more specifically, to that particular kind of metaphor which evokes a mental picture of something "acting" or moving. Quintilian uses the word, without translating it into Latin, as a component of that force, or *vis*, which is present in all effective speech. For him the word connotes action, and the presence of the quality itself assures us that nothing we say is flat or tame: "et cuius propria sit virtus non esse, quae dicuntur, otiosa." Thus by both Aristotle and Quintilian, ἐνέργεια is used to describe a particular stylistic quality which is forceful because it succeeds in communicating the active, the living, the moving in all the "energy" of its original actuality.[24]

The second phrase of Johnson's definition of *energy*, "force of signification," includes more than style, and sanctions the use of the word for a comparable quality in the thought that lies behind the stylistic expression. Julius Caesar Scaliger had similarly extended the classical meaning: "Efficaciam Graeci ἐνέργειαν vocant. Ea est vis orationis repraesentantis rem excellenti modo. Intelligo nunc non verborum virtutem, sed Idæarum, quae rerum species sunt. Nam tametsi in verbis esse videtur: tamen in rebus ipsis est primò." Puttenham, going even farther than Scaliger, had confined the use of ἐνέργεια to the *meaning* of words — to the "certaine intendments or sence of such wordes & speaches inwardly working a stirre to the mynde" or to such ideas as "wrought with a strong and vertuous operation." [25]

But Johnson's definition goes beyond either Aristotle and Quintilian, on the one hand, or Scaliger and Puttenham, on the other. It makes *energy* also synonymous with "spirit" and "life," which, as we have seen, are primarily qualities of the mind. This meaning the Oxford English Dictionary recognizes in its third definition of *energy*: "vigour or intensity of action, utterance, etc. Hence as a personal quality: The capacity and habit of strenuous exertion." This is perhaps the most radical extension of meaning (outside scientific contexts) that this word has undergone in its long and complicated history. It can now refer to personal qualities or to an artistic effect resulting from personal qualities. For this particular meaning, the first example given by the Oxford Dictionary comes from Coleridge. But this is surely too late, for Johnson (and there must have been many others) consistently used *energy* to describe the operation of imaginative genius — its power to animate and amplify knowledge and experience, which would otherwise remain inert and unattractive.

Such language in and of itself may not do much to illuminate

Johnson's criticism. But in his tributes to mental energy and vigor, he assures his reader that he admired the *mens divinior* and recognized that there was a grace beyond the reach of mechanical criticism. And that fact must be weighed in any final evaluation of Johnson. He saluted those "felicities which cannot be produced at will by wit and labour, but must arise unexpectedly in some hour propitious to poetry." [26] Although that may have been the concession of a man prevailingly rational and empirical, it is nevertheless made gladly.

In this discussion of Johnson's conception of genius, I have not wished to claim that he approved of the *furor poeticus* or of any kind of wild, irregular, titanic, and primitive genius. He might not have conceded that such men exist outside of Bedlam, and if they did he would certainly not have found them capable of any kind of excellence. On one occasion, in the year 1775, when Johnson was sixty-six years of age, he said to Boswell, "Sir, as a man advances in life, he gets what is better than admiration — judgment, to estimate things at their true value." Boswell remained unconvinced and insisted that "admiration was more pleasing than judgment, as love is more pleasing than friendship. The feeling of friendship is like that of being comfortably filled with roast beef; love, like being enlivened with champagne." Could anything be more typical of Boswell? And could anything be more typical of Johnson than his reply? "No, Sir; admiration and love are like being intoxicated with champagne; judgment and friendship like being enlivened." [27]

No one can understand Johnson's criticism, especially what he had to say about poetic genius, who fails to see that he cherished in others that *vivida vis animi* which is so unmistakably present in him. He probably never asked himself where fancy is bred, but he doubtless would have placed in the head what others have placed in heart, blood, bowels, and reins. He considered a mind stimulated to poetical production a mind energized and invigorated with all its faculties operative — "a mind active, ambitious, and adventurous, always investigating, always aspiring; in its widest searches still longing to go forward, in its highest flights still wishing to be higher; always imagining something greater than it knows, always endeavouring more than it can do." [28] I find it remarkable that Johnson wrote that sentence, but it is perhaps even more remarkable that it was written about Alexander Pope.

III

If the sentence just quoted about the mind of Pope is no more than a stroke of fine rhetoric, the definition of genius, cited earlier, as "that energy which collects, combines, amplifies, and animates," does illuminate the relationship between mental power and antecedent experience and makes relevant to a consideration of Johnson's conception of genius everything that was said in the first chapter about the primacy of experience and knowledge in the achievement of intellectual certainty and excellence. All of the verbs in this elucidation of genius (except perhaps *animates*) point directly to the materials of life and outside experience without which the mind gropes uncertainly in the dark and without which it can exercise none of its powers. Although he did say of Goldsmith, whom he admired, that his genius was great but his knowledge was small, it requires no profound knowledge of Johnson to realize that he was not fully satisfied with that state of affairs. He was much more enthusiastic when he found, as he did in Shakespeare, that genius was combined with both judgment and knowledge.

Thus it was very high praise indeed for Johnson to have said of Dryden's compositions that they are "the effects of a vigorous genius operating upon large materials," since that comment brings together those two aspects of mental achievement that are both indispensable, faculties of the highest power and the materials from life and experience. "It is the proper ambition of the heroes in literature to enlarge the boundaries of knowledge by discovering and conquering new regions of the intellectual world." [29]

One of the most striking features of Johnson's frequently repeated character of the poet is the prominence he gives to the empirical faculty and to knowledge. He often insists that the mind of the poet must be stocked with fresh and immediate observations of nature and men. Baconian philosophy and Lockean psychology provided him with a new touchstone for determining the rank of a poet: has he, like the natural philosopher, collected accurate and extensive data? has he exercised the empirical faculty in gathering from abroad? have the senses stocked the mind with fresh and original impressions of reality? As Imlac says, "No kind of knowledge [is] to be overlooked by the poet": mountains, deserts, forests, flowers, crags, pinnacles, rivulets, summer clouds, plants, animals, minerals, and meteors, as well as men, manners, and books, must all "concur to store his mind with inexhaustible variety."

It was, of course, no new thing for a critic to require that a poet be learned. The Italian humanists, the French classicists, and Ben Jonson, Sidney, Milton, Dryden, and Dennis had urged that he be the master of all virtues and of all systems of thought. But if one compares Ben Jonson's character of the poet with Samuel Johnson's, one finds that, although both stress the importance of humanistic knowledge of the minds and actions of men, the earlier critic emphasizes the written tradition, oratory, and civil prudence, whereas the later critic emphasizes sense-observation, firsthand investigations of nature, and travel. Of such empirical search, Ben Jonson says nothing. Samuel Johnson had inherited the traditions of the scientific revolution initiated by Bacon and the psychological revolution initiated by Hobbes and Locke and applied them to literature.[30]

No discussion of Johnson on genius would be complete or accurate without making clear this important point, which should always be considered in connection with everything that Johnson said about the *mens divinior* and the noble and aspiring mind of the poet. The quest of Johnson's poet (how unlike the Neoplatonic quest of, say, Shelley's Alastor!) is a quest for impressions of and information about nature and life. Johnson is always preoccupied with the poet's mental stores and with how the shelves of the mind are stocked. The mind of the poet, like any other mind, can make use only of what has already been supplied. If he awaits the power of nature or the stirrings of inner genius apart from experience, he waits in vain, for "the power of nature is only the power of using to any certain purpose the materials which diligence procures, or opportunity supplies. Nature gives no man knowledge, and when images are collected by study and experience, can only assist in combining or applying them. *Shakespeare*, however favoured by nature, could impart only what he had learned . . ."[31]

That comment on what was then the more than century-old controversy concerning the learning of Shakespeare, which had arisen from Ben Jonson's comment that the bard had "small Latin and less Greek," is doubly significant in view of the fact that Johnson had accepted Richard Farmer's conclusions that Shakespeare's "*Studies* were most demonstratively confined to Nature and his own *Language*": "Dr. Farmer," said Johnson, "you have done that which was never done before; that is, you have completely finished a controversy beyond all further doubt."[32]

But if the controversy about the nature and extent of Shakespeare's learning had itself been completely finished, it was still important for Johnson to resist any attempt to make the classically unlearned bard a natural seer or a rude, unlettered prophet, through whom inspiration, if not learning, flowed as through a vessel. Farmer's conclusions might well have been grist for Edward Young's mill, for Young had said what it was becoming fashionable to believe, that "to neglect of learning, genius sometimes owes its greater glory."[33] If that were true, Johnson's whole system of empirical rationalism must collapse and the force of his entire critical position evaporate. He therefore had to make it clear that there was no such thing as an intellectual and literary *natura naturans*. "Nature gives no man knowledge. . . . Shakespeare . . . could impart only what he had learned . . ." No statement of Johnson illuminates his conception of the relation of genius to experience more clearly than that.

CHAPTER IV

Nature

WHEN Johnson in one of his best-known sentences praised Shakespeare as "the poet that holds up to his readers a faithful mirrour of manners and of life," he repeated a metaphor that he had used fifteen years before in a context of censure: "If the world be promiscuously described, I cannot see of what use it can be to read the account; or why it may not be as safe to turn the eye immediately upon mankind as upon a mirror which shews all that presents itself without discrimination." [1] In his Dictionary he defined a *mirror* as (1) "A looking-glass; anything which exhibits representations of objects by reflection," and (2) a "pattern; for that on which the eye ought to be fixed; an exemplar; an archetype." These two definitions of *mirror*, like the two usages quoted above, point to two conceptions of literary representation, the kind that tends to be literal and the kind that is produced by selection and generalization in accordance with some regulative ideal or principle. If these meanings are extended to that which is represented — as they have been and legitimately may be — it becomes apparent that nature as the source of art may be viewed under two aspects: nature as life, reality, or particular experience; and nature as some kind of general order.

Both these conceptions, which may seem to be contrary and

antithetical, but are not, I think, contradictory, are accepted as equally valid by Johnson. He may in certain contexts stress one rather than the other, but it will not be found that he is fully satisfied as a critic unless the author has somehow managed to accommodate both. Let us first consider the conception of nature as particular reality.

I

Johnson's Dictionary defines *nature* in its literary sense as "Sentiments or images adapted to nature, or conformable to truth and reality," and *naturalness* as "Conformity to truth and reality; not affectation." These meanings are made more explicit in a comment made in 1756, the year following the first edition of the Dictionary: "What is meant by 'judge of nature' [a phrase in an epitaph by Pope which Johnson is evaluating] is not easy to say. Nature is not the object of human judgment; for it is vain to judge where we cannot alter. If by nature is meant, what is commonly called *nature* by the criticks, a just representation of things really existing and actions really performed, nature cannot be properly opposed to *art*; nature being, in this sense, only the best effect of *art*." [2]

"Things really existing and actions really performed": such a conception of nature is a broad one, including both external and human nature, but it is no broader than human experience, upon which, as we have seen in Chapter I, Johnson founded knowledge, certitude, and all manner of excellence. Richard Hurd perceived that it was exactly this conception of nature which he had to attack in recommending literature which was more imaginative, original, and subjective than what was currently accepted, and which was created in the poet's own world, "where experience has less to do, than consistent imagination": "A poet, they say, must follow *Nature*; and by Nature we are to suppose can only be meant the known and experienced course of affairs in this world." [3]

It should not be surprising that one of Johnson's basic requirements for art is that it be a representation of nature so conceived. What other position would be expected of one whose incredulity, according to Mrs. Thrale, "amounted almost to disease," who warned of "the dangerous prevalence of imagination," who said that "there is no crime more infamous than the violation of truth," who praised those critics who founded beauty upon truth, and who "inculcated upon all his friends the importance of perpetual vigilance against the slightest degrees of falsehood; the effect of which, as Sir Joshua Reynolds observed to me, has been, that all who were of his *school* are distinguished for a love of truth and accuracy, which they would not have possessed in the same degree, if they had not been acquainted with Johnson." [4] Given both his temperament and his empirical epistemology, it was perhaps inevitable that these austere standards of honesty should be applied to belles-lettres and that even the most exalted literature should be scrutinized with a sharp and realistic eye.

Had the truthfulness of poetry been the much debated issue in his time that it had been a century or two earlier, Johnson could not have resolved the question in the manner of Sir John Harrington, who wrote in 1591, "Poets neuer affirming any [ideas] for true, but presenting them to vs as fables and imitations, cannot lye though they would . . ." [5] If poetry ought to be a just (that is, according to his Dictionary, an "exact," "proper," and "accurate") representation of nature (that is, "things really existing and actions really performed"), it follows that a poet *can* lie — profoundly, mischievously, even viciously. It is, in fact, always one of the poet's most besetting temptations to bear false witness. In the Dictionary — and these are not the only occasions on which that monumental work bears the impress of its author's vigorous personality — *fiction* means not only "The act of feigning or inventing," but also "A falsehood, a lye"; a *fable* means not only "a feigned story intended to enforce some moral precept" but also "A vitious or foolish fiction" and "A lye" — a sense made stronger in the fourth edition by Johnson's addition of the angry phrase, "a vicious falsehood"; *romantick* means not only "resembling the tales of romances, wild" and "fanciful, full of wild scenery" but also "improbable, false." The gratuitously redundant and rhetorical quality of some of these definitions points to Johnson's impatience with romantic absurdities, puerile enchantments, and outmoded pagan mythology and to his acceptance of the law of literary probability.

Johnson's acceptance of this literary doctrine is so well known and so clearly expressed and the examples of it are so voluminous that it is unnecessary to develop it at length. It is an important and logical consequence of his adherence to reality, which always provides presumptive evidence against the supernatural and the remote; against, indeed, almost anything that is not readily available to the mind as experience. Nevertheless he often mitigated the rigors of his position and occasionally accepted even the supernatural and the fantastic.[6] And although he sometimes does violence to artistic intention by irrelevantly calling attention to minute factual, historical, and geographical improprieties and anachronisms — a kind of obsession with him — he did have some notion of probability as a pattern of formal relationships implied, stated, and realized within the confines of a single work of art and seems to have distinguished such *aesthetic* probability from *natural* and *historical* probability. "Poetical action," he said, "ought to be probable upon certain suppositions"; "philosophic nonsense" could under certain aesthetic conditions be "poetical sense."

Thus some of his strictures upon improbability arise not so much from an excessively literal-minded application of the principle of natural probability as from some kind of appreciation of formal and structural considerations. He objected to the appearance of the ghost in *Hamlet* not because a ghost is "out of nature" and therefore inadmissible in poetry and drama but because "the apparition left the regions of the dead to little purpose; the revenge which he demands is not obtained but by the death of him that was required to take it . . ." He accepted Horace's rule that on certain occasions supernatural intervention may be aesthetically necessary, and his objection to the appearances of gods and goddesses in Gay's *Trivia* is that they are not called for by the exigencies of the action. "An honest blacksmith might have done for Patty what is performed by Vulcan. The appearance of Cloacina is nauseous and superfluous; a shoeboy could have been produced by the casual cohabitation of mere mortals. Horace's rule is broken in both cases; there is no 'dignus vindice nodus,' no difficulty that required any supernatural interposition. A patten may be made by the hammer of a mortal, and a bastard may be dropped by a human strumpet." [7]

These modifications of the doctrine of literal probability are important and ought to be noticed, but the principle that reality is a test of art remains intact. It may be asked why that principle seems to provide strength more often than limitation and how the critic without ever departing from it achieved the vigor and subtlety that very often are pre-eminently his, even though it must be conceded that at the touch of this cold philosophy many charms did indeed fly away. The answer lies in the fact that what Johnson lost in one dimension he gained in another. If he did not achieve sublimity and height, he did achieve what may be of equal value — comprehensiveness, range, and even profundity.

It is never to be forgotten that Johnson's *nature* was coterminous with all reality, inanimate and intellectual. Within it there was air to breathe, space to roam, and treasures to dig up. He was fully as censorious of those who failed to sound its depths as he was of those who ignored its boundaries. "It seems natural for a young poet to initiate himself by Pastorals, which, not professing to imitate real life, require no experience, and, exhibiting only the simple operation of unmingled passions, admit no subtle reasoning or deep enquiry." "I know not that there can be found in [Nicholas Rowe's] plays any deep search into nature, any accurate discriminations of kindred qualities, or nice display of passion in its progress; all is general and undefined." [8]

In both these utterances Johnson is invoking nature and reality in behalf of profundity, subtlety, sophistication, and complexity. His criticism raised the curtain upon the penetrating researches and the ample vistas of Shakespeare's contemplation of life just as surely as it lowered it upon the "fairies, genii, giants, and monsters" of William Collins — those "flights of imagination which pass the bounds of nature . . ." [9]

"In *Much ado about nothing*, the father of *Hero*, depressed by her disgrace, declares himself so subdued by grief that *a thread may lead him*. How is it that grief in *Leonato* and lady *Constance* [who says in *King John*, 'To me, and to the State of my great Grief, / Let Kings assemble'], produces effects directly opposite, and yet both agreeable to nature? Sorrow softens the mind while it is yet warmed by hope, but hardens it when it is congealed by despair. Distress, while there remains any prospect of relief, is weak and flexible, but when no succour remains, is fearless and stubborn; angry alike at those that injure and at those that do not help; careless to please where nothing can be gained, and fearless to offend when there is nothing further to be dreaded Such was this writer's knowledge of the passions." [10]

And such was Johnson's criticism at its realistic best, criticism that is valuable or not, illuminating or not, in direct proportion to the critic's experience of men and life, just as the original literary excellence is correspondingly attributable to similar experience of the author. It is a pity that the notes of Johnson's edition of Shakespeare are not better known, for in them there is perhaps the best expression in the English language of what always has been and doubtless always will be the layman's approach to literature, an approach which, in all truth, nearly everyone follows, gladly or grudgingly, at some time or other.

Such tag-lines as "This is according to nature" or "This sentiment is drawn from nature" or "Richard speaks here the language of nature" [11] are signals to the reader that the critic is about to match the author's experience with his own and to draw the reader's attention to that fund of common but varied experience from which the literary effect is drawn. Johnson was never under the impression that in such instances he was commenting upon the work as a whole — its form, its structure, or its total effect. He once referred to the presence of real life and experience in a particular passage as *"touches* of nature." [12] The phrase is far from being original with him. Anyone familiar with the criticism of the seventeenth and eighteenth centuries knows that such phrases as *"touches* of nature" or *"strokes* of nature" were frequently used and that they were very often described as lively or vivacious. *Lively* had several synonyms, according to Johnson's Dictionary: "brisk," "vigourous," "vivacious," "gay," "airy," "strong," "energetick." But the only meaning of direct relevance to literary criticism, as indicated by the fact that for this meaning alone Johnson used examples from criticism, is this: "representing life," for the adjective, and "with strong resemblance of life," for the adverb. To illustrate each, Johnson used a sentence from Dryden. For the adjective he quotes this comment from Dryden's translation of Du Fresnoy: "Since a true knowledge of nature gives us pleasure, a *lively* imitation of it in poetry or painting must produce a greater." For the adverb he quotes a sentence from Dryden's Preface to *The State of Innocence*: "That part of poetry must needs be best, which describes most *lively* our actions and passions, our virtues and our vices."

The association here of the word *lively* with nature is significant, as is also its association with painting. The Horatian phrase *ut pictura poesis* had suggested to innumerable critics that one of the most valuable lessons poetry could learn from the sister art of painting was the ability to reproduce with lifelike efficacy the sensuous objects of external nature. If Wordsworth is right that poetry between *Paradise Lost* and the *Seasons*, with a few minor exceptions, "does not contain a single new image of external nature; and scarcely presents a familiar one from which it can be inferred that the eye of the Poet had been steadily fixed upon his object," [13] it was surely not from lack of critical precept. To the general critical acclaim of the vivid sensuous particular, Johnson added his own voice. He praised Thomson's eye as one that "distinguishes in every thing presented to its view whatever there is on which the imagination can delight to be detained" and his mind as one that "at once comprehends the vast, and attends to the minute." He praised Shakespeare as "an exact surveyor of the inanimate world," and he censured Milton for failing to capture "the freshness, raciness, and energy of immediate observation." [14]

But he would certainly not have confined *liveliness* to sensuous representation, for psychological data and all human experience could also imbue a work of art with the liveliness and vivacity of ideas and impressions fresh from the living world. *Liveliness* for Johnson was not an original stroke of the creative and subjective imagination; representations had to be *just*, that is, "Exact; proper; accurate." Since he interpreted Dryden's use of the word *lively* to mean "lifelike," he would not have considered his predecessor's definition of a play ("a just and lively image of human nature")[15] as an antithesis in which *just* referred to rational instruction and *lively* to imaginative pleasure. The combination of *just* and *lively* was a kind of emphatic redundancy, for to Johnson a work of art is *lively* only to the extent that it is *just*. A literary effect is original not in the sense that it is creative and has never existed before in its new form, but in the sense that it is natural, reproduced accurately from the original or primary source, life and experience.

It would be pleasant to dwell on Johnson's comments on these touches of nature that appear everywhere in the pages of Shakespeare: on the "petty perverseness" of Rosalind in *As You Like It*, who "finds faults in her lover, in hope to be contradicted"; on the combination of deformity, envy, and ambition in the future King Richard III; on the "pain of deformity" in Falstaff, who "may affect to make sport with it among those whom it is his interest to please" but who is "ready to revenge any hint of contempt upon one whom he can use with freedom."[16] Thus does Johnson everywhere dig out the Shakespearean ore. In all such cases the commentator is writing from life, just as he supposed the dramatist to have done before him.

He himself often returns an echo from the sentiment before him. His criticism is seldom more endearing than when Johnson the man takes the pen from the hand of Johnson the critic. The English monarch's soliloquy beginning, "Upon the King!" in *Henry V* (Act IV, Scene i) led Johnson to comment as follows: "There is something very striking and solemn in this soliloquy, into which the king breaks immediately as soon as he is left alone. Something like this, on less occasions, every breast has felt. Reflection and seriousness rush upon the mind upon the separation of a gay company, and especially after forced and unwilling merriment." [17] This is surely "drawn from nature," if one may apply to the critic himself the phrase he often used to call attention to comparable effects in the work of art before him. The terrible reality that lay behind this comment was fully known only to Johnson himself. But one is inclined to remember that memorable occasion when Johnson, "in order to support himself, laid hold of one of the posts at the side of the foot pavement, and sent forth peals so loud, that in the silence of the night his voice seemed to resound from Temple-bar to Fleet-ditch" — "huge laughter," in the words of Max Beerbohm, whose echoes "come ringing down the ages."

That occasion immediately followed a social evening in which the merriment about Langton's will had about it, to say the least, something "forced and unwilling," and preceded those midnight hours of solitude and anguish in which Johnson records that his memory seemed fallacious, that he suffered from fever and inflammation in his useful eye, that his nights gave him no rest, and that he was not certain whether, as he says, "I have not lived resolving till the possibility of performance is past. . . . God help me, I will yet try." [18]

II

Because Johnson believed that experienced reality was in such large measure the source and test of art, one can apply to him the words of R. G. Collingwood and say that he tends to view art as "a reduplication of perceptible objects, whose value, so far as it has a value, is therefore the same in kind as the value of the object which it reduplicates." [19] Yet any one familiar with Johnson must be aware that his conception of nature cannot be confined to empirical reality alone, which carries with it no implicit values. *Nature* was also used to refer to general order and rational principle. He once said that "there is more thought in the moralist than in the historian. There is but a shallow stream of thought in history." [20] In Johnson's thought history is often virtually synonymous with nature as particular reality, which we have been discussing, and morality with general nature, which we are about to discuss.

Principles of order arise usually from philosophy, morality, and religion and tend to affect one's conception of nature and reality. Johnson was an unrelenting moralist and a fervent Christian, and he once censured modern pastoral poets, who relied upon outmoded mythological allusions, for ignoring "the change which religion has made in the whole *system of the world*." The phrase I have underlined Johnson often used synonymously with *nature*, and it might therefore seem plausible to some that his conception of reality was ordered and modified to a significant degree by his theology and his morality. For that reason, a brief inquiry must be made into those aspects of his religion and his philosophy which are relevant to literary criticism.

One of his pre-Boswellian biographers, John Hawkins, found him to have rejected the philosophy of Shaftesbury, which "makes virtue to consist in a course of action conformable to what is called the moral sense," and the philosophy of Wollaston, for whom virtue consists in "acting, in all cases, according to truth, and treating things as they are," but to have accepted the philosophy of Samuel Clarke, who "supposes all rational agents as under an obligation to act agreeably to the relations that subsist between such, or according to what he calls the fitness of things." [21] In claiming that Johnson disagreed with Clarke only on the Trinity and "fell in with the scheme of fitness," Hawkins had surely forgotten *Rasselas*, where the philosopher who recommends "due regard to the fitness arising from the relations and qualities of causes and effects" is given the self-satisfied complacency "of a man that had co-operated with the present system" — a sage whom one "should understand less, as he heard him longer." [22] Moreover, Hawkins ignores the whole point and main emphasis of all Johnson's moral writings, that external nature is too much subject to chance and that human life is much too complicated and at times too whimsical to be explained by any purely rationalistic doctrine, natural or moral. Johnson was acting typically and with full regard to his basic premises when he ridiculed the idea of the Great Chain of Being, when he called the metaphysics of Descartes "precarious," when he attacked the "sophistries" of Hobbes, Leibniz, Spinoza, and Bolingbroke, and when he laughed at the speculative Platonism of Henry More.[23]

The simple truth is that Johnson's thought cannot be identified with any of the popular cosmologies of the seventeenth and eighteenth centuries. Yet since Johnson was a Christian, he did, of course, accept (but only in its most general terms and without much insistence upon it) the teleological principle of ultimately good and rational purpose in the universe. He asserted, in reviewing a volume of letters by Newton, that the world could have been produced only "by a voluntary and meaning agent," and he concluded one of his essays by urging that "nothing in reality is governed by chance, . . . but the universe is under the perpetual superintendence of Him who created it . . ."[24] He thought that God might give instructive notices to man through the events of history and that nature was monitory, reminding man that as the seasons pass life becomes shorter and the need of repentance more urgent.

When considering Johnson's religion as a whole, the reader carries away an impression that it is intensely personal and real but at the same time in intellectual content general and somewhat rationalistic. But simple and vague though his religion may have been theologically, it was for him a lifelong preoccupation, an unrelenting and demanding thing with which he could never be finished. In a passage that is surely partly autobiographical, he says that the doctrines that appear in Milton (the redemption of man, the need of repentance, and the future judgment) were such as affect one's whole life and entire being: "these truths . . . have been taught to our infancy; they have mingled with our solitary thoughts and familiar conversation, and are habitually interwoven with the whole texture of life."[25]

In his writings about religion Johnson is usually silent about symbol and ritual; the cosmological drama of creation, fall, redemption; the contest with evil; and millennial or heavenly bliss. The nature of his contemplation of the Deity is typical of his whole religious attitude. For one thing there is little ontological argument about the existence of God. He occasionally liked to argue among his closest friends in the manner of legalistic apologetics based upon the universal testimony of men and the eyewitness accounts of the apostles. Moreover, most references to God are made in the most general and impersonal terms possible. In the Dictionary God is called simply "The Supreme Being" — the title which Johnson seems most often to have used. God is "the great Lawgiver of the universe," an "unbounded Being," "a sovereign Protector," before whom man is impotent. As mere men "we live and act under the eye of our Father and Judge, by whom nothing is overlooked or forgotten." [26]

Although he does not completely neglect the more amiable traits of the Deity, he gives them little or no emphasis and is careful to point out that God's forgiving goodness and His gracious fatherhood mean, not that He will be infinitely good to individuals, but that His purposes will ultimately prevail. The emphasis is normally upon the justice of God and the conditional nature of the salvation of man, for whom the verdict is concealed until all the evidence is finally and irrevocably reviewed after death. God was considered to be self-sufficient, independent, sovereign. "It seems . . . probable," he once said in a sermon written for his friend, John Taylor, "that this inclination [the desire for society] is allotted to all rational beings of limited excellence, and that it is the privilege only of the infinite Creator to derive all his happiness from himself." [27] The ways of God are past tracing out. The reason, for example, why the Europeans are more powerful and more knowing than the Asiatics lies hidden in the mystery of God's independent action, in "the unsearchable will of the supreme being." And the appropriate human response to an absolutely sovereign God is an emotion compounded largely of reverence and awe. Nekayah's comment in *Rasselas* conveys the most typical religious emotion of Johnson himself: "But the being whom I fear to name, the being which made the soul, can destroy it." [28]

This twofold quality of Johnson's religion, that in itself it was inscrutable but that it provoked responses of overwhelming awe and fearsome reverence, has significant consequences for literary criticism, the most important of which is that religion and poetry are effectually divorced. The two belong to different spheres, involving means of expression so diverse as to make them incompatible. The themes which the mind dwells upon in devotion are awful and incomprehensible; poetry must deal with the easily comprehensible. The mood of religion is overwhelming and direct; poetry requires leisure and control. In devotion the appropriate expression is a simple cry for mercy; in poetry there are the embellishments of wit and fancy. "The good and evil of Eternity are too ponderous for the wings of wit; the mind sinks under them in passive helplessness, content with calm belief and humble adoration." [29] If T. E. Hulme is right in saying that romanticism is "spilt religion" and that concepts "right and proper in their own sphere" are poured out like "a pot of treacle over the dinner table," [30] then Johnson is one of the least "romantic" of all English writers.

To this radical discontinuity between personal religion and most kinds of poetry we shall return in considering Johnson's concept of the sublime. But Johnson's religion had another consequence more relevant to our present discussion of nature. Fontenelle once described the world as a grand opera. No view could be further from Johnson's, whose universe had neither angels nor devils, neither a heroic Christ nor a magnificently rebellious Satan. Johnson's religion, at least in its theological and cosmological aspects, gave him no symbol, no ritual, no mythological machinery, no epic or tragic personages, no pageantry. It provided very little that was available to the fine arts. The realm of religion was colorless, general, austere, and inscrutable. Johnson marveled at the "energetick operations" by which Milton was able, from "the few radical positions which the Scriptures afforded him," to elaborate the pomp and pageantry of *Paradise Lost*.[31]

Humanistic, stoical ethics and Christianity have often been at odds. In Johnson's view they were not, chiefly because he felt that the Christian revelation was given not to annihilate pagan morality but to complete it by adding to it the doctrine of immortality and of future rewards and punishments. Those doctrines gave ultimate sanction to morality, but they did not destroy its rational foundations. Reason, although ultimately powerless to break the chains of passion and habit, could lead man a considerable piece along the way. To Johnson, as to Locke and most thinkers of the period, religion and reason were not antithetical but complementary. And faith was not mysticism or inward light but acceptance of testimony and even sense-evidence upon the highest possible authority.

Johnson, moreover, could accept classical morality (but always within the Christian framework of ultimate supernatural sanction and authority) because he seems not to have accepted fully or perhaps even to have understood the doctrine of original sin or total depravity in its extremer forms. The *Christian's Magazine* had emphasized the doctrine of the Fall when it said that the important difference between Deism and Christianity lay in the fact that the Christian, unlike the Deist, who believes in natural goodness, is "persuaded, that man has fallen from the state of *innocence*" and "that being now weak through sin, he stands in need of grace . . ." [32] But this is not Johnson's emphasis: in his Dictionary definition of *Deism* he made the Deist's refusal to accept revelation the chief divergence from Christianity.

Although he found that "human life is everywhere a state, in which much is to be endured, and little to be enjoyed" and although his view of man's moral position is austere and realistic, it is not melancholy. He does not speak of man's absolute dilemma and of his desperate corruption without supernatural grace. He rejected both the law of progress and the law of decay, although he perceived clearly the importance of the latter notion to seventeenth-century thought. Instead of total corruption he found in human nature a balance of virtues and vices. As he said in one of his earliest works, "Wherever human nature is to be found, there is a mixture of vice and virtue, a contest of passion and reason: and . . . the Creator doth not appear partial in his distributions, but has balanced in most countries their particular inconveniences by particular favours."

But this "mixture of vice and virtue" in human nature and society Johnson never allowed to excuse human perversity or to encourage the notion that man was bound to sin that grace might abound. The principle of Swift, that men are "grateful in the same degree as they are resentful," Johnson rejected indignantly because it "supposes man to act from a brute impulse, and pursue a certain degree of inclination, without any choice of the object; for, otherwise, though it should be allowed that gratitude and resentment arise from the same constitution of the passions, it follows not that they will be equally indulged when reason is consulted . . ." Johnson's morality kept man rational and free, and no doctrine was allowed to destroy those basic premises. "He that thinks reasonably must think morally": it therefore follows that "virtue is the highest proof of understanding, and the only solid basis of greatness; and that vice is the natural consequence of narrow thoughts; that it begins in mistake, and ends in ignominy."

Such views were, of course, not consonant with the conception of the total corruption of human nature. Although Johnson would never have equated ignorance and vice, he interpreted human corruption in such a way as to preserve intact the foundations of rational morality and argued that virtue and knowledge, vice and ignorance were related analogically. "Mankind are universally corrupt, but corrupt in different degrees; as they are universally ignorant, yet with greater or less irradiations of knowledge. How has knowledge or virtue been increased and preserved in one place beyond another, but by diligent inculcation and rational enforcement?" [33]

It is important to see that Johnson's view of human nature is a kind of median one. He neither despaired with the cynics nor sunned himself in the light of supernatural grace. Nor, of course, did he believe that this was the best of all possible worlds and that man was on a kind of evolutionary escalator which willy-nilly would bring him to moral perfection. Nature provided neither automatic perfection nor automatic corruption. But it did provide psychological and moral universals which are available to human reason. When Johnson referred to "the general system" of nature and to "unavoidable concatenation," [34] he did not refer specifically to Christian cosmology or Christian theology or to any system of speculative metaphysics. He referred to those general principles of rational and stoical morality — the wisdom of self-knowledge, the need of controlling and directing the passions — softened by Christian charity and given ultimate sanction by Christian revelation. He also referred to the permanence and immutability of human nature, whose elementary passions have always been the same and have always operated in essentially the same way. Such moral and psychological universals Johnson found within nature. But he never explained or clarified them fully. They always remain general and basic. They are the simple assumptions of common sense, without which there could be neither morality, language, nor art.

III

How, then, does art instruct? It instructs by performing its essential function, that is, by imitating nature in its two large aspects. Art instructs by representing lifelike and particular reality, extensive in its range and various in its forms; and by representing, or at least implying, moral and psychological truth, which is general, rational, and normative. Johnson considered Shakespeare the greatest English poet, for he was above all others "the poet of nature" both particular and general. The plays of Shakespeare exhibit "the *real* state of sublunary *nature*, which partakes of good and evil, joy and sorrow, mingled with endless *variety* of proportion and *innumerable* modes of combination; and expressing the course of the *world*, in which the loss of one is the gain of another . . ." Such are his representations of reality, rich in particularity, complexity, and contradiction. At the same time he was supremely the poet of general nature. He "thinks only on men" and presents "the genuine progeny of common humanity," who "act and speak by the influence of those general passions and principles by which all minds are agitated, and the whole system of life is continued in motion."

By Johnsonian standards Shakespeare must be, in spite of occasional and incidental lapses from the strictest morality, the most moral of poets precisely because he is the most natural. Only a poet of nature allows the mind to "repose on the stability of truth": "he who has mazed his imagination, in following the phantoms which other writers raise up before him, may here be cured of his delirious ecstasies, by reading human sentiments in human language, by scenes from which a hermit may estimate the transactions of the world, and a confessor predict the progress of the passions." In this, Johnson's central conception of the way in which art instructs, morality is neither a kind of didactic appendage, artificially attached to the work, nor any kind of direct homiletical appeal. Art is moral because it is the mirror of life, which in its variety and reality is always instructive; and because it is a representation of general nature, which is itself morally constituted into "standing relations and general passions."[35]

How has it happened, then, that Johnson has impressed many as the most crudely and directly didactic of all great critics? The reason lies, I think, in the fact that from the time of Coleridge to the present there has been a tendency to forget Johnson's basic position and to judge him only by his own lapses from it. The fault is in part his own, for his attacks upon Fielding, Swift, Voltaire, Chesterfield, and Bolingbroke on moral and religious grounds were so unforgettably and vigorously expressed that they have taken on the force of fundamental aesthetic principle. Sometimes, too, as Coleridge was fond of pointing out, Johnson completely lost sight of the dramatic situation before him and actually misread a passage in order to administer a severe moral rebuff. In such cases he destroyed art without conferring very much benefit upon morality.

Nowhere is his morality more obtrusive, artificial, and irrelevant than in his comment on Iago's words, "She did deceive her father, marrying you": "This and the following argument of *Iago* ought to be deeply impressed on every reader. Deceit and falsehood, whatever conveniences they may for a time promise or produce, are, in the sum of life, obstacles to happiness. . . . The same objection may be made with a lower degree of strength against the imprudent generosity of disproportionate marriages." [36] Thomas Rymer at his worst equalled that, but he would have had difficulty outdoing it. It not only blandly disregards the motives of Iago's remark and its specific dramatic context but it bases the tragic issue upon Desdemona's "deceit" and "imprudence" and thus destroys the fundamental moral and dramatic relationships of the play: the malignity of Iago, the innocence of Desdemona, and the helplessness of Othello. Fortunately such was not Johnson's final estimate of Shakespeare's masterpiece.

Such lapses arise, it would seem, from Johnson's acute moral sensibility and from his at times almost overpowering sense of moral obligation. But they are not central to Johnson's criticism, nor do they usually appear in the most crucial places. He was as far from believing that the moral wholesomeness of their works made Savage, Watts, and Blackmore great poets as he was from believing that Shakespeare's specific departures from Christian morality, which are dutifully pointed out and deplored, obviated his being not only the greatest but the most moral of poets. Moreover, although highly sensitive morally, Johnson was far from being a prude. He liked the *Beggar's Opera* and thought that people had vastly overrated its tendency to mischief. Homer was a great natural and moral poet in spite of the crude and barbarous manners and morals he occasionally portrayed. And although at times he did insist upon poetic justice, he defended the violation of it in Addison's *Cato* on the grounds of nature and reality and thus answered the strictures of Dennis: "Whatever pleasure there may be in seeing crimes punished and virtue rewarded, yet, since wickedness often prospers in real life, the poet is certainly at liberty to give it prosperity on the stage. For if poetry is an imitation of reality, how are its laws broken by exhibiting the world in its true form? A stage may sometimes gratify our wishes; but, if it be truly the *mirror of life*, it ought to shew us sometimes what we are to expect." [37]

There are in Johnson's criticism, then, two large conceptions of nature, each of which may at various places and under various conditions receive primary emphasis but both of which are usually operative, especially in accounting for works of literary art that have attained the stature of classics. Nature as particular reality carries with it no principle of universal value or formal organization. But it is instructive in that it is sober and unfanciful and keeps one's feet firmly planted on the ground; and it is of aesthetic value in that it provides touches of liveliness and vivacity without which literary art remains dull and unattractive. Nature as ordered reality introduces universal psychological truth, the uniform and unchanging constitution of man's mind and emotions, and also those radically simple but fundamental moral truths which must provide the subject matter of all permanent literary art. Nature so conceived is neither creative nor dynamic. It neither progresses nor retrogresses, neither develops nor declines. In itself it has no principle of growth and decay. It is unlike the φύσις of Aristotle since it is not an active force realizing its own implicit ends and applying form to matter in a series of entelechies. Nor is Johnsonian nature Platonic or Neoplatonic, since it implies no ascending scale of spiritual value and no system of appearance and reality. But although it is not in and of itself a life-giving principle, it serves literature well in both its general fixity and its particular reality as criterion and standard, as foundation and source.

If, then, nature as reality and truth does not disclose itself, how is it made available to art? Only through the continuing and deepening *experience* of the artist, who must unveil nature since she will not do it for herself. There are, to be sure, a few truths which Johnson felt were not available to normal human experience — the miracles, for example, and the future state of the soul. Of them, said Johnson, "we were not sure, till we had a positive revelation." But after revelation, he felt, they virtually entered the realm of observed reality since we then had them on unimpeachable human testimony. Yet those religious truths, we have seen, are not very important for literature. It may be fairly said that all the artist needs to know he can know through experience. But that empirical search must be arduous and unrelenting. As both Imlac and Rasselas perceive, it is a labor: the poet ranges, observes, wanders, converses, learns, estimates, traces. The verbs all come from the tenth chapter of *Rasselas*, the portrait of the ideal poet. The process is an empirical one: as the poet perseveres, he enters into nature. He ultimately will "rise to general and transcendental truths, which will always be the same . . ." But he must rise to them; they will not descend to him. It is in this way — and in this way alone — that art can attain moral validity.[38]

CHAPTER V

Pleasure

JOHNSON'S sententiously expressed definitions of poetry — "the end of poetry is to instruct by pleasing," "poetry is the art of uniting pleasure with truth, by calling imagination to the help of reason"[1] — are variants of the Scaligerian formula that the end of poetry is *docere cum delectatione*. Such conventional definitions unquestionably sprang from a desire to subordinate pleasure to instruction. But these definitions do in effect sanction pleasure as the *sine qua non* of poetry — a fact which Johnson's didacticism should never be allowed to obscure. Judged by post-Coleridgean standards, his theoretical conception of literary pleasure may seem to be inadequate and even casual; but judged, as it more properly should be, against the weighty tradition of didacticism that lay impressively and authoritatively behind it, it appears not only whole-hearted and vigorous but at times even subtle and penetrating. It more than overbalances those homiletical moments, upon which we remarked in the last chapter, when he dutifully, bluntly, and sometimes crudely "stooped to truth and moralized" his comment.

Consider the following tribute to literary pleasure, for example, which is not only eloquent and sincere but is the very foundation upon which much of his criticism rests: "Works of imagination excel by their allurement and delight; by their power of attracting and detaining the attention. That book is good in vain which the reader throws away. He only is the master who keeps the mind in pleasing captivity; whose pages are perused with eagerness, and in hope of new pleasure are perused again; and whose conclusion is perceived with an eye of sorrow, such as the traveller casts upon departing day." That encomium upon one of the chief ends of poetry is immediately followed by a bold challenge to traditional criticism to recognize what had in fact happened and to make pleasure the criterion of critical justice. "By his proportion of this predomination [that is, "allurement," "delight," "pleasure"] I will consent that Dryden should be tried; of this, which, in opposition to reason, makes Ariosto the darling and the pride of Italy; of this, which, in defiance of criticism, continues Shakespeare the sovereign of the drama." [2]

Johnson had, to be sure, the moralist's objections to some kinds of pleasure, scruples which were not always absent from his literary criticism; but it would be naive and wrong to think that conscience cannot coexist with aesthetic sensibility. It may well be that such critics as Mr. Eliot, Mr. Auden, and Professor Pottle, who look to religion and morality for absolute and transcendental values, have greater interest in the principle of pleasure in poetry than critics of a humanistic and secular stripe, who find it necessary to place such values within the purview of art. In any event it is unthinkable that, however exalted his conception of poetry, Johnson would have acquiesced in what Mr. Eliot once called Shelley's consecration or Arnold's ordination of the poet.

Johnson once said that "as there is no necessity for our having poetry at all, it being merely a luxury, an instrument of pleasure, it can have no value, unless when exquisite of its kind." [3] This comment, provoked as it was by Boswell's more than usually insistent questioning and by Johnson's greater than usual impatience with such importunity, is not, of course, a careful or final statement of the critic's position. But it is not so untypical as it may at first appear to those who remember only the didactic Johnson. Even within the rigid logic of his definitions — in which instruction is made the common aim of all writing and pleasure the differentiating aim of poetry — pleasure is accorded the dignity of being that without which poetry would cease to exist or would at least lose its reason for existing.

Johnson's conception of pleasure, which, like most of his critical theory, must be reconstructed from his practice and therefore from many divergent contexts, is a complicated one. He would probably have never submitted it to full and complete definition. The ensuing chapters of this study will be concerned with it as it appears in language and formal structure; in such qualities as beauty, sublimity, and pathos; in wit, novelty, variety, and familiarity. This chapter is devoted to matters preliminary to such specific investigations: (1) the general characteristics of literary pleasure; (2) the relations between pleasure and nature, especially as they appear in the theory of generality; and (3) the theory of the imagination.

I

"Whatever professes to benefit by pleasing must please at once. The pleasures of the mind imply something sudden and unexpected; that which elevates must always surprise. What is perceived by slow degrees may gratify us with the consciousness of improvement, but will never strike with the sense of pleasure." [4] This passage is reminiscent of Aristotle, who denied that speed and slowness are relevant to pleasure, who said that "while we may *become* pleased quickly as we may become angry quickly, we cannot *be* pleased quickly," and who compared pleasure to the act of seeing: "Seeing seems to be at any moment complete, for it does not lack anything which coming into being later will complete its form; and pleasure also seems to be of this nature. For it is a whole, and at no time can one find a pleasure whose form will be completed if the pleasure lasts longer." [5] Johnson too seems to have conceived of pleasure as being something like a particular visual perception — sudden, authentic, complete in itself, and immediate in its effect. This view may explain his impatience with that kind of subtle, analytical, and therefore gradually and even painfully perceived pleasure which the metaphysical poets demanded of their readers. Johnson is interested in the immediate and general effects upon the mind which can easily be dissipated by too much disquisition, elaboration, and indirection. Poetry "must please at once." How else, indeed, could it be expected to awaken an echo in every human breast?

Johnson does not always appear to be fully aware of the Aristotelian point of view that each activity has a pleasure proper to it; therefore he does not pursue as often as one would wish that critic's suggestions about pleasures peculiar to literature as a whole and also to its various types. Perhaps he was deterred by annoyance with the post-Renaissance traditions of generic criticism. But he does discriminate kinds and degrees of pleasurable activity. In defining *diversion* ("sport; something that unbends the mind by turning it off from care"), he was careful to distinguish it from amusement and pleasure: "Diversion seems to be something lighter than *amusement*, and less forcible than *pleasure*." In defining the verb *amuse* ("to entertain with tranquillity; to fill with thoughts that engage the mind, without distracting it"), he drew the same threefold distinction: "To *divert* implies something more lively, and to *please*, something more important. It [to *amuse*] is therefore frequently taken in a sense bordering on contempt." *Pleasure* ("delight; gratification of the mind or senses") and *to please* ("to delight; to gratify; to humour . . . to satisfy; to content . . . to favour") refer to something of a much higher order than either diversion or amusement.

In morality pleasure can have the pejorative meaning of "loose gratification," but in purely literary contexts it is a term of the very highest praise. Thus when Johnson finds "poetical pleasure" and "poetical terrour" in Milton and the power of pleasing many and pleasing long in Shakespeare, he is conferring distinction of the most exalted kind. But when he encounters a "lucky trifle" (like the *Dove* of Anacreon or the *Sparrow* of Catullus) which "genius now and then produces," he feels that he is concerned with the merely diversionary, with "flowers fragrant and fair, but of short duration" or with "blossoms to be valued only as they foretell fruits." Or when he describes *Coriolanus* as "one of the most *amusing* of our author's performances" (the word seems egregiously ill-chosen unless one remembers Johnson's definition of *amusement*), he means that the play is acceptable but not great. It arouses and holds curiosity and provides variety of incident and character, but the fact that there is "perhaps too much bustle in the first act, and too little in the last" keeps it from being fully pleasurable.[6]

Johnson does not always follow these particular distinctions from his Dictionary with exact and scrupulous care, but they are helpful reminders that he graduates his praise and that there are planes of excellence in the literary pantheon. They are therefore an indication of both tolerance and austerity. Johnson admitted the lower forms of pleasure (*Vive la bagatelle!*) but only on their proper levels. In his literary heaven there were many mansions for the many excellencies below the very highest. Consider his evaluation of Addison's poetry, which, he says, "has not often those felicities of diction which give lustre to sentiments, or that vigour of sentiment that animates diction; there is little of ardour, vehemence, or transport; there is very rarely the awfulness of grandeur, and not very often the splendour of elegance. He thinks justly; but he thinks faintly." The several qualities here enumerated as being beyond Addison's poetic grasp are all components of literary pleasure. "Yet, if he seldom reaches supreme excellence, he rarely sinks into dulness, and is still more rarely entangled in absurdity. . . . There is in most of his compositions a calmness and equability, deliberate and cautious, sometimes with little that delights but seldom with any thing that offends." [7] If Addison's poetry could not produce pleasure, it did at least provide what Johnson, had he remembered the definition in his Dictionary, might have called amusement, for *to amuse* was "to entertain with tranquillity."

These gradations imply not only tolerance but also the very severest requirements. Powerful currents were necessary to set the mighty frame of the Great Cham rolling with genuine pleasure, and when he felt them his language was commensurate with the force of the stimulus. *Anne Killigrew* is "undoubtedly the noblest ode that our language ever has produced. The first part flows with a torrent of enthusiasm. 'Fervet immensusque ruit.' " [8] Such response seems somewhat stronger than the coolly judicious appraisals of Pope's men of sense who "approve" but do not "admire." Mrs. Thrale wrote that Johnson's "idea of poetry was magnificent indeed, and very fully was he persuaded of its superiority over every other talent bestowed by heaven on man." [9] It was thus quite inevitable that he found intolerable that dull tissue of didactic verse that was so assiduously produced in his day. He did not deign to dignify Green's *The Spleen*, Dyer's *The Fleece*, or Grainger's *The Sugar-Cane* with the name poetry. He even withheld the title from another most characteristic eighteenth-century production: "You may find wit and humour in verse, and yet no poetry." Poetry, whatever it is, must be something that "towered above the common mark." [10]

In administering his famous *coup de grâce* to the dramatic unities of time and place Johnson opposed to mere regularity and correctness "the nobler *beauties* of variety and instruction." [11] The phrase is suggestive because it bears the implication that one of the most important characteristics of literary pleasure is that it cannot be separated from instruction. It had been one important tendency of neoclassical criticism, while admitting both as necessary ends of art, to isolate the function of each. The moral was the pill; pleasure was the sugar-coating. Bossu, in a famous dictum that was approved almost *ad nauseam* in the eighteenth century, but perhaps as often disagreed with, had asserted that the epic poet must first find the moral truth and then accommodate fable, character, and sentiment to that truth. Huetius had applied the same principle to the fictional romance. "The principal End of *Romance* . . . is the Instruction of the Reader; . . . but because the Mind of Man naturally hates to be inform'd and (by the Influence of Self-Conceit) resists Instruction; 'tis to be deceived by the Blandishments of Pleasure; and the Rigor of Precept is to be subdued by the Allurements of Example." [12]

To that point of view Johnson pays frequent lip service. But the deeper one probes into his essential meanings, the more one is convinced that his reconciliation of the two in the conventional manner is superficial and verbal and does not illuminate his real thought and intention. For one thing, this traditional view makes of literary pleasure only an external embellishment, an attractive gloss and coating, a verbal overlaying; and that in no way seems consistent with the vigorous and manly approbation of pleasure which fell frequently and naturally from his lips and of which we have given examples earlier in this chapter. Moreover, such a view of pleasure is much too restricted for Johnson, who did not depend exclusively for pleasure upon aesthetic form, embellishment, or texture. All knowledge, all learning, nature in both its empirical particularity and its moral generality, and the vigorous operation of the mind expressed in any kind of activity — all these he found pleasurable. Biography, at its most literal and minute, was to him especially delightful and instructive; and he praised well-written histories and books of travel in much the same terms that he applied to poetry itself.[13]

All this reminds one of Aristotle. Among such sources of pleasure as variety and rarity, the Greek philosopher had placed learning and wonder and had thus related the two:

"Learning things and wondering at things are also pleasant as a rule; wondering implies the desire of learning, so that the object of wonder is an object of desire; while in learning one is brought to one's natural condition. . . . Again, since learning and wondering are pleasant, it follows that such things as acts of imitation must be pleasant — for instance, painting, sculpture, poetry — and every product of skilful imitation; this latter, even if the object imitated is not itself pleasant; for it is not the object itself which here gives delight; the spectator draws inferences . . . and thus learns something fresh."[14]

We do not fully understand Johnson's theory of pleasure or many of his particular literary judgments unless we realize that for him what was pleasurable was also instructive and that what was instructive was also pleasurable. In commenting upon the "chief scene of inchantment" in *Macbeth*, he praised not only the poet's power to evoke emotion but also the extraordinary historical judgment that accompanied it. Shakespeare's poetic fire did not destroy his fidelity to the details of current belief in selecting the ingredients of the witches' unholy brew.[15] Johnson once expressed admiration for a work that can hardly be classified as belles-lettres, Bishop Warburton's *Divine Legation of Moses,* by saying of it that "you are always entertained. He carries you round and round, without carrying you forward to the point; but then you have no wish to be carried forward." The delight Johnson took in reading a book in any form whatever that was written with a "mind full of reading and reflection" is one of his most important intellectual predispositions.[16] He grazed in many pastures. The very catholicity of his taste may have prevented him from evolving a clear-cut and precise definition of the pleasure peculiar to literary art.

II

Johnson's conception of literary pleasure might have been more exclusively aesthetic had nature itself been conceived of as providing the beautiful as well as the true and the good and thus giving its sanction to the Platonic triad. But for him it did not do so. His nature was *la vraie nature,* never *la belle nature.* Nature, as we have seen, provided a stream of particular experience appropriated into the mind empirically, general moral law made perceptible by experience and by right reason, and a human psychological constitution uniform and invariable in its basic responses. But there is no evidence that it provided general beauty or any kind of aesthetic ideal toward which the artist must strive as toward perfection. His first and only extended discussion of the theoretical concept of beauty is empirical; its burden, although stated cautiously, is that beauty is not static, abstract, absolute, or even general, but "relative and comparative," and that the very meaning of the term shifts with the shifting tides of sensibility and with the growth of knowledge and experience.

"It has been long observed, that the idea of beauty is vague and undefined, different in different minds, and diversified by time or place. It has been a term hitherto used to signify that which pleases us we know not why, and in our approbation of which we can justify ourselves only by the concurrence of numbers, without much power of enforcing our opinions upon others by any argument but example and authority. It is, indeed, so little subject to the examinations of reason, that Paschal supposes it to end where demonstration begins, and maintains, that without incongruity and absurdity we cannot speak of *geometrical beauty*.

"To trace all the sources of that various pleasure which we ascribe to the agency of beauty, or to disentangle all the perceptions involved in its idea, would, perhaps, require a very great part of the life of Aristotle or Plato. It is, however, in many cases apparent, that this quality is merely relative and comparative; that we pronounce things beautiful because they have something which we agree, for whatever reason, to call beauty, in a greater degree than we have been accustomed to find it in other things of the same kind; and that we transfer the epithet as our knowledge increases, and appropriate it to higher excellence, when higher excellence comes within our view.

"Much of the beauty of writing is of this kind; and therefore Boileau justly remarks, that the books which have stood the test of time, and been admired through all the changes which the mind of man has suffered from the various revolutions of knowledge, and the prevalence of contrary customs, have a better claim to our regard than any modern can boast, because the long continuance of their reputation proves that they are adequate to our faculties, and agreeable to nature." [17]

Such is Johnson's idea of beauty, which is not a Platonic but a complex Lockean idea, in which it is difficult "to disentangle all the *perceptions* involved." It is therefore a psychological idea, for he speaks of it as an "agency" which produces "pleasure" that is universal and permanent only if the response is constant and lasting — if, that is, the work itself "proves adequate to our faculties and agreeable to nature." But until that takes place, "we transfer the epithet as our knowledge increases, and appropriate it to higher excellence, when higher excellence comes within our view." Absolutes existed for Johnson on other levels. In matters of pleasure and taste he tended to be a psychological relativist, for whom truth was not beauty nor beauty truth. He would certainly not have understood the incantation of the "Attic shape," the "fair attitude."[18]

From this crucial passage it must be concluded, I think, that the much discussed principle of generality in Johnson does not include an idea of general beauty, either in nature or in the mind of man. Beauty is a shifting and adaptable term of empirical comparison. What, then, does generality mean? It is, first of all, as the previous chapter on nature attempted to demonstrate, primarily a term of moral and psychological signification, referring to basic moral law and to the uniform and unalterable constitution of human nature.

This had important implications, in Johnson's view, for literary style: his *Ramblers* were addressed to those only "whose passions left them leisure for abstracted truth, and whom virtue could please by its naked dignity."[19] "Abstracted truth" and "naked dignity" are phrases of moral meaning, but they suggest the type of literary style that most appropriately should convey such truth and express such dignity. Edmund Burke, who attempted to be empirical and inductive in his aesthetics and whose central political tenet was that "abstract ideas of right" and "mere general theories of government" were no better than "arrant trifling" and that "liberty inheres in some sensible object," admits that in most rhetorical contexts "generalities . . . are apt to heighten and raise the subject." He associated them with "fiction," "invention," and "imagination."[20]

Johnson's own poetic practice suggests that he surely shared the sensibility of his age, which found the generalized diction, the personifications, and the abstract ideas of reflective and didactic poetry to be emotionally and aesthetically evocative and even sublime and elevated, imbuing literary art with that kind of "Homerick majesty" that arose only from an "open display of unadulterated nature."[21] His own poetry also suggests, as do his essays, that he conceived generality to be primarily moral and humanistic in origin, chiefly concerned with moral and humanistic effects. It was only secondarily and derivatively aesthetic. There was such a thing, to borrow a phrase Boswell used to describe the effects of London, as "dissipating variety"; its best antidote was general truth generally expressed. Therefore in literary works a character of nature was always preferable to a character of manners, since only that character drawn upon the lines of fundamental humanity could instruct and please over a long period of time and under various historical and cultural conditions. Nothing could account for the permanence of Homer except the fact that "his positions are general, and his representations natural, with very little dependence on local or temporary customs, on those changeable scenes of artificial life, which, by mingling original with accidental notions, and crowding the mind with images which time effaces, produce ambiguity in diction, and obscurity in books." [22]

Because this was Johnson's fundamental desideratum for all art, the requirement of generality guided not only the selection of subject matter and the presentation of fictional character but also all manner of natural and psychological description. "The fault of Cowley, and perhaps of all the writers of the metaphysical race, is that of pursuing his thoughts to their last ramifications, by which he loses the grandeur of generality. . . . Thus all the power of description is destroyed by a scrupulous enumeration . . ." [23] This does not mean that the metaphysical poets failed because they did not imitate a static ideal of general beauty. It does mean that they failed because their excessive particularity dissipated the emotion that ought to have been conveyed. It is the "*power* of description" which is destroyed by "scrupulous enumeration." Consider Johnson's comment on Edgar's speech to Gloucester while overlooking the precipice near Dover, the speech beginning, "How fearful / And dizzy it is, to cast one's eyes so low!"

"The description is certainly not mean, but I am far from thinking it wrought to the utmost excellence of poetry. He that looks from a precipice finds himself assailed by one great and dreadful image of irresistible destruction. But this overwhelming idea is dissipated and enfeebled from the instant that the mind can restore itself to the observation of particulars, and diffuse its attention to distinct objects. The enumeration of the choughs and crows, the samphire-man and the fishers, counteracts the great effect of the prospect, as it peoples the desert of intermediate vacuity, and stops the mind in the rapidity of its descent through emptiness and horrour." [24]

I have argued that Johnson's adherence to the principle of generality arose from two of the most firmly held of his critical tenets. The first is his belief that literary art should imitate general nature. The second is his belief that literary art is the communication of ideas and emotions and that nothing should be allowed to pervert that fundamental aim. This is, of course, not to say that the principle of generality is a fixed and unalterable aesthetic principle. Far from it. It should always be remembered that Johnson required art to represent particular nature in all its variety as well as the ordered moral and psychological law of general nature. He therefore often praised the particular and the specific, and occasionally censured the "general and undefined" as dull and uninstructive. In certain kinds of writing and under certain psychological conditions the general was, of course, preferable, for particularity could destroy the emotional effect desired and could divert attention from general truth. Similarly (but less frequently perhaps) the opposite was true. It was the task of the writer to determine how general and how particular his work should be in order for it to attain (1) effectiveness and (2) permanence.

In attempting to understand what Johnson meant by generality, it is well for us to remember that, except only in the realm of the most basic and universal moral and psychological truth, he was usually Lockean and empirical. Therefore a general idea did not mean an aesthetic ideal fixed in nature and possessing the highest order of reality. A general idea was for Johnson a *complex* idea, that is, in the words of his Dictionary, "composite; of many parts; not simple; including many particulars"; or, in the words of Locke, which Johnson quoted to illustrate this definition: "Ideas made up of several simple ones, I call *complex*; such as beauty, gratitude, a man, the universe; which though complicated of various ideas, or *complex* ideas made up of simple ones, yet are considered each by itself as one." Thus an abstraction was not a *donnée* of nature but something "separated from something else." To *abstract* in Johnson's Dictionary meant "to take one thing from another," "to separate ideas," and "to reduce to an epitome." In the words of Johnson's mentor, Isaac Watts, abstraction "signifies a withdrawing some Parts of an Idea from other Parts of it."[25]

It is against this epistemological background that one must view Johnson's notions of the general, which is arrived at inductively and empirically. The *general* he defined in his Dictionary as "The whole; the totality; the main, without insisting on particulars." Imlac's famous tulip is not a Platonic Tulip and certainly not an Ideal Flower. The poet does not "number the streaks of the tulip," since it is his wish, in the words of the definition of *general* just cited, to present "the main, without insisting on particulars" and thus he remarks "general properties and large appearances." But the particular is important as that from which the general has been derived and as that upon which all description must ultimately depend. Plato in the *Phaedo* had advised the poet to choose such particulars as remind the reader of universals; Johnson urged the poet "to exhibit, in his portraits of nature, such prominent and striking features, as recall the original to every mind . . ."[26] Plato wanted the particular to reveal the general and universal; Johnson wanted the general to recall the particular. Plato's point of view is metaphysical; Johnson's psychological.

Having said that Johnsonian generality in contexts other than the moral was made up of and derived from particulars and that therefore his notion of the abstract and the general is always rooted in the empirical and sensational, it is only fair to add that the weight of his approval was usually applied to what was generalized rather than to what remained in its particular, specific, and original condition. He may well have admitted the truth of Joseph Trapp's remark that "Generals, being always the same, grow cold and lifeless, by their too frequent Repetition"; but he would certainly not have agreed with Thomas Gray that "*Circumstance* [that is, particular detail] ever was, and ever will be, the life and the essence both of oratory and of poetry." Gray's

Homer was "the father of *circumstance*." Johnson's Homer was that and more. He was "the father of *all* poetical beauty." That included "wonderful multiplicity," "every thing, in or out of nature, that can serve the purpose of poetry," but above all else the ability "to appropriate to particular persons qualities which are common to all mankind." [27]

III

Johnson defined *imagination* as "Fancy; the power of forming ideal pictures; the power of representing things absent to one's self or others." He defined *fancy* as "Imagination; the power by which the mind forms to itself images and representations of things, persons, or scenes of being." He defined *fantasy* as "Fancy; imagination; the power of imagining." His practice also reveals that he found these terms practically synonymous. Why indeed should he have attempted, like Coleridge, to distinguish them in order to discover a faculty more autonomous and powerful than imagination-fancy had proved to be? He believed that excellence of any kind arose only when a single faculty was subordinate to the whole mind and only when the whole mind was itself subordinate to antecedent experience and investigation of external reality. The natural bent of his own mind and the unmistakable emphasis of his psychology made it an irrelevant and even an impudent quest to search within the mind itself for a faculty powerful enough to explain literary excellence.

Hume's well-known statement of the empirical position on the imagination is an excellent summary of the basic theory to which Johnson adhered. Under it the imagination could never be conceived of as an instrument of insight into the transcendental, unseen order which lies behind and gives meaning to the real world.

"But though our thought seems to possess this unbounded liberty, we shall find, upon a nearer examination, that it is really confined within very narrow limits, and that all this creative power of the mind amounts to no more than the faculty of compounding, transposing, augmenting, or diminishing the materials afforded us by the senses and experience. When we think of a golden mountain, we only join two consistent ideas, *gold*, and *mountain*, with which we were formerly acquainted. A virtuous horse we can conceive; because, from our own feeling, we can conceive virtue; and this we may unite to the figure and shape of a horse, which is an animal familiar to us." [28]

Yet a theoretical statement does not explain Johnson's paradoxical practice: his vigorous praise of inventive genius and his equally vigorous denigration of the imaginative faculty. In both praise and censure he seems to have found the faculty to be considerably more powerful for good or evil than its position in empirical epistemology seems to suggest. How shall these divergent strains in his comments upon the imagination be reconciled? A survey of all that he said about it will reveal that his attack occurs more prominently in his earlier than in his later works. It was in his periodical essays and in *Rasselas* that he was wont to call the imagination "licentious and vagrant," wild, unrestrained, vehement, and rapid, and to associate it with youth and inexperience, with lyrics and with pastoral verse, to which he was either hostile or indifferent. There is, I think, somewhat less of this in the *Lives of the Poets*, where he praises the inventive genius of Milton and the fiery energy of Dryden and almost regularly places the *mens divinior* above the lower orders of genius; the "pleasing captivity" and "allurement" of literary delight above correctness, elegance, and refinement. But this shift of emphasis does not involve any important change in conception or in literary program, for the grounds of Johnson's earlier censure remained to the very end, just as the basis of his admiration was implicit within his critical system from the very beginning.

These two points of view, each predominant at various times, spring from a double conception of the imagination, which is not made fully clear in his definitions of that faculty. James Beattie discriminates them carefully. "Imagination, in the modern philosophical language, seems to denote two things: 1. That power of the mind which contemplates *ideas* (that is, *thoughts* or *notions*) without referring them to real existence, or to past experience; 2. That power which combines ideas into new forms or assemblages." [29] It was the imagination of Beattie's first meaning that Johnson feared, censured, and attempted to bridle. He considered the *fantastical* (defined in his Dictionary as the "Irrational; bred only in the imagination. . . . Subsisting only in the fancy; imaginary. . . . Unreal; apparent only; having the nature of phantoms. . . . Capricious; humourous; unsteady; irregular. . . . Whimsical, fanciful; indulgent to one's own imagination") and the *visionary* ("Affected by phantoms; disposed to receive impressions on the imagination. . . . Imaginary; not real; seen in dreams; perceived by the imagination only") to be mischievous effects of the imagination operating apart from reality.

"The dreamer retires to his apartments, shuts out the cares and interruptions of mankind, and abandons himself to his own fancy; new worlds rise up before him, one image is followed by another, and a long succession of delights dances round him. He is at last called back to life by nature, or by custom, and enters peevish into society, because he cannot model it to his own will. . . . The infatuation strengthens by degrees, and like the poison of opiates, weakens his powers, without any external symptoms of malignity." [30]

The brief portrait of the dreamer was drawn in 1751. It was embodied in that terrible example of "the dangerous prevalence of imagination" in *Rasselas*, the obsessed and paranoiac astronomer, who sat "days and nights, in imaginary dominion, pouring, upon this country and that, the showers of fertility, and seconding every fall of rain with a due proportion of sunshine." The fear expressed in this portrait was no academic one with Johnson. Of that we may be certain, even though it may never be known exactly what it was that he feared.

" 'There is no man, whose imagination does not, sometimes, predominate over his reason, who can regulate his attention wholly by his will, and whose ideas will come and go at his command. No man will be found, in whose mind airy notions do not, sometimes, tyrannize, and force him to hope or fear beyond the limits of sober probability. All power of fancy over reason, is a degree of insanity. . . .

" 'To indulge the power of fiction, and send imagination out upon the wing, is often the sport of those who delight too much in silent speculation. . . . The mind dances from scene to scene, unites all pleasures in all combinations, and riots in delights, which nature and fortune, with all their bounty, cannot bestow.'"[31]

The man who wrote those lines deeply and harrowingly feared that "dangerous prevalence" within himself, for he was a man of violent and powerful imagination,[32] who often prayed for strength and sanity to overcome it. The consequences for literary criticism are, I think, obvious. Johnson could easily and naturally conceive of art as illusion, of the imagination as creative, and of literary pleasure as overwhelming and potent. But he could never have felt that such a conception was in any way desirable, nor could he have found acceptable or even possible "a willing suspension of disbelief" for the reason that, under circumstances powerfully imaginative and emotive, the will is sometimes powerless to regulate attention and belief. A man's ideas will not "come and go at his command." What Bacon expressed casually Johnson must have felt deeply, that "it is not good to stay too long in the theatre."

Anyone familiar with that side of Johnson, revealed intimately and even terrifyingly in his *Prayers and Meditations* (that side illuminated so well by Professor Bronson's epithet, "Johnson Agonistes"), must conclude, I think, that his literary realism, his conception of literary imitation as likeness and as an "attempt to resemble" nature, and his insistence that the spectators in viewing it are always in their senses, was as much the imposition of a starkly necessary discipline by a highly imaginative and violently emotional man as it was an insight of plain common sense. Under no other conditions could emotion and imagination be made manageably instructive and pleasurable.

These reflections arise from considering Johnson's lifelong opposition to the imagination as an instrument of delusion and even of literary illusion. What the imagination could do positively will appear in our subsequent discussions of language, metaphor, the emotions, and especially wit, in connection with which Johnson's conception of invention, originality, and novelty will be considered. In this more general discussion of imaginative pleasure the reader is asked to remember what has been discussed in Chapters I and III: the nature of Johnson's empiricism and his conception of genius as being the heightened power of all the faculties of the mind cooperating to produce excellence. It is therefore impossible to separate with any degree of accuracy what is purely imaginative from what is purely rational in literary production. Such analysis, in the oversimplified manner of the facultative psychology which Johnson's argument seems to reject, ignores the fact that genius was total intellectual power and that the part could never be satisfactorily set off against the whole.

It should not, of course, be supposed that Johnson was the first — or the last [33] — to express this important insight. A careful examination of Dryden's crucial definitions reveals that, however often he may have paid lip service to currently popular separations of wit and judgment, of fancy and reason, his very language betrays the impossibility of disuniting them. Thus *"wit written* is that which is well defined, the happy result of *thought,* or product of *imagination."* Even that traditional rhetorical classification of poetic creation into the three acts of "invention" ("finding of the thought"), "fancy" ("the variation, deriving, or moulding, of that thought"), and "elocution" ("the art of clothing and adorning that thought . . . in apt, significant, and sounding words") Dryden interprets to be a single imaginative act from beginning to end, since "the quickness of the imagination is seen in the invention, the fertility in the fancy, and the accuracy in the expression." [34]

Similar attention to Johnson's language reveals that he had seized upon Dryden's intuition and made it his own. To the fiery and energetic Homer, often considered by the seventeenth and eighteenth centuries as a natural genius and as one in whom the imagination predominated, Johnson attributed the invention of the epic — "the art of poetical narration, . . . the texture of the fable, the variation of incidents, the interposition of dialogue, and all the stratagems that surprise and enchain attention." But all these arose from his "vigour and amplitude of *mind."* Milton, characterized by Johnson as prevailingly "sublime" in both mind and works, is also a "thinker for himself": "there is more thinking in him and in Butler, than in any of our poets." Observe the quality of language in Johnson's description of the effect of the *imagination* in Milton's greatest work. "The *thoughts* which are occasionally called forth . . . are such as could only be produced by an imagination in the highest degree fervid and active, to which materials were supplied by incessant *study* and unlimited *curiosity*. The heat of Milton's *mind* might be said to sublimate his *learning*, to throw off into his work the spirit of *science*, unmingled with its grosser parts." [35] Thus does Johnson's very language leap from one psychological category to another, from reason to fancy, from imagination to thought, across the boundaries artificially set up by neoclassical criticism.

I have already cited Johnson's comment that there were moments "propitious to poetry." He has nowhere in his formal criticism described in detail what those moments were like. One may be sure that he did not believe with Shelley that "the mind in creation" is "as a fading coal, which some invisible influence, like an inconstant wind, awakens to transitory brightness . . ." It is not at all certain that his conception of invention included, as Mr. Eliot thought Dryden's did, "the sudden irruption of the germ of a new poem, possibly merely as a state of feeling." Johnson was tolerant of various methods of composition — perhaps of all except one, that notion of Gray "that he could not write but at certain times, or at happy moments; a fantastick foppery, to which my kindness for a man of learning and of virtue wishes him to have been superior." Nevertheless, he did admit that in Milton's life there were "transient and involuntary excursions and retrocessions of invention," but he did so reluctantly, insisting that such "inequality" was natural. "The mechanick cannot handle his hammer and his file at all times with equal dexterity; there are hours, he knows not why, when 'his hand is out.' "

Johnson paused to write a couple of pages on Pope's habit "to write his first thoughts in his first words, and gradually to amplify, decorate, rectify, and refine them." Such method he found to lead to "*poetical prudence*," of which he certainly did not disapprove but which with equal certainty he did not usually practice himself, except in some of his poetry and in *Irene*, the successive refinements and purifications of which led to the unhappy results that were all too obvious even to the author himself. The *Lives of the Poets* he wrote "in my usual way, dilatorily and hastily, unwilling to work, and working with vigour and haste." Only this can be said with certainty, that poetry arises from a mind stocked with knowledge and that it attains the power of evoking pleasure only when the writer is "able to animate his mass of knowledge by a bright and active imagination." Whether "a man may write at any time, if he will set himself *doggedly* to it" or whether he must await "the lucky moments of animated imagination" to achieve "those felicities which cannot be produced at will by wit and labour" (the phrases all come from Johnson) is perhaps an impossible and frivolous inquiry.[36]

But propitious moments did come. "When I first entered Ranelagh," Johnson said to Boswell in 1777, "it gave an expansion and gay sensation to my mind, such as I never experienced any where else. But, as Xerxes wept when he viewed his immense army, and considered that not one of that great multitude would be alive a hundred years afterwards, so it went to my heart to consider that there was not one in all that brilliant circle, that was not afraid to go home and think; but that the thoughts of each individual there, would be distressing when alone." Although Johnson does not say that this was the occasion that inspired his greatest poem, his comment was elicited by Boswell's talking of "the doom of man . . . as displayed in his 'Vanity of Human Wishes' " — a poem which, like all of Johnson's most characteristic creations, may have sprung from many such recollections and many such reflections.

Whatever it inspired, this occasion, which Johnson describes after a lapse of perhaps thirty years, has in it all the ingredients of a state of mind "propitious to poetry." There is, first, the "expansion and gay sensation" experienced at the first sight of Ranelagh, of which Johnson had said some five years before this recollection that the "*coup d'œil* was the finest thing he had ever seen." This heightened sensibility is followed by a recollection of Xerxes's famous comment. Then the reflection is darkened by a sable emotion ("it went to my heart to consider") and is universalized (as the mind glances back to the original "gay sensation" by thinking of "all that brilliant circle") into the common and inescapable doom of man. Johnson here does not speak as a literary critic, but he does describe, perhaps by a kind of happy inadvertence, a state of heightened consciousness antecedent to that type of poetry which he felt to be most deeply satisfying. [37]

CHAPTER VI

Language and Form

PERHAPS the prose style of no other English writer has received the minutely analytical attention that has been deservedly paid to Samuel Johnson's. This chapter differs from such studies[1] in purpose: its aim is to consider his theory of language — and also his theory of structure and form — in order better to understand his literary criticism, not in order to describe or evaluate his own literary practice.

I

Johnson once said, "Why, Sir, I think every man whatever has a peculiar style, which may be discovered by nice examination and comparison with others . . ." Such a view — *le style, c'est l'homme*, style is *mentis character, oratio imago animi* — is perhaps as old as the theoretical consideration of language and writing. But Johnson never implied, as many others have, that literary expression is either subjective or organic, obeying only the laws and impulses of its own growth; for he said that distinctiveness is attained not naturally but through the diligent acquisition of a "habit of expression," possible only by "a daily imitation of the best and correctest authors." "The style of an author," said Gibbon, "should be the image of his mind, but the choice and command of language is the fruit of exercise."

It is, moreover, not only individual character that determines style. In the manner of classical rhetoricians, Johnson recognized various types or "levels" of style, each of which became a kind of determining cause: "All polished languages have different styles: the concise, the diffuse, the lofty, and the humble." Such distinctions, along with the conception of individuality, tended to predispose the critic to tolerance of various manners of expression: "One loves a neat style, another loves a style of more splendour. In like manner one loves a plain coat, another loves a laced coat; but neither will deny that each is good in its kind." Johnson paid tribute to Swift's "good neat style," which Hume, typical of many in his day, said he could approve but never admire, since it had "no harmony, no eloquence, no ornament; and not much correctness." Johnson's approbation of Swift's style is a measure of his tolerance, since it is the tribute of a man whose own style possessed to an eminent degree those qualities which Hume found Swift's to lack. Style, like everything literary and indeed like everything human, Johnson found to be a complicated matter, diverse in both excellence and fault; and to these complicating varieties the critic accommodated his judgments. It would be most untrue to say that he had in mind a single and uniform stylistic ideal which guided his evaluation.[2]

Nevertheless he did have standards. Four of the most important of them appear in the four adjectives of his commendation of the historian Knolles, whose style he found to be "pure, nervous, elevated, and clear."[3]

1. The ideal of *pure* diction led Johnson to attempt in his *Ramblers* "to refine our language to grammatical purity, and to clear it from colloquial barbarisms, licentious idioms, and irregular combinations." In critical practice he censured Hume's Gallic style, the style of Pope's later verse ("infected" perhaps by the French idioms of Bolingbroke), and Milton's "perverse and pedantick principle" of using "English words with a foreign idiom." He praised the "genuine Anglicism" of Addison's prose.[4]

2. *Nervous* he defined in the Dictionary as "Well strung; strong; vigorous." He also said that the word *nerve* "is used by

the poets for sinew or tendon"; *nervous*, therefore, when applied to style, may have borne the vague, metaphorical meaning of sinewy and supple, adaptable and flexible; but I think its primary meanings are the ones he suggests in the definition: strong and vigorous. It is therefore related to the Greek quality ἐνέργεια, which I have discussed in another connection and which Johnson usually conveyed by such words as *forcible, animated, energetic*. A genuine virtue even though it could easily be vitiated by being associated with "uncouthness," the "nervous" style arose from the imagination ("that energy that amplifies and animates"), from fidelity to nature (which produced "liveliness"), from rhetorical emphasis and grammatical position, and from importance and dignity of subject matter.

It was also unquestionably associated with another quality, perspicuity, which in his appraisal of Knolles Johnson separated from it. In discussing poetical energy, F. W. Bateson has said: "What is not so clear is that the 'energy' of the poetry is closely dependent upon the 'perspicuity' of the diction. The Augustan achievement was by shearing words of their secondary and irrelevant associations to release the full emphasis of their primary meanings. The connotations, instead of blurring the denotations, reinforced them. The poetry of Dryden and Pope differs therefore from earlier and later English poetry in that it is not a poetry of suggestion but of statement."

All these meanings, however complicated they make the conception, are present in stylistic energy, force, or vigor; but there is another association which is pre-eminently Johnsonian and neoclassical and which perhaps illumines its peculiar effectiveness: its association with brevity and succinctness. Johnson was fully aware of this association, for he defined *sententious* as "short and energetick," *sententiously* as "with striking brevity," and *sententiousness* as "brevity with strength." Energy was thus what Dryden felt it to be, carrying great weight with ease. It arose from resistant tautness, condensation, compression.[5]

3. The stylistic ideal of *elevation* will be discussed in connection with sublimity in the next chapter and as the opposite of

"low" and "familiar" words in the ensuing discussion of poetic diction. It will suffice to say here that, although often separated from elegance, it was a general requirement for making literary language distinct from useful, everyday language. It thus epitomized the ideals of grace, urbanity, ornament, cadence, and indeed that whole *curiosa felicitas* amenable to some rhetorical principles but in its essence beyond the reach of art.

4. The requirement of *perspicuity* was for Johnson and his age a *sine qua non*. Obscurity "counteracts the first end of writing," and "every piece ought to contain in itself whatever is necessary to make it intelligible." Although it was recognized that "obscurity and clearness are relative terms," that "hard words" were often necessary to express profound and subtle meanings, and that clarity was never to be equated with shallow thinking or vulgarization, there was not the slightest appreciation of inherent ambiguity, unresolved paradox, or deep-lying irony of meaning.[6]

These four, along with the far from absolute standard of generality, discussed earlier, are Johnson's stylistic ideals. Each one is invoked in relevant contexts usually without explanation. Sometimes one of the standards is used; sometimes several of them; and sometimes all of them. Each of these ideals not only possesses isolated value; it is also modified, complicated, and enriched by its association with each of the others, with antithetical and contradictory qualities, and even with its closely annexed faults. Thus each takes its place in a complicated pattern of meaning and adornment, of pleasure and instruction. Subject to such qualifications as these, the requirements are sufficiently clear and well known.

There is one problem, however, that deserves more careful attention, the much discussed and much misunderstood matter of poetic diction. Johnson's only extended discussion of it occurs in the *Life of Dryden*.

"Every language of a learned nation necessarily divides itself into diction scholastick and popular, grave and familiar, elegant and gross; and from a nice distinction of these different parts arises a great part of the beauty of style. But if we except a few minds, the favourites of nature, to whom their own original rectitude was in the place of rules, this delicacy of selection was little known to our authors: our speech lay before them in a heap of confusion, and every man took for every purpose what chance might offer him.

"There was therefore before the time of Dryden no poetical diction: no system of words at once refined from the grossness of domestick use and free from the harshness of terms appropriated to particular arts. Words too familiar or too remote defeat the purpose of a poet. From those sounds which we hear on small or on coarse occasions, we do not easily receive strong impressions or delightful images; and words to which we are nearly strangers, whenever they occur, draw that attention on themselves which they should transmit to things." [7]

The passage is as important for what it neglects to say as for what it affirms. It is related (but not integrally, I think) to Johnson's acceptance of the familiar theory of neoclassical literary history that the line of greatest technical development in English verse began with Waller and Denham and culminated in Dryden and Pope. But that development was chiefly, as Johnson saw it, a development in versification, and this is the only passage in which he speaks, at any length, of diction in connection with it. Moreover, this passage recommends diction of the middle register — words neither too familiar nor too remote. Such language possesses semantic and psychological efficacy: it calls attention to "things" and it evokes "strong impressions or delightful images." Johnson's is therefore what Mr. Bateson calls a "negative" and not a "positive" theory of poetic diction, less important for what it recommends than for what it forbids. In Mr. Bateson's words, the Augustan poets "tended therefore to avoid familiar words because of the unmanageable range of their associations and unfamiliar words for the opposite reason that they had next to no associations at all."

Such a theory separated Johnson from those who attempted to achieve dictional beauty by widening the differences between prose and poetry — the imitators of Milton, Spenser, and the Greeks. Johnson's recommendation of this kind of middle diction also separated him from those who looked upon the language of poets as an arsenal or storehouse of poetical words, epithets, similes, and metaphors, even though he did say that Pope in his *Iliad* had left "a treasure of poetical elegances to posterity." It is much too broad and much too medial to be so conceived. Johnson did, to be sure, attach considerable value to poetical ornaments for their own sake; but so redoubtable a foe of artificial imitation could scarcely have approved the practice of drawing stock adjectives ending in *y*, participial epithets, or any of the conventional features of poetic diction from even Pope's elegant store. Indeed, on one occasion at least, Johnson censured Pope himself because "he now and then admits an epithet rather commodious than important." [8]

To look upon Johnson's poetic diction as a kind of color-box prepared by Dryden and Pope for the use of subsequent poets is either to ignore or obscure his theory of words. Like Locke before him, he considered them conventional and arbitrary signs of things in nature or of ideas in the mind, possessing only a subordinate instrumental value. His poetic diction excluded those words which "draw that attention on themselves which they should transmit to things." "To our language may be, with great justness, applied the observation of Quintilian, that speech was not formed by an analogy sent from heaven. It did not descend to us in a state of uniformity and perfection, but was produced by necessity, and enlarged by accident, and is, therefore, composed of dissimilar parts, thrown together by negligence, by affectation, by learning or by ignorance." "I am not yet so lost in lexicography," he said in the Preface to his Dictionary, "as to forget that *words are the daughters of earth, and that things are the sons of heaven.* Language is only the instrument of science, and words are but the signs of ideas . . ."

Thus words cannot be valuable per se. There can be no fixed vocabulary of literary excellence. Poetical words, like all others, are efficacious (1) if they denote things and ideas and (2) if they provide appropriate and pleasurable associations. This twin principle governs the rejection (1) of "terms of art" as too remote in denotation and (2) of "low" words as too familiar (and there-fore disgusting and unmanageable) in connotation. For the latter group an invariable and universal rule would be an impertinence. One's only recourse is to experience. "No word is naturally or intrinsically meaner than another; our opinion therefore of words, as of other things arbitrarily and capriciously established, depends wholly upon accident and custom. . . . Words become low by the occasions to which they are applied, or the general character of them who use them; and the disgust which they produce, arises from the revival of those images with which they are commonly united." With the particular censures of some words as "low" which Johnson's experience of life and society led him to make one may well disagree, but he must be credited with a profound insight into the relativism of connotative language and with the statement of a flexible principle that bids the poet look into his own experience and write.[9]

II

It was in connection with versification rather than with diction or language as a whole that Johnson seems to have been an orna-mentalist and to have attempted a separation of pleasure from instruction. Metrical and rhymed language provided the kind of overlaid adornment that could exist independent of meaning. Too often he tended to separate the pleasures of the ear from the pleasures of the mind. He did not always perceive clearly that those pleasures should be intimately and organically related. The basic principle that governed the delights of the ear, thus inde-pendently conceived, was simply this: variety in uniformity. The basic quality was uniformity since without it variety would be meaningless or licentious. "The great pleasure of verse arises from the known measure of the lines and uniform structure of the stanzas, by which the voice is regulated and the memory re-lieved." [10] It was usually "uniform structure" and "known meas-ure" that Johnson emphasized, but never fully with *l'esprit géométrique* of Fontenelle. There was also the subordinate quality of variety: "The great source of pleasure is variety. Uniformity must tire at last, though it be uniformity of excellence. We love to expect; and, when expectation is disappointed or gratified, we want to be again expecting. For this impatience of the present, whoever would please must make provision. The skilful writer *irritat, mulcet*; makes a due distribution of the still and animated parts." [11]

This is Johnson's basic theory of versification. Stated in such general terms as these, it could govern any formal metrical scheme. Diversity of application results from a greater or less emphasis upon its contradictory constituents, uniformity or variety, and from the particular way in which the claims of each are adjudicated. Johnson rejected the sonnet (to the degree that this judgment was based upon principle and not upon mere dislike and impatience) because it was too restrictive. "The fabrick of a sonnet, however adapted to the Italian language, has never succeeded in ours, which, having greater variety of termination, requires the rhymes to be often changed." Besides, sonnets often dealt with trivial subjects, like love, in an artificial and affected manner. The Spenserian stanza was also unsuitable to the English tongue. It required so many rhymes that the sense was often disturbed, and it was "tiresome to the ear by its uniformity, and to the attention by its length." [12]

Johnson's preference of the rhyming couplet to blank verse is somewhat more complicated. It is not that rhyme is more difficult and therefore imposes greater discipline upon an otherwise licentious imagination — "imagination in a poet," Dryden had said, "is . . . so wild and lawless, that like an high-ranging spaniel, it must have clogs tied to it . . ." — but rather that Johnson expected verse to provide its own independent and adjunctive pleasure. "Blank verse *left merely to its numbers* has little operation either on the ear or mind: it can hardly support itself without bold figures and striking images." It fails "unless sustained by the dignity of the subject" or by excessive enrichment of the language. This argument, in which Johnson had been anticipated by Addison, is ingenious and perhaps oversubtle. Johnson has his cake and eats it too. Rhyme is more artificial but it allows the rest of the verse to remain more natural. Blank verse is more natural but its intrinsic plainness forces the author to make subject and diction unnecessarily artificial. He was fully aware, I think, of the separation of music and meaning that such a view necessarily entailed. He agreed with Milton that "rhyme is no necessary adjunct of true poetry": "perhaps of poetry as a mental operation metre or musick is no necessary adjunct." But he was careful to add that "it is however by the musick of metre that poetry has been discriminated in all languages. . . . Poetry may subsist without rhyme, but English poetry will not often please; nor can rhyme ever be safely spared but where the subject is able to support itself." [13]

Johnson thus attempted to separate metre and music from "poetry considered as a mental operation." It may therefore seem strange and inconsistent that he came very close to looking upon prosody as a "science." "Considering the metrical art simply as a science, and consequently excluding all casualty, we must allow that triplets and alexandrines inserted by caprice are interruptions of that constancy to which science aspires." [14] The severity of this emphasis upon uniformity, which at times all but eclipses the principle of variety, is somewhat tempered by the next sentence: "And though the variety which they produce may very justly be desired, yet to make our poetry exact there ought to be some stated mode of admitting them." Nevertheless, the principle remains, in all truth, severe enough. Its consequences are applied with ruthless consistency in appraising metrical history. Now that the system of versification initiated by Waller and Denham and refined by Dryden has been perfected by Pope, "to attempt any further improvement of versification will be dangerous. Art and diligence have now done their best, and what shall be added will be the effort of tedious toil and needless curiosity." [15]

Nothing could be clearer or more dogmatic. The meaning cannot be explained away. But one important qualification must be made: Johnson is speaking only of versification. When all the elements of that complicated phenomenon, literary pleasure, are considered, Pope stands, for all the excellence of his versification, below Dryden, and both stand below Milton and Shakespeare.

Nevertheless, the force of Johnson's position on metrics is clear. Prosody had already attained what criticism as a whole was far from having attained, the stability and regularity of an intellectual discipline. Debarred by natural endowment as much as by lack of desire, Johnson could never have been a metrical experimenter and pioneer like Donne and Coleridge. He was content to work within the prosodic system of his own day, which was a severely limited one and which, of all possible English systems, was the most amenable to stability and regularity. He apparently followed Bysshe in basing his prosody upon syllables, for he defined versification as "the arrangement of a certain number of syllables according to certain laws." His prosodic system excluded, for all practical purposes, a metrical foot of three syllables and was primarily concerned with duple rhythms, iambic in beat and varied by occasional and cautiously introduced substitutions. It ordered the consonants and vowels in such a way as to achieve smoothness "by tempering the mute consonants with liquids and semivowels" and by avoiding "collisions of consonants," the "openings of vowels upon each other," and excessive sibilance. It restricted all pauses to only the five middle syllables: those that concluded the sense should properly fall on strong syllables, but those that only suspended it might fall on weak syllables. It considered the fourth and sixth to be the most satisfactory syllables upon which to rest, especially the sixth. "Some passages which conclude at this stop, I could never read without some strong emotions of delight or admiration."

Such a metrical system was highly amenable to "scientific" regularity. To musical effects modulated within its restrictive limits Johnson's ear was very sensitive. To other effects it was deaf. His own verses reveal that he could make of the end-stop couplet a form of power and originality, fully capable of conveying what a recent student of the eighteenth-century couplet has described as "a solemn stateliness, a slow-paced resonance, a uni-

versality in meaning, and a tone of 'pathos in isolation' that, at
its best, is unique." But he was not equipped to follow the subtler
cadences of Milton's lyrics; and he had no hint of Coleridge's
perception that "to read Donne you must measure *Time,* and
discover the *Time* of each word by the sense of Passion." [16]

No one will censure Johnson for his tastes, and everyone
capable of hearing its stately music will be grateful for the
achievement of his verse. But why did he as a critic of versification forsake his usual tolerance and sanity in order to erect the
system of Pope into the law and gospel of versification? He may
have felt that it represented the genius of his age, from which
it was dangerous to depart even under the guidance of the greater
works of Milton and Shakespeare. If so, he was walking in paths
made plain for his feet by Dryden. On one occasion at least he
praised metrics as that which "shackles attention, and governs
passions." If the heroic couplet could indeed do that, one can
understand the strength of Johnson's loyalty.

But I suspect that, however much he may have invoked the
pomp and severity of science to support the versification he liked
best, he was really aware that he was actually speaking only of
aural perception: "if I can give any credit to my own ear," he
says in praising the rest upon the sixth syllable. "I suspect this
objection to be the cant of those who judge by principles rather
than perception," he says of those who wished Pope to break
his lines and vary his pauses. "But where the senses are to judge,
authority is not necessary, the ear is sufficient to detect dissonance
. . ." It may be that Johnson shared Campion's view that "the
eare is a rationall sence and a chief iudge of proportion . . ." But
I doubt it. It would have been more in keeping with the tentative
and skeptical cast of his mind in matters purely aesthetic to have
believed with Addison that "Musick is of a Relative Nature, and
what is Harmony to one Ear, may be Dissonance to another."

The truth seems to be that Johnson was fully capable of separating the pleasures of the ear from the larger and more complicated pleasures of the mind and the imagination; when he did so
he found that the music of the heroic couplet was so deeply

satisfying as to seem almost inevitable. It was then that he felt that "the essence of verse is order and consonance" and that Dryden's and Pope's was "the most perfect fabrick of English verse." At other times, when impressed with the fact that such judgments are after all not rationally principled but merely the perceptions of the sense of hearing, he might not have objected too strenuously had someone said that his whole system of metrical criticism was a grand rationalization of his own auricular pleasures.[17]

III

Critics have always been aware that words in literature must somehow express both visual beauty and beauty of sound. Dr. Johnson was no exception, even though he of course appreciated most the poetry of statement and had no conception at all of purely sensuous art. The Oxford English Dictionary records no use of the word *sensuous* between Milton's in 1644 and Coleridge's in 1814, and nothing more effectively measures the distance between Coleridge and Johnson in this matter than to compare their respective interpretations of Milton's meaning of *sensuous* in his famous description of poetry as "simple, sensuous, and passionate." Coleridge, who felt that if these words had been properly understood "a whole library of false poetry would have been either precluded or still-born," says that sensuousness "insures that framework of objectivity, that definiteness and articulation of imagery, and that modification of the images themselves, without which poetry becomes flattened into mere didactics of practice or evaporated into a hazy, unthoughtful, daydreaming . . ."[18] Johnson cites Milton's comment to illustrate *sensuous* in his Dictionary — a word which he classifies as "not in use" and which, so far as I know, he himself never used. But he understands the word to mean "Tender; pathetick; full of passion." Since, as will appear in the next chapter, he associated the tender and the pathetic as critical terms, he naturally assumed that Milton was using a kind of emphatically redundant triplet when he required poetry to be "simple, sensuous, and passionate."[19]

If Johnson's misunderstanding of the term is typical of the

period as a whole, it would appear that the word *sensuous* did not become current until Coleridge revived it, partly because it was associated with the emotions (and for them other words, including that characteristic eighteenth-century creation *sentimental*, were adequate) and partly because words like the somewhat restricted *picturesque* and the more general *descriptive* were considered sufficient to convey as much of physical sensation as was then deemed proper in literature. Nevertheless, the eighteenth century did prepare the ground for the nineteenth in this as well as in other respects; in its own way it did appreciate the sensuous qualities of language.

It was reserved for nineteenth- and twentieth-century France and England, for Shelley, Pater, the pre-Raphaelites, Baudelaire, Mallarmé, Verlaine, Ezra Pound, and Wallace Stevens, to attempt to make poetry approach the condition of music. The earlier period was not interested in the accommodation of the sense to the sound (Johnson's comment on the rhapsodies of Ossianic verse may give some clue to the neoclassical reaction to that) but in the accommodation of the sound to the sense, of which Johnson once said that "there is nothing in the art of versifying so much exposed to the power of the imagination . . ."

Such resemblances he found to be of two kinds. The first is general:

"To revolve jollity and mirth necessarily tunes the voice of a poet to gay and sprightly notes, as it fires his eye with vivacity; and reflection on gloomy situations and disastrous events, will sadden his numbers, as it will cloud his countenance. But in such passages there is only the similitude of pleasure to pleasure, and of grief to grief, without any immediate application to particular images. The same flow of joyous versification will celebrate the jollity of marriage, and the exultation of triumph; and the same languor of melody will suit the complaints of an absent lover, as of a conquered king."

Such general resemblances suggest the Greek musical modes in purpose and effect. They also suggest the relations between music and libretto in early operas and oratorios.

The second type of resemblance is particular, "comprised in the sound of some emphatical and descriptive words, or in the cadence and harmony of single verses," "in the adumbration of particular and distinct images by an exact and perceptible resemblance of sound" — an effect not unlike Mozart's use of the horns in the orchestra to suggest cuckoldry in the libretto of the *Marriage of Figaro* and *Così Fan Tutte*. These particular echoes of the sense Johnson found to be "sometimes studied, and sometimes casual."

"How the Verse labours!" said Joseph Trapp of Vergil's piling of Ossa on Pelion, and comments like that stud the pages of eighteenth-century criticism. But it was Pope more than any other prominent English writer who had recommended such effects in his criticism and exemplified them in his verse. At the end of the sixth volume of the first edition of his *Iliad* there had appeared "A Poetical Index," arranged topically under the conventional heads of fable, characters or manners, speeches or orations, descriptions or images, similes, and versification. There were also many subtopics under each general topic, and reference was made to appropriate lines in the text. Under the topic of versification in this index (which seems designed to make of the translation what it actually became, a thesaurus of "poetical beauties") appeared a subtopic entitled "Expressing in the Sound the Thing describ'd." It listed many kinds of phenomena, physical and spiritual, natural and psychological; and each item referred the reader back to the line of translated verse in which the quality, whatever its nature, was sonantly expressed. Thus haste was expressed in an abrupt verse without conjunctions; disappointment in a verse "full of breaks"; a stormy sea in a verse "broken and disordered." Pope had attempted to accommodate the versification to such an assortment of things as panting, relaxation of the limbs in death, old age, the quivering of feathers in the sun. In one note he says that although Homer had in one of his descriptions enumerated the various parts of the body over which the blood flowed from thigh to foot, "the Author's Design [was] only to image the streaming of the Blood." To Pope it therefore seemed equivalent to make it "trickle thro' the Length of an *Alexandrine* Line." [20]

Under the aegis of Pope such criticism had become licentious, extreme, and very popular. Johnson's Dick Minim was perhaps not the only critic who was an investigator of such beauties and who was particularly delighted when he found the sound an echo to the sense or when he discovered that a line "is *crack'd* in the middle to express a crack, and then shivers into monosyllables." Although one may remember Dick Minim's cant the longest of all Johnson's discussions of the subject, it would be inaccurate to consider his position one of scornful protest and nothing more. He found such resemblances more often chimerical than not, it is true; but his real purpose was to separate the valid from the invalid and thus to refine the position of Pope into one of greater value.

What kind of verbal and metrical resemblances did he accept and what kind did he reject? He accepted such naturally onomatopoetic words as *thump, rattle, growl, hiss, buzz,* and *jar,* but found that they were "but few, and the poet cannot make them more . . ." He also accepted as verbally and metrically possible the representation of sound, motion, and duration of time. "The representative power of poetick harmony consists of sound and measure; of the force of the syllables singly considered, and of the time in which they are pronounced. Sound can resemble nothing but sound, and time can measure nothing but motion and duration."

But beyond that he would not go. "A *boundless* verse, a *headlong* verse, and a verse of *brass* or of *strong brass*, seem to comprise very incongruous and unsociable ideas. What there is peculiar in the sound of the line expressing *loose care* I cannot discover; nor why the *pine* is *taller* in an Alexandrine than in ten syllables." Milton's line "so stretch'd out huge in length the archfiend lay" is not "a *long* form described in a *long* line; but the truth is, that length of body is only mentioned in a *slow* line, to which it has only the resemblance of time to space, of an hour to a maypole." Pope had lengthened his line to suggest the speed and lightness of the "swift Camilla": "Flies o'er th' unbending corn, and skims along the main." When, as Johnson says, he had "enjoyed for about thirty years the praise of Camilla's lightness of foot, [he] tried another experiment upon *sound* and *time*," and produced another alexandrine to express the stately dignity of Dryden's poetry: "The long majestick march, and energy divine." "Here are the swiftness of the rapid race and the march of slow-paced majesty exhibited by the same poet in the same sequence of syllables, except that the exact prosodist [by counting the elided *the* as a complete syllable in the first example] will find the line of *swiftness* by one time longer than that of *tardiness*." [21]

Johnson's conclusion about a critical problem which he investigated in several of his *Ramblers* and in several paragraphs of the *Life of Pope* is this: "Beauties of this kind are commonly fancied; and when real are technical and nugatory, not to be rejected and not to be solicited." Poetical language may therefore be properly sensuous when it is closely allied to meaning and when this fundamental fact is never lost sight of: that it is the function of language to *mean* and not to *be*, to point beyond itself not primarily through its sounds but through its images and its meanings to real things, to ideas of real things, and to real concepts existing in the mind. Rigid adherence to this principle of Locke (who had denied any natural connection between the sound of a word and what it signifies, for "then there would be but one language amongst all men" [22]) placed a severe limitation upon the plastic power of imaginative language. But it also reveals that Johnson had something of Lessing's insight into the limits imposed upon each art by the nature of its medium.

The same awareness appears in his consideration of the relations between poetry and painting, another matter of great concern to his age. Always wary of instruction by analogy and comparison (which could all too easily reason from parallels which are "fortuitous and fanciful"), Johnson did accept as "literal and real" the often urged parallels between painting and poetry. These, he found, are "two arts which pursue the same end, by the operation of the same mental faculties, and which differ only as the one represents things by marks permanent and natural [painting], the other by signs accidental and arbitrary [poetry]." The common end of the two arts was unquestionably the representation of nature; and the identical faculties employed, the reason and the imagination. The difference lay only in the medium peculiar to each.

What does the acceptance of this parallel imply for literary criticism? Johnson enjoyed and recommended poetry that was exactly and accurately visual: "One of the great sources of poetical delight is description, or the power of presenting pictures to the mind." Description should be descriptive and not argumentative or evocative. "The general fault [of Dryden in *Annus Mirabilis*] is that he affords more sentiment than description, and does not so much impress scenes upon the fancy as deduce consequences and make comparisons." "When Virgil describes the stone which Turnus lifted against Aeneas, he fixes the attention on its bulk and weight" — a virtue which Cowley does not possess, for he "gives inferences instead of images, and shews not what may be supposed to have been seen, but what thoughts the sight might have suggested."

But the differences between these sister arts are no less important than the resemblances, even though they lie only in the means employed. "It is not very easy to find an action or event that can be efficaciously represented by a painter. He must have an action not successive but instantaneous; for the time of a picture is a single moment." Since this is true, painting can teach poetry very little about form and structure. There is no evidence that Johnson's version of the *picturesque* in poetry extended beyond those "lively strokes of nature" which should appear in description. He said nothing of contemporary attempts to imitate verbally the prospects of Salvatore Rosa, Claude, and Poussin by selecting and arranging the details with the eye of a painter and attempting to introduce foreshortening and perspective. Pope had approved of Boivin's attempts to represent the shield of Achilles in design, since he had found contrast, perspective, and even the three unities in the Homeric descriptions. William Whitehead had adorned Warton's *Virgil* with an elaborate design, elaborately explained and justified, of the shield of Aeneas. Although Johnson's fervent admiration of Homer may well have extended to his description of the shield of Achilles, he may well have admired the descriptive effects alone and not discovered in it any structural or formal implications whatsoever. "The painter, whose work is partly intellectual and partly manual, has habits of the mind, the eye and the hand, the writer has only habits of the mind."

One may draw the conclusion that Horace's *ut pictura poesis* was an important critical principle in Johnson, but only to the extent that poetry was descriptive. The dictum was relevant to poetry considered as a representation of particular nature but not to poetry considered as a representation of general moral or intellectual nature. Only as the former could poetry legitimately learn the lessons of concreteness, objectivity, and vivacity from its sister art.[23]

IV

Our present conception of imagery includes but does not always distinguish two functions of language, that of introducing sensuous concreteness and that of making comparisons.[24] Dr. Johnson recognized both but carefully distinguished them. His definition of imagery does not include comparison. Imagery consists of "representations in writing, such descriptions as force the image of the thing described upon the mind." The imagination was in part conceived of as the image-making faculty; and an idea was defined as a "mental image." Imagery, although of course it included the sensuous, was therefore not exclusively confined to it. When Johnson praised Gray's *Elegy* for its "happy selection of images" or Milton's *L'Allegro* and *Il Penseroso* because "the images are properly selected and nicely distinguished" or when he wrote late in life that one of the comforts of having old friends is that they have "many images in common," he probably referred in all these cases to mental pictures of reality, both phenomenal and intellectual. Imagery referred to what we have

114

discussed earlier as "lively touches of nature" in descriptions.[25] In Pope's "Poetical Index" to the *Iliad* one of the sections is entitled "Descriptions or Images," under which were included these items: "Descriptions of Places, . . . Persons, . . . Things, Military Descriptions, Descriptions of the Internal Passions, or of their visible Effects." Observe that this list, which seems to treat imagery and description as synonymous, includes representation of such objective matters as *places* and such subjective ones as *internal passions* and that comparison is not directly alluded to in any of these items. There is no evidence that Johnson's conception of imagery was any broader or more subtle, or that he ever departed from his Dictionary definition of imagery as "representations" or "descriptions."

For comparison Johnson used other terms. He defined *metaphor* as follows: "The application of a word to an use to which, in its original import, it cannot be put: as, he *bridles* his anger; he *deadens* the sound; the spring *awakes* the flowers. A metaphor is a simile comprized in a word; the spring putting in action the powers of vegetation, which were torpid in the *winter*, as the powers of a sleeping animal are excited by awaking him." A *trope* was defined as "A change of a word from its original signification; as, the clouds *foretel* rain for *foreshew*," and is thus conceived of as almost identical with metaphor. A *simile* was "A comparison by which any thing is illustrated or aggrandized" — a definition which does not define so much as it describes the double function of a simile, to make clear and to endow with beauty. A *catachresis* is, in the definition in Smith's *Rhetorick* which Johnson adopts for his own, "the abuse of a trope, when the words are too far wrested from their native signification, or when one word is abusively put for another for want of the proper word; as, *a voice* beautiful to *the ear*." Thus catachresis is conceived of as the abuse of a function which is usually legitimate in metaphor and simile. An *allegory* appears to be an extended metaphor: "A figurative discourse, in which something other is intended, than is contained in the words literally taken; as, *wealth is the daughter of diligence, and the parent of authority*."

The words thus defined imply no necessary or inevitable antitheses between the sensuous and the spiritual, between the material and immaterial — except perhaps in allegory, where personification appears to be involved. They compare the literally sensuous and the metaphorically sensuous ("the silk had blue flowers on a red *ground*")[26] or the metaphorically sensuous and the literally spiritual ("he *bridled* his anger"). Perhaps other relations between the abstract and the concrete, the general and the specific, the spiritual and the material, may be involved, but such relations are apparently not essential to the nature of the metaphor and the simile. The common quality is the comparison involved in transferring the meaning from original or primitive signification to other meanings or in bringing together for purposes of comparison two otherwise disparate or unrelated sets of data. It should thus be clear why metaphors and similes were in a peculiar way supposed to represent the operation of the imagination, since that faculty was in part defined as the power of joining the miscellaneous data provided to the mind by the senses and by reflection, just as it was the function of the judgment to separate them.

Johnson does not seem to have considered the symbol of great literary importance. Among the several definitions of *symbol* in the Dictionary is one that might have some relevance to linguistic comparison: "that which comprehends in its figure a representation of something else." But in his critical practice there is no search of literary texts for recurring images or metaphorical habits that might symbolically reveal meanings. Johnson usually looked at one figure at a time in its immediate context. If he discovered patterns of imagery and metaphor, he remained silent about them. It would, of course, have been surprising if the symbol had been accorded any great value by a critic who was prevailingly empirical and rational, who derived little or no aesthetic value from his religion, and who relied upon words for denotative and direct meanings in specific contexts. The poetry of statement is not usually congenial to symbol or myth.

Johnson, like most of his contemporaries, appears to have preferred the simile and the allegory to the briefer metaphor, although he recognized the basic affinities between them. The reasons for this preference must await close investigation of eighteenth-century rhetorical and poetic theory and habit, but it would appear that the admiration for the ancient epic, the desire for clarity, and a taste for grandeur and elevation in comparisons made the simile more congenial. The metaphor, by virtue of its swiftness and condensation, could easily become "broken," [27] as Johnson would say, or "mixed," as we would say, and thus vitiate one of the prime purposes of literature, the accurate and realistic representation of nature. It could less easily be controlled, its "tenor" and "vehicle" could be more easily confused, it seemed to be more emotional than rational, and it was often felt to be characteristic of excited and even demented speech.[28] The slower and statelier simile seemed by its very nature to be exempt from some of these faults.

Johnson has most helpfully stated his conception of the perfect simile. If we fully understand that conception, we shall perhaps better understand his position with respect to the comparative function of language. "A simile, to be perfect," he said in 1781, "must both illustrate and ennoble the subject; must shew it to the understanding in a clearer view, and display it to the fancy with greater dignity . . ."[29] Although in didactic poetry a simile that illustrates but does not ennoble is admissible and in heroic poetry a simile that ennobles but does not illustrate is admissible, perfection requires both. The prime requisites, then, are perspicuity and majesty, clarity and grandeur, the rational and the imaginative. But no purpose is served in separating them: in the best literary effects, as we have seen, instruction and pleasure, reason and fancy have a tendency to fuse, even though Johnson is at times capable of viewing them separately. Instead of separating them, it is therefore better to consider the basic requirements for attaining at once both these qualities of clarity and nobility.

1. The first technical or instrumental requirement is that the two elements of comparison be brought together from a distance.

Wit, in one of its many meanings, was "a kind of *discordia concors*; a combination of dissimilar images, or discovery of occult resemblances in things apparently unlike." The fact that this definition occurs in connection with his famous censure of the metaphysicals should warn us that Johnson perhaps was not fully congenial to "occult" resemblances, but it should not obscure the fact that he not only approved but insisted upon as requisite to successful comparison the union of dissimilars. "A poetical simile is the discovery of likeness between two actions in their general nature dissimilar, or of causes terminating by different operations in some resemblance of effect. But the mention of another like consequence from a like cause, or of a like performance by a like agency, is not a simile, but an exemplification. It is not a simile to say that the Thames waters fields as the Po waters fields; or that as Hecla vomits flames in Iceland, so Aetna vomits flames in Sicily. . . . A simile may be compared to lines converging at a point and is more excellent as the lines approach from a greater distance: an exemplification may be considered as two parallel lines which run on together without approximation, never far separated, and never joined."

This brilliant definition makes of the simile a subtle and sophisticated imaginative effect, requiring observational range, perceptual acuity, and good judgment. It was ever in Johnson's mind. He thus denied that Addison's much admired comparison of Marlborough to an angel, in the *Campaign*, was a simile at all, since Marlborough is "so like the angel in the poem that the action of both is almost the same, and performed by both in the same manner." It "gives almost the same images a second time." He said of one of Dryden's comparisons, "There is so much likeness in the initial comparison that there is no illustration"; he said of another, "This is little better than to say in praise of a shrub that it is as green as a tree, or of a brook, that it waters a garden as a river waters a country." Even Vergil failed in comparing the ship-race with the chariot-race: "land and water make all the difference." When, in Ovid's *Metamorphoses*, "Apollo running after Daphne is likened to a greyhound chasing a hare, there is nothing gained; the ideas of pursuit and flight are too plain to be made plainer . . ." This requirement, though difficult, is in no way mysterious. The elements of a comparison should come from a great distance, not the more brilliantly to display the learning and ingenuity of the author but the better to clarify his meanings.[30]

2. The other technical requirement is somewhat antithetical. Although in the perfect simile the two elements of the comparison ought to come together from a great distance, they should both originate in reality. Together they become metaphorical, imaginative, artistic — a construction of the mind. But when considered separately, as they originally were before the artist brought them together, they must be real. Therefore, Johnson considers a comparison seriously faulty that is metaphorical (i.e., unreal, untrue, fabulous) on one side and literal on the other. Both sides should be drawn from life and reality. They become metaphor only when brought together.

All this becomes clear if we look closely at Johnson's censure of comparisons which he felt were imperfect in this respect. He censures both Dryden's and Pope's odes for St. Cecilia's Day for concluding with the same fault: "the comparison of each is literal on one side, and metaphorical on the other." He says of Dryden's: "The musick of Timotheus, which 'raised a mortal to the skies,' had only a metaphorical power; that of Cecilia, which 'drew an angel down,' had a real effect . . ." Johnson here speaks as a Christian. The power of the pagan Timotheus could only be metaphorical; the power of the Christian saint must be actual. A comparison which equates the two is, in Johnson's view, "vicious." Johnson was here not examining the comparison itself so much as the origin of each side. Even when not impious, the practice of bringing together the real and the unreal could easily become ludicrous. This he makes abundantly clear in his censure of Cowley's *The Mistress.*

"Love is by Cowley as by other poets expressed metaphorically by flame and fire; and that which is true of real fire is said of love, or figurative fire, the same word in the same sentence retaining both significations. Thus, [and here he quotes Addison's *Spectator* no. 62 on mixed wit] 'observing the cold regard of his mistress's eyes, and at the same time their power of producing love in him, he considers them as burning glasses made of ice. Finding himself able to live in the greatest extremities of love he concludes the torrid zone to be habitable. Upon the dying of a tree, on which he had cut his loves, he observes that his flames had burnt up and withered the tree.'

"These conceits Addison calls mixed wit, that is, wit which consists of thoughts true in one sense of the expression, and false in the other. Addison's representation is sufficiently indulgent: that confusion of images may entertain for a moment, but being unnatural it soon grows wearisome. Cowley delighted in it, as much as if he had invented it; but, not to mention the ancients, he might have found it full-blown in modern Italy."

This passage, in which Johnson accepts Addison's concept of the undesirability of mixed wit, makes fully clear his objection to comparisons literal on one side and metaphorical on the other. It is a "confusion of images," in which the same word does double duty as literal and metaphorical, obscuring the meaning, mixing the false and the true, the unreal and the real, and vitiating the chief end of literature, the production of "just representations" of nature.

The passage may also provide a clue to Johnson's preference of the simile to the metaphor. The metaphor could too easily lead to a confusion of reality with unreality because the same words were, in so condensed a form of expression, expected to serve at once as literal and metaphorical; in the simile, however, it was easier to keep the "tenor" and the "vehicle" distinct.

But the real point is that both the referent and the analogue should represent reality. Then the simile truly illustrates: real is compared with real, truth with truth. Johnson finds Pope's famous comparison of a student's intellectual progress with the journey of an Alpine traveler in the *Essay on Criticism* (II, 19–32) to be "perhaps the best that English poetry can shew." It is both illustrative and ennobling; it has no useless parts; the picture of the journey "affords a striking picture by itself"; the analogue comes from a considerable distance and therefore does not exactly parallel the original idea. But we may assume that the simile is perfect also because both mental progress and mountain climbing in the Alps are equally real, although they represent different kinds of reality.

We are now in a position to understand what Johnson says about Denham's famous and influential lines,

> O could I flow like thee, and make thy stream
> My great example, as it is my theme!
> Though deep, yet clear; though gentle, yet not dull;
> Strong without rage, without o'erflowing full.

Johnson's comment is this: "The lines are in themselves not perfect, for most of the words thus artfully opposed are to be understood simply on one side of the comparison, and metaphorically on the other; and if there be any language which does not express intellectual operations by material images, into that language they cannot be translated." He does not find the comparison impious, like Dryden's and Pope's, or ludicrous, like Cowley's. But he does not find it perfect, because it is not fully clear. The wit is somewhat mixed. One side of the comparison, when considered alone, is somewhat ambiguous. The assertion about the river is clear; but the assertion about the poet himself is not. "Without o'erflowing full" is literally true of the river; what does the phrase mean when it is transferred metaphorically to the poet? Since no words in the comparison literally and clearly explain the poet's mental operations, they can be understood only by analogy. The words have no literal and exact meaning which is independent of the river itself. That meaning may be clear to us because of the conventions of our language: material metaphors for immaterial operations are frequent enough. But a language without those associations would not convey the poet's meaning. What Denham says about the river and the mind is in this respect not unlike what Cowley said about real fire and the fire of love: the same word in the same sentence is both simple and metaphorical. Denham's is not a ludicrous conceit.

But to be completely clear, the poet should have used words that referred exclusively and literally, not metaphorically and analogically, to the mental operation itself. Johnson knew what Denham was illustrating because by his time both Aristotle's mean and Horace's *nil admirari*, considered as desirable poetic qualities, had become clichés. But anyone without that experience and without the benefit of a language in which material images expressed intellectual qualities would not have learned that by reading only these lines.[31]

V

Johnson gave considerable thought to the relations between subject matter and organization, between ultimate literary ends and literary form. Although he accepted both descriptive and didactic poetry as pleasurable and instructive, he felt that neither, by its very nature, could provide a satisfactory form of organization. Neither was sufficiently capable of assisting the memory or of exciting curiosity "by suspense or expectation." "The great defect of *The Seasons* is want of method; but for this I know not that there was any remedy. Of many appearances subsisting all at once, no rule can be given why one should be mentioned before another . . ." Exactly the same objection was raised to Pope's *Windsor Forest*; the defect lay in the very nature of descriptive poems: "because as the scenes, which they must exhibit successively, are all subsisting at the same time, the order in which they are shewn must by necessity be arbitrary, and more is not to be expected from the last part than from the first."

The same formal and methodical weakness characterized didactic verse, as Johnson shrewdly and penetratingly observed. Sequence was necessary but it was inevitably arbitrary. In commenting on Pope's *Essay on Criticism*, he observed: "Almost every poem, consisting of precepts, is so far arbitrary and immethodical, that many of the paragraphs may change places with no apparent inconvenience; for of two or more positions, depending upon some remote and general principle, there is seldom any cogent reason why one should precede the other." A thesis poem does not organically grow; its meanings do not unfold. The proposition is stated and then illustrated. For that kind of verse very few formal considerations of great subtlety are necessary: "for the order in which [the ideas] stand . . . ," said Johnson, "a little ingenuity may easily give a reason." The only end is perspicuity, and "where there is no obscurity it will not be difficult to discover method." Excellence lies within the sentence or at most within the paragraph and arises from utterance compressed into neatness, generalized into meaning, and illustrated with appositeness and nobility.[32]

But as Professor Tillotson has said, you exercise reason either as intuition or as *reasoning*.[33] If you express the sententiae of *a priori* right reason, you arrange your precepts and insights in no inevitable order; your problem is chiefly one of selection and illustration. But if you attempt to prove something either inductively or deductively, you must then proceed in the manner of stepwise argumentation and lengthen your development and provide careful transitions. Johnson was clearly aware of the diverse implications for form and method of intuitive reason and of disquisition. In the comment upon form in didactic poetry, cited in part from the *Life of Pope* in the preceding paragraph, he was thinking of the former. He quotes Hooker, who describes the processes of deductive inference: "It is possible that, by long circumduction, from any one truth all truth may be inferred." Johnson continues:

"Of all homogeneous truths at least, of all truths respecting the same general end, in whatever series they may be produced, a concatenation by intermediate ideas may be formed, such as, when it is once shewn, shall appear natural; but if this order be reversed, another mode of connexion equally specious may be found or made. Aristotle is praised for naming fortitude first of the cardinal virtues, as that without which no other virtue can steadily be practised; but he might, with equal propriety, have placed prudence and justice before it, since without prudence fortitude is mad; without justice, it is mischievous."

This must mean that method, form, and order are somewhat specious and arbitrary when you draw conclusions from and apply generally accepted and assumed truth. Then common sense flashes out its applications in any kind of order that meets the test of clarity.

Literary form is not, however, exclusively related to deductive, intuitive, or *a priori* insights. Johnson also recommended that methodical reasoning and connected, inductive argumentation determine the form of the essay and even of the lyric. F. W. Bateson has distinguished three types of lyrical form and made each characteristic of an epoch in English literary history.[34] In the repetitive form, illustrated by a sonnet of Wyatt and typical of Elizabethan expression, a proposition is first stated and then variously repeated in order to draw out its lessons and applications. This type of organization we have discussed in the preceding paragraphs. The organic form (in which the theme grows with the poem and is not fully perceived until its completion) is exemplified by Carew and the metaphysicals. Concerning this manner of proceeding Johnson seems to have been silent. The logical form, illustrated by a song of Congreve and typical of the eighteenth century, is developed by rational and discursive gradation. There is little doubt that Johnson found such logical form to be the most satisfying of all and that he judged the organization of lyrical poetry and the essay from the point of view of their stepwise logical progressions.

"The imagination of the first authors of lyrick poetry was vehement and rapid, and their knowledge various and extensive. Living in an age when science had been little cultivated, and when the minds of their auditors, not being accustomed to accurate inspection, were easily dazzled by glaring ideas, they applied themselves to instruct, rather by short sentences and striking thoughts, than by regular argumentation; and, finding attention more successfully excited by sudden sallies and unexpected exclamations, than by the more artful and placid beauties of methodical deduction, they loosed their genius to its own course, passed from one sentiment to another without expressing the intermediate ideas . . .

"From this accidental peculiarity of the ancient writers the criticks deduce the rules of lyrick poetry, which they have set free from all the laws by which other compositions are confined . . .

"A writer of later times [perhaps Montaigne] has, by the vivacity of his essays, reconciled mankind to the same licentiousness in short dissertations; and he therefore who wants skill to form a plan, or diligence to pursue it, needs only entitle his performance an essay, to acquire the right of heaping together the collections of half his life without order, coherence, or propriety. . . . To proceed from one truth to another, and connect distant propositions by regular consequences, is the great prerogative of man. Independent and unconnected sentiments flashing upon the mind in quick succession, may, for a time, delight by their novelty, but they differ from systematical reasoning, as single notes from harmony, as glances of lightning from the radiance of the sun." [35]

This passage is highly revealing because it finds the same logical method of proceeding applicable to the lyric and the essay. But because it makes system, order, and gradation crucial, it does not therefore seem fully consistent with Johnson's comment upon form in didactic poetry, in which "many of the paragraphs may change places with no apparent inconvenience; for of two or more positions, depending upon some remote and general principle, there is seldom any cogent reason why one should precede the other." The two points of view may be reconciled by discriminating the two related but diverse literary ends introduced in this section, both of which are rhetorical. When known truth is recommended, form is not crucial to persuasion; but when new or less familiar truths are presented, it is. To be convincing, they must be developed in methodical argument.

If the point of view of Jean Le Clerc is typical of logicians and rhetoricians of the late seventeenth and early eighteenth centuries, it was felt that the modern scientific revolution had developed a logical method unknown to the ancients and applicable to many forms of discourse. Here, said Le Clerc, "we very much surpass the Ancients," although there are still many who do not know the rules of mathematical and empirical science. "These Rules had continued as it were hidden among the Geometricians till the time of *Descartes*, who first discover'd the great Use that might be made of them upon all occasions. Since the Discoveries that have been made in our Age about them, several Persons have enlarged and even rectified his Thoughts; as we may see in the *Logic* of the *Port-Royal*, and the *Search* after Truth." [36] This type of logic, which Johnson recommended,[37] may have influenced the form and structure of lyrical poetry and the essay, which were not carefully separated from the rhetorical and persuasive arts.

Johnson's theoretical conception of epic and dramatic structure is in no way original. The fable should be unified, single, complete, and concatenated. "Whoever purposes, as it is expressed by Milton, *to build the lofty rhyme*, must acquaint himself with this law of poetical architecture, and take care that his edifice be solid as well as beautiful; that nothing stand single or independent, so as that it may be taken away without injuring the rest; but that, from the foundation to the pinnacles, one part rest firm upon another." [38]

He would certainly, had he given it any thought, have rejected the Gothic design, which Hurd had found in Spenser. The unity of Spenser's *Faerie Queene*, said Hurd, "consists in the relation of it's several adventures to one common *original*, the appointment of the Faery Queen; and to one common *end*, the completion of the Faery Queen's injunctions." This unity Hurd distinguished carefully from "the classic Unity, which consists in the representation of one entire action." Spenser's Gothic method of design is "an Unity of another sort, an unity resulting from the respect which a number of related actions have to one common purpose. In other words, It is an unity of *design*, and not of action." Such unity of design Hurd illustrated by the Gothic garden, in which the "walks were distinct from each other" but had "their several destinations, and terminated on their own proper objects. Yet the whole was brought together and considered under one view by the relation which these various openings had, not to each other, but to their common and concurrent center." [39]

Such a conception of unity for fable and plot, resembling the popular axial design of a garden, Johnson would have rejected.

It was not linear and developmental, complete within itself, providing a beginning, a middle, and an end, each of which arose out of what had preceded but out of nothing else. Had he given it thought, he might have found that Hurd's Gothic unity was not unlike the kind of unity found in that didactic poetry which presents a series of unconnected truths that open not upon one another but upon a single assumption from which each is derived. Such form might provide unity; it could never achieve any high degree of coherence.

However inevitable and natural the poetical architecture called classical had at first seemed to be, Johnson apparently shifted somewhat his reasons for supporting it. He came to view it not as an inevitable law of natural symmetry and proportion valuable for its own sake but as an instrument of pleasure. This change of emphasis appears in his two discussions of the form of *Samson Agonistes*, separated by an interval of some twenty-eight years.[40] The change is, I think, fully apparent, even though the conclusion reached is virtually the same in both (that the drama lacks a "middle," but does possess a satisfactory beginning and end) and even though some allowance must be made for the fact that the first discussion is an entire essay and the second a few brief sentences.

In the earlier treatment Johnson not only develops at length Aristotle's famous dictum that a plot must have a beginning, middle, and end, but recommends it as an "indispensable" law. Its justification is that it provides just, necessary, and "consequential" regularity. The only hint of its psychological effect comes in the single phrase that describes the catastrophe, when "the mind is left in repose, without expectation of any further event." But what is incidental in the first discussion is made primary in the second. Aristotle is not named and his "indispensable law," although alluded to, is not presented as necessary and natural. Because "the intermediate parts have neither cause nor consequence, neither hasten nor retard the catastrophe," *Samson* therefore "wants that power of attracting attention which a well-connected plan produces." Of the "power of attracting attention" through form, nothing at all was said in the earlier discussion. Alone, this is perhaps not significant, but taken in connection with similar shifts of emphasis noted earlier,[41] it points to an increasing preoccupation with psychological criticism. Literary form is validated by the response of the reader. If it "surprised" and "enchained" attention, it was good form; if not, it was bad. Whatever the formalists might say of the plots of Shakespeare, Johnson found the interest of the reader sufficient justification:

"His plots, whether historical or fabulous, are always crouded with incidents, by which the attention of a rude people was more easily caught than by sentiment or argumentation; and such is the power of the marvellous even over those who despise it, that every man finds his mind more strongly seized by the tragedies of *Shakespeare* than of any other writer: others please us by particular speeches, but he always makes us anxious for the event, and has perhaps excelled all but *Homer* in securing the first purpose of a writer, by exciting restless and unquenchable curiosity and compelling him that reads his work to read it through."[42]

CHAPTER VII

The Beautiful, the Pathetic, and the Sublime

THE words *beautiful, pathetic, sublime* and their synonyms appear often in Johnson's discussions of literary pleasure. Although I do not know that all three are ever used together in one sentence, the sublime and the pathetic, on the one hand, and the sublime and the beautiful, on the other, are among Johnson's most frequently recurring doublets. Each word becomes an important term of aesthetic meaning, clearly distinguished from the others; each expands under the pressure of contemporary theory; each is complicated and enriched by the vigorous personality of its user; and each is used as a tool of practical criticism to help account for the distinguishing excellence of a great English poet. For Johnson, Pope's poetry exemplified the beautiful, Shakespeare's the pathetic, and Milton's the sublime.

I

That extended discussion of the theoretical concept of beauty which was quoted in full and analyzed in an earlier chapter[1] introduces, in *Rambler* no. 92, a discussion of the "accommodation of the sound to the sense." In the series of essays on Milton and on related topics[2] from which it comes, both the sources and the effects of beauty are unmistakably associated with the following words and phrases: pleasure, agreeableness, elegance, harmony, "symmetrical elegance and easy grace" of verse, embellishment of language. Vague though the abstract conception of beauty may have been, these were for Johnson the basic and permanent associations of the term.

There are also other connotations (chiefly apparent in the passages Johnson selects for illustration and comment) which he, like many leading critics of his age, was later to separate from beauty and associate specifically with sublimity. In discussing what in this series of essays is referred to as the poetical beauty of suiting sound to sense, the critic selects passages from Homer and Milton that describe the "dreadful and astonishing," the "crush of men against a rock," the "creaking of hell-gate," "the hideous name" of death (all suggestive of qualities which he himself was later to distinguish from beauty) as well as "fountains," "melodious murmurs," "angelic harmony" (suggestive of qualities which he was always to associate with beauty).

The definitions of beauty that appeared in the Dictionary express the same associations: "1. That assemblage of graces, or proportion of parts, which pleases the eye. . . . 2. A particular grace, feature, or ornament . . ." The word *elegance* (later used by Johnson as a synonym for beauty) is defined as follows: "Beauty of art; rather soothing than striking; beauty without grandeur." [3] The last definition implies an antithesis between the sublime and the beautiful but conceives of beauty as a generic term referring to a quality which could either *soothe* or *strike*, which was either *elegant* or *grand*. There is no clear separation of the concepts; they are considered aspects of the same general quality.

That was to change after the appearance in 1757 of Burke's *A Philosophical Inquiry into the Origin of our Ideas of the Sublime and the Beautiful,* in which the author clearly separated the two terms on the basis of the object or the scene in nature that produced the emotion and on the basis of the emotion itself. Johnson, who was later to express approval of Burke's treatise and the method it used, apparently accepted the distinction in terminology as a useful one. In Imlac's "character" of the poet in the tenth chapter of *Rasselas*, published two years after the appearance of Burke's treatise, the careful distinction between the dreadful and the beautiful, between the "awfully vast" and the "elegantly little," is the Burkean antithesis. In this passage appear those familiar natural phenomena that Burke and others after him regularly cited as means of evoking the sublime (mountains and deserts, crags and pinnacles) as well as those that aroused the agreeable and milder pleasures of the beautiful (trees and flowers, rivulets and clouds). What was implicit in the *Rambler* essays on versification and in the definitions in the Dictionary has here been made explicit. The two conceptions of sublimity and beauty have been clearly separated.

Thereafter they appear together often, but only in antithetical doublets. Even where synonyms are used, the contrast is clear enough. Thomson, for example, "comprehends the vast, and attends to the minute," and describes all of nature whether "pleasing or dreadful"; the verse of Collins could at times produce "sublimity and splendour"; Milton suggests two important and genuine sources of poetry, "pleasure and terrour," "poetical pleasure" and "poetical terrour"; in Addison there is "very rarely the awfulness of grandeur, and not very often the splendour of elegance"; and in the *Life of Waller*, the poet is referred to as one who describes "the beauty and the grandeur of Nature." These examples [4] are by no means exhaustive, but they provide a fairly good indication of the stylistic manner in which the contrast is drawn and of the synonyms which are substituted for one or the other or for both members of the antithesis.

Johnson appears to have contemplated nature through the lenses of this critical perception. Phrases that suggest Burke's distinction occur in his letters to Mrs. Thrale during his journey to the Western Islands. The Minster at York combines both qualities; it is "an edifice of loftiness and elegance." But the Cathedral at Durham "rather awes than pleases, as it strikes with a kind of gigantic dignity . . ." From Skye he writes: "You are perhaps imagining that . . . I am surveying nature's *magnificence* from a mount, or remarking her minuter *beauties* on the flowery bank of a winding rivulet"—a passage which repeats almost verbatim the distinction first clearly made by Johnson in *Rasselas* some fourteen years before and which also associates with the concept the very same natural objects that Imlac had mentioned in the earlier work.[5]

From the examples cited thus far of Johnson's treatment of the concept of beauty, it should be apparent that he thought of it both in the older rhetorical sense in connection with numbers and language and also in its more contemporary relation to certain types of natural data and their appearance in descriptive verse. Rhetorical beauty—the beauty of language, of resemblance between sound and sense, of elegance and grace in verbal embellishment—remained for him the very core and center of his doctrine of aesthetic beauty. It evoked in him the very emotion that it was traditionally intended to—that of agreeableness and rational pleasure. But the newer associations of the term with external nature are also present, and as critic he demanded that the poet be sensitive to both the "elegantly little" and the "awfully vast" in nature and that he be able to represent these effects in descriptive verse. Whenever Johnson was faced with the task of evaluating nature poetry, he found the distinction useful. It became for him a convenient means of classifying natural descriptions, and he often inquired whether the poet writing this genre of verse had attended to both awful grandeur and minute beauty. But even though present, these newer associations remained subordinate. In the *Life of Thomson* the final evaluation of even so thoroughly picturesque a poet is made on other grounds. Thus, while Thomson is praised for having observed nature with a clearly observant eye and with a "mind that at once comprehends the vast and attends to the minute" and that presents "the whole magnificence of nature whether pleasing or dreadful," the very highest praise is reserved for the originality of his imagination.

Although he seems to have followed the contemporary fashion in broadening the concept for at least minor critical purposes, it is for the traditional and exclusively literary beauty of language and numbers that Johnson reserves his enthusiasm. Such beauty, which rests in the sound and its ability to evoke imagery, does not perhaps differ so widely from natural beauty in its effect upon the beholder or reader as might at first appear. There is, of course, a superficial distinction between what appeals to the eye and what appeals to the ear. Beauty was often associated primarily with visual objects and their effects. As Lord Kames pointed out, "the term *beauty*, in its native signification, is appropriated to objects of sight: . . . the agreeableness denominated *beauty* belongs to objects of sight." [6] But however much the critics of his day, under the influence of Newton's *Optics*, may have associated the beautiful with objects of sight and their colors, Johnson did not adhere to what for Kames was the "native signification." In the Dictionary he admitted beauty of form as being coordinate with beauty of sight; in his early essays on versification he associated the word with language and referred frequently then and later to the "beauties" of poetic sound. One is tempted to ask if, after all, the agreeable emotion produced by an elegant phrase or conceit differed very much from that loving and tender emotion produced, according to Burke, by the small, the smooth, the delicate, and the polished objects of sight and touch. Although Johnson was not enough of a theoretical psychologist of beauty to have said so, the fact that such words as *beauty, elegance, grace, agreeableness, pleasure,* and *delight* are used interchangeably for both rhetoric and the loveliness of nature strongly suggests an implicit psychological connection.

However that may be, it is to rhetorical beauty that Johnson responded most strongly, and it is Pope who becomes for him its great exemplar. In isolating that quality in the poetry of Pope, he applies, with unmistakable enthusiasm and verve, and in language that is richly metaphorical, this canon of aesthetic value. He of course praises Pope for other reasons too. He gives him the qualities of invention, imagination, and good judgment, but he concludes the paragraph in which these qualities are enumerated with a brief and perhaps climactic statement of the poet's ability to create the kind of beauty under discussion. Pope "had colours of language always before him ready to decorate his matter with every grace of elegant expression . . ."

It is on the presence of that ability in Pope that Johnson rests, if not his whole case for Pope, at least his whole *aesthetic* case. Steele's comment that the "Temple of Fame" has "a thousand beauties" leads Johnson to add that "every part is splendid; there is great luxuriance of ornaments." The *Essay on Criticism* would itself have placed Pope "among the first criticks and the first poets": it is full of "particular beauties" and among its many embellishments are "splendour of illustration." The *Rape of the Lock* has "the power of pleasing"; *Eloise* is "one of the most happy productions of human wit"; *Dr. Arbuthnot* is a "union of scattered beauties"; of the *Dunciad* "the beauties . . . are well known." And so on. The evaluation of a particular poem nearly always brings into play Johnson's canon of rhetorical beauty — the excellence in poetry of elegance, exquisiteness, grace, and embellishment.[7]

One suspects, from his insistent recurrence to these qualities in Pope, that Johnson was grinding a critical axe. For one thing, Pope's reputation had begun to decline when Johnson undertook an appraisal of him. In 1756 Joseph Warton had distinguished between "a Man of Wit," "a Man of Sense," and "a True Poet." He said that only "a creative and glowing imagination" can make a poet and that "the Sublime and the Pathetic are the two chief nerves of genuine poesy." He had then asked: "What is there transcendently Sublime or Pathetic in Pope?" To that problem Johnson appears to be addressing himself in his *Life of Pope*. He is forced to concede part of the argument: he is no more able than Warton to find the sublime or the pathetic in Pope. And yet he is for Johnson a very great poet indeed. "If Pope be not a poet, where is poetry to be found?" By strong implication he takes issue with Warton's assertion that the sublime and the pathetic are "the two chief nerves of genuine poesy." There is at least one other — rhetorical beauty — the expression of which was in itself an achievement of the very highest poetical genius.

This view appears nowhere more forcibly in the *Life of Pope* than in Johnson's defense of the translation of the *Iliad*. Homer possessed "awful simplicity," "artless grandeur," "unaffected majesty" — qualities that Johnson and most contemporary critics called "sublime." In Pope's hands, however, the sublime has become the beautiful, the elegant, the embellished; and that transformation Johnson is prepared to defend with vigor:

"I suppose many readers of the English *Iliad*, when they have been touched with some unexpected beauty of the lighter kind, have tried to enjoy it in the original, where, alas! it was not to be found. Homer doubtless owes to his translator many Ovidian graces not exactly suitable to his character; but to have added can be no great crime if nothing be taken away. Elegance is surely to be desired if it be not gained at the expence of dignity. A hero would wish to be loved as well as to be reverenced.

"To a thousand cavils one answer is sufficient; the purpose of a writer is to be read, and the criticism which would destroy the power of pleasing must be blown aside. Pope wrote for his own age and his own nation: he knew that it was necessary to colour the images and point the sentiments of his author; he therefore made him graceful, but lost him some of his sublimity." [8]

The passage obviously turns on the familiar distinction between sublimity and beauty. With the latter term Johnson here, as in his more theoretical statements, associates elegance, embellishment, color, grace, and the agreeable power to please. The defense of Pope rests on a taste for that kind of beauty.

Johnson's relish for Popean beauty appears with almost equal obviousness and force in his criticism of the *Essay on Man*. A vigorous defense of Pope as a poet, the passage about to be cited becomes a direct answer to Warton, since the case rests on the grounds of poetic beauty and on those grounds alone. To Warton, who had attempted to make of Pope a man of sense and wit but not a poetical genius because he was incapable of the sublime and the pathetic, Johnson says in effect: Pope was not always a man of sense; in fact, he was something of a fool for accepting the ideas of Bolingbroke without fully understanding them. The ideas of the *Essay* are partially digested commonplaces. "Having exalted himself into the chair of wisdom [Pope] tells us much that every man knows, and much that he does not know himself . . ." The attack on Pope's *ideas* in the poem, on the "metaphysical morality" which was for the poet obviously "a new study," is somewhat reminiscent of Johnson's annihilation of Soame Jenyns. But the crucial point is that in spite of commonplace ideas, in spite of the conspicuous absence of sublimity and pathos, Johnson still finds that Pope is a genius (one is tempted to use Warton's phrase a "transcendent genius") because of his extraordinary powers of embellished and eloquent language:

"This *Essay* affords an egregious instance of the predominance of genius, the dazzling splendour of imagery, and the seductive powers of eloquence . . .

"Surely a man of no very comprehensive search may venture to say that he has heard all this [the ideas of the poem] before, but it was never till now recommended by such a blaze of embellishment or such sweetness of melody. The vigorous contraction of some thoughts, the luxuriant amplification of others, the incidental illustrations, and sometimes the dignity, sometimes the softness of the verses, enchain philosophy, suspend criticism, and oppress judgement by overpowering pleasure." [9]

Seldom did Johnson write with such aplomb about a purely aesthetic quality. It was at once his response to a challenge and his statement of a creed.

In the case of the beautiful, unlike that of the sublime, Johnson as man and moralist imposed few, if any, restraints on his taste. He was not unaware that the kind of neoclassic beauty that he found ablaze in Pope could lose its heat and light and become frigidly correct. Matthew Prior, for example, although he could achieve elegance (and even sublimity) was at times dull. And tediousness, as Johnson said in connection with Prior, is "the most fatal of all faults" — a power which, like Pope's personified Dulness in the *Dunciad*, "propagates itself." But this fault, however fatal it might be in achieving a literary effect, certainly represented no moral danger. It was a threat neither to orthodox religion nor to a man's emotional stability. And if Johnson was aware that Popean beauty, when it was not impregnated by wit and fancy, could easily become tedious, he must have felt that

that was preferable to a "dangerous prevalence of imagination," with which neoclassical elegance cannot often have been associated even when it was most fully enjoyed. When he found rhetorical beauty, Johnson was free to enjoy it to the full. It set up no conflict or tension within him. The pleasure it aroused was almost unadulterated, and he could read Alexander Pope with "perpetual delight."[10]

II

In the Dictionary Johnson defined *pathetic* as follows: "Affecting the passions; passionate; moving." This definition in no way hints at his very special uses of the word, nor does it in itself suggest what is perhaps the most important preliminary fact about the concept in Johnson, namely, that in resistance to one of the most significant aesthetic tendencies of his century, he consistently separated the pathetic from the sublime. Samuel H. Monk has commented that Longinus's hints that the sublime could not exist apart from the pathetic

"form the nucleus of much that was written and thought in the eighteenth century as to the relation of the sublime to the pathetic. Although Longinus does not consider emotion as absolutely necessary to sublimity, he nevertheless habitually associates the two, since the orator's task was to persuade by affecting the emotions of his audience as well as by convincing their reason. The presence of emotion in art is the point of departure for the eighteenth-century sublime, and indeed the study of art as the evoker of emotion is perhaps even more characteristic of the aesthetic thought of the period than the study of the rules."[11]

Johnson's practice was regularly to resist this fusion of the pathetic and the sublime. He always kept the terms in separate critical compartments. Influenced by the tendencies to which Professor Monk alludes only in the sense that he seldom thought of the one without thinking of the other, he sharply distinguished them even when they appeared, as they often did, in a stylistic doublet. Of Waller, Johnson says that "he is never pathetick, and very rarely sublime." Having described the inability of Cowley and the metaphysicals to represent or move the affections, he adds: "Nor was the sublime more within their reach than the pathetick" — a clear indication that Johnson had moved from one concept to the other. Later he uses almost the same phrase about Cowley that he had used in the *Life of Waller*: "It will be found that . . . he is never pathetick, and rarely sublime . . ." He censures the metaphysicals for producing the one when they intended the other: "Their expressions sometimes raise horror [i.e., the sublime], when they intend perhaps to be pathetick." But it is in the *Life of Milton* that he most clearly distinguishes the two terms: "As human passions did not enter the world, before the Fall, there is in the *Paradise Lost* little opportunity for the pathetick; but what little there is has not been lost. . . . But the passions are moved only on one occasion; sublimity is the general and prevailing quality in this poem . . ." There is no mistaking the sense of these passages.[12] The two qualities might conceivably appear together, but I know of no case in which Johnson saw them both present to any important extent in any single work.

It is possible by going back to *Rasselas* to see that the distinction is part of a larger one. Early in his career Johnson had, to be sure, used the pathetic in its older rhetorical sense, distinguishing it from the familiar and the solemn and locating it in the "animated Oration." But more useful and certainly more characteristically Johnsonian is the distinction clearly made by Imlac, who in the following phrases anticipates the distinction we have illustrated from the *Lives of the Poets*: "The province of poetry is to describe *nature* and *passion*"; "My desire of excellence impelled me to transfer my attention to *nature* and to *life*"; "But the knowledge of *nature* is only half the task of the poet; he must be acquainted, likewise, with all the modes of *life*."

These sentences partition Imlac's discourse and provide its transitions. In the words *nature* and *life*, which give to this crucial passage its very form and meaning, lies the old distinction between external nature and human nature — a distinction which dictated the separation of the sublime and the pathetic. As Imlac's speech makes abundantly clear, *nature* includes the sublime and *life* includes the pathetic. Under *nature* Johnson discusses qualities regularly associated with the beautiful and also those regularly associated with the sublime (mountains, deserts, "whatever is dreadful," "the awfully vast"). Under *life* he discusses the human mind, right and wrong, laws and opinions, and "the *passions* in all their combinations" (i.e., the pathetic). Therefore in the often recurring doublet, "the sublime and the pathetic," the part is frequently allowed to stand for the whole. The more general antithesis is "nature and life." On one occasion at least *passion*, in a kind of synecdoche, takes the place of *life*: Johnson refers to the distinction in the phrase, "by nature or by passion." [13]

This is the basic affiliation of the term *pathetic*: it refers in its broadest signification to the representation of human life in art, to a selective imitation of Aristotle's ἤθη, πάθη, and πράξεις. It thus at times becomes almost as much an ethical as an aesthetic term. Since the passions are coextended with rational nature, since they can be malignant or noble, their representations in art must of course meet the standards of morality and rationality, of universality and permanence. But there is, besides this broad ethical meaning, a more restricted aesthetic sense in which Johnson uses the term to refer to the simple and quiet emotions of human tenderness and domestic love. Both usages appear in the frequent antitheses between the sublime and the pathetic: (1) as a part of the philosophical distinction between external nature (whose grander aspects can evoke sublimity) and human life (which includes the passions), and (2) as an aesthetic contrast of mood and feeling between that which arouses terror and awe (the sublime) and that which arouses sympathy and tenderness (the pathetic).

It is this latter meaning that prevails in the discussion of pathos in the drama of Dryden, of whom Johnson says somewhat dogmatically that he is "with all his variety of excellence, not often pathetick; and had so little sensibility of the power of effusions purely natural that he did not esteem them in others. Simplicity gave him no pleasure . . ." This passage is important not only because it denies to Dryden the ability to express the pathetic to any great extent, but also because it hints at the reason and suggests strongly the emotions Johnson associates with this aesthetic quality. The pathetic is associated with "effusions purely natural" and with simplicity, but not with forced violence and emotional turbulence. Because "Dryden's was not one of the 'gentle bosoms'," he could not achieve this quality. "With the simple and elemental passions, as they spring separate in the mind, he seems not much acquainted. . . . Love, as it subsists in itself . . . was too soft and subtle to put his faculties in motion. He hardly conceived it but in its turbulent effervescence with some other desires . . ." [14]

If because of such effervescence and violence Dryden as dramatist did not qualify as an exemplar of the pathetic, Shakespeare most certainly did. For Johnson he was supremely the poet of the pathetic, both in its broadly ethical and humanistic meaning and in the narrower aesthetic sense which I have been discussing. Just as the word *pathetic* belongs to the representations of all of life in literature and could not therefore escape an ethical connotation, so its great exemplar illustrates the large and central moral qualities that all enduring representations of life must possess. In the more restricted aesthetic sense in which it was used in the *Life of Dryden*, the pathetic was also abundantly present in Shakespeare. Although subordinated to the pleasures of the mind, the pleasures of the emotions do exist as the simple and "elemental" emotions of pity, joy, and sorrow which Johnson always associated with the pathetic, which have immemorially been associated with laughter and tears, and which he found conspicuously absent from the dramas of Dryden. In arousing these gentle and tender emotions Shakespeare became for him the poet of the pathetic but never, in any important degree, the poet of the beautiful or the sublime. Each of the following passages illustrates his discovery of the pathetic in Shakespeare:

"*Shakespeare* has united the power of exciting laughter and sorrow not only in one mind, but in one composition. Almost all his plays are divided between serious and ludicrous characters, and, in the successive evolutions of the design, sometimes produce seriousness and sorrow, and sometimes levity and laughter.

.   .   .   .

"Through all these denominations of the drama, Shakespeare's mode of composition is the same; an interchange of seriousness and merriment, by which the mind is softened at one time, and exhilarated at another. But whatever be his purpose, whether to gladden or depress, or to conduct the story, without vehemence or emotion, through tracts of easy and familiar dialogue, he never fails to attain his purpose; as he commands us, we laugh or mourn, or sit silent with quiet expectation, in tranquillity without indifference.

.   .   .   .

"The force of his comick scenes has suffered little diminution from the changes made by a century and half, in manners or in words. As his personages act upon principles arising from genuine *passion*, very little modified by particular forms, their pleasures and vexations are communicable to all times and to all places; they are natural, and therefore durable; the adventitious peculiarities of personal habits, are only superficial dies, bright and pleasing for a little while, yet soon fading to a dim tinct, without any remains of former lustre; but the discriminations of true *passion* are the colours of nature; they pervade the whole mass, and can only perish with the body that exhibits them . . ." [15]

Such is the "pathos" that Johnson found in Shakespeare. One weeps with those that weep and rejoices with those that rejoice. There is no violence, no naked, primitive energy. When there were emotional excesses — as in the conclusion of *Lear* or in the "extrusion" of Gloucester's eyes — Johnson left the play unread until he revised it as an editor. And he was willing to accept the revision of Nahum Tate.

Johnson's tendency to see the pathetic as one of Shakespeare's most characteristic and successful literary effects appears prominently in some of the specific comments that he made as a Shakespearean editor. From the pomp and splendid pageantry of *Henry VIII* he selects for special commendation "the meek sorrows and virtuous distress of *Catherine*," which appeared in scenes "which may be justly numbered among the greatest efforts of tragedy," and he makes the extraordinary statement that Act IV, Scene ii of this play, in which Katherine discusses her own fate and that of Cardinal Wolsey, is, "above any other part of *Shakespeare's* tragedies, and perhaps above any scene of any other poet, tender and pathetick, without gods, or furies, or poisons, or precipices, without the help of romantick circumstances, without improbable sallies of poetical lamentations, and without any throes of tumultuous misery." The same strong sensibility for the pathetic led him to praise *Timon of Athens* as "a domestick Tragedy," which "strongly fastens on the attention of the reader."

It was the presence of the pathetic in the bourgeois and sentimental drama which caused him to praise excessively several rather indifferent examples of that genre. He accounted for the century-long success of Otway's *Orphan* ("a domestick tragedy drawn from middle life") on the same grounds: "Its whole power is upon the affections, for it is not written with much comprehension of thought or elegance of expression. But if the heart is interested, many other beauties may be wanting, yet not missed." He welcomed the continuing presence on the stage of Rowe's *Jane Shore*, which, as a play of "domestick scenes and private distress, lays hold upon the heart." Mrs. Thrale reports that Johnson did not like to speak often of "the pathetic in poetry" — perhaps he felt that it was inconsistent with his character as the Great Cham — but he did not deny Hannah More's implication that he wept at the death of Jane Shore, although he did rebuke his friend, then thirty-seven years old, as "a saucy girl" for her impudence. She also recalls that Johnson took her by the hand at dinner and repeated "with no small enthusiasm" many passages from Rowe's *Fair Penitent*, another domestic tragedy, which Johnson called one of the most pleasing on the stage.[16]

There can, I think, be no doubt of his taste for the pathetic as it has been here defined or of the fact that Shakespeare is for him one of its greatest exemplars. The significant corollary of his emphasis on the tender and the pathetic in Shakespeare is that he tends to dilute whatever violence appears in the plays. Convincing evidence of this lies in his comment on the age-old problem of why the spectacle of tragedy and human suffering pleases. The critic found that extreme emotion in all dramatic art was softened and mollified by the time it reached the spectator. "The reflection that strikes the heart is not, that the evils before us are real evils, but that they are evils to which we ourselves may be exposed. If there be any fallacy, it is not that we fancy the players, but that we fancy ourselves unhappy for a moment; but we rather lament the possibility than suppose the presence of misery, as a mother weeps over her babe, when she remembers that death may take it from her." Fiction, by diluting the emotional intensity and mitigating the pain of reality, helps to keep terror and all the intenser emotions within the bounds of the bearably pathetic. Dramatic terror is successful if it sinks the spectator in dejection; dramatic pity, if it mollifies him with "tender emotions." It is significant that Johnson calls such literary effects "soft and pathetic." [17]

Such modulated emotion may seem somewhat inconsistent with the robust and vigorous Samuel Johnson, who once wrote of a passage in *Macbeth* that he "that peruses *Shakespeare*, looks round alarmed, and starts to find himself alone." But for whatever reason, the fact is that having separated the sublime from the pathetic, having kept each in a separate category, and having decided to praise Shakespeare as the poet of human nature and as the exemplar of the tenderly pathetic, Johnson had little to say about the dramatist's powerful emotional and imaginative effects. It was, of course, no new thing to conceive of pathos as tender, natural, simple, and soft. Critics as diverse as Pope and Wordsworth, Hume and Tolstoy, have made the same associations, and they still cling to the term. The force and originality of Johnson's conception lay rather in its application to Shakespeare.

To call Shakespeare "pathetic" was to give him a cultivated Vergilian quality: Joseph Warton had said that "the *pathetick* was the grand, distinguishing characteristic of the Roman poet's genius and temper"; and Thomas Sheridan implied as much when he told Boswell and Erskine that he thought Ossian "excelled Homer in the Sublime and Virgil in the Pathetic." Shakespeare had more often been likened to that natural and sublime genius Homer. Dryden had praised the English bard as fiery, masculine, and bold, whose works moved terror rather than pity. Addison had commented on his extravagant fancy, the wild and solemn force of his bold, untutored mind. Dennis, who perhaps more than any other critic of the first half of the century had tended to fuse the sublime and the pathetic, considered him a master of terror. Although Theobald found that Shakespeare could draw nature in miniature, he was perhaps more impressed with the dramatist's ability to raise his description to "that Pitch of Grandeur, as to astonish you with the Compass and Elevation of his Thought," and Maurice Morgann said that we feel rather that "we are possessed by him, than that we possess him." But Johnson's Shakespeare allows the mind to repose on the stability of truth and softens the heart with pathos and tenderness, dejection and laughter. The reason for this critical emphasis will appear more clearly when we consider the highly individual way in which Johnson responded to the sublime.[18]

III

Johnson's Dictionary gives several definitions of *sublime*: "1. High in place; exalted aloft. . . . 2. High in excellence; exalted by nature. . . . 3. High in stile or sentiment; lofty; grand. . . . 4. Elevated by joy. . . . 5. Haughty; proud . . ." The term clearly possessed meanings outside criticism, and Johnson often used the word both literally and metaphorically for anything that was lofty. But he used it most often and most significantly as a term of aesthetic meaning.

It has been observed that Johnson lists it as a substantive in his Dictionary and epitomizes in one sentence the history of the word in English since Boileau: "*The sublime* is a Gallicism, but now naturalized." Yet in the definition of the substantive Johnson expresses little more than the traditional rhetorical meaning, which came to be outmoded in favor of the subjective and the emotional sublime, the sublime that ravishes and transports. Johnson is content to designate *the sublime* as "The grand or lofty stile," a definition which he illustrates from Pope's famous tribute to Longinus ("and is himself the great sublime he draws") and from Addison, who concentrates on the source of the sublime in the work of art itself: "The *sublime* rises from the nobleness of thoughts, the magnificence of the words, or the harmonious and lively turn of the phrase; the perfect *sublime* arises from all three together." Johnson continued to use the word to refer to this kind of rhetorical elevation from the very beginning of his literary career to its end.

His comments on Longinus, although brief, point to a kind of moderate, neoclassic esteem. As a preface to Zachary Pearce's commentary on the Four Evangelists, Johnson wrote comments which he interpolated into the autobiography of that learned divine. These passages have only recently been attributed to Johnson and therefore appear in no edition of his complete works. They have not, in fact, been reprinted since 1777, when they appeared anonymously. Johnson comments as follows: "Longinus, whose name had been long known only to men of abstruse erudition, till he was introduced by his translator Boileau, among the witty and the elegant, had now for about half a century enjoyed great popularity, quoted by every poet and every critick, and deciding upon faults and beauties of stile with authority contested only by *Huetius* and *Le Clerc*." [19] Johnson's Longinus is an *arbiter elegantiarum*, deciding upon beauties and faults in the conventional manner, and is in no way related to the inspirer of lonely romantic geniuses agonized with ecstasy and terror.

Quite apart from Longinus, Johnson has much to say about the high style, which is appropriate to the epic, to some kinds of moral discourse, and to any subject that was sufficiently elevated and noble in purpose and theme. It is the critical club with which he beats down the metaphysicals, who could attain neither the sublime nor the pathetic because they were analytical, oversubtle, fragmentary, and therefore incapable of the "grandeur of generality." "Sublimity is produced by aggregation, and littleness by dispersion. Great thoughts are always general, and consist in positions not limited by exceptions, and in descriptions not descending to minuteness." [20] In this famous evaluation of the metaphysical school, it is, I think, the rhetorical sublime which Johnson uses as an instrument of critical appraisal. His definition of the sublime in this passage ("that comprehension and expanse of thought which at once fills the whole mind, and of which the first effect is sudden astonishment, and the second rational admiration") does indeed suggest the emotional sublime at times. Nevertheless, the passage makes no mention of what he stresses in connection with the sublimity of Milton, namely "poetical terrour"; and the subsequent discussion shows that he is thinking chiefly of style and imagery.

But as every student of the eighteenth century knows, the rhetorical sublime did not suffice for criticism and was therefore extended to include the lofty and the great in nature — the dark, the obscure, the terrible, the grand — which overpowered the imagination and evoked the harrowing emotions of terror and fear. Johnson's conception of the sublime was similarly extended. It should almost go without saying that he was by his very nature singularly susceptible to those emotions which the term came to include. He was agitated as few others by the contemplation of death; he was awed by his religion; his devotional life was crossed with terror and despair. And he was not so indifferent as he has been made out to be to the grandeur of nature. In both his own and in Boswell's records of the tour to the Hebrides there is revealed a Johnson who was awed by the naked wildness of the Western Islands. In that most romantic of countries, Wales, he described Sir Rowland Hill's seat at Hawkestone as "a region abounding with striking scenes and terrifick grandeur." He was made solemn by the "extent of its prospects, the awfulness of its shades, the horrors of its precipices, the verdure of its hollows, and the loftiness of its rocks. The Ideas which it forces upon the mind, are the sublime, the dreadful, and the vast. Above, is inaccessible altitude; below, is horrible profundity." [21]

As I have pointed out earlier, it was doubtless under the influence of Burke that Johnson came to separate the two concepts of sublimity and beauty from one another and to make a more careful association of each term with a special kind of natural phenomena; but "the sublime, the dreadful, and the vast" were certainly present in his imagination from the very beginning. In his Dictionary he does not neglect this type of emotion, and in some of his *Rambler* essays he actually attempts to express it. But it is in *Rasselas*, his first major work after Burke's treatise, that he most clearly reveals his awareness of this type of aesthetic effect. Imlac on the sea introduces the notion of "pleasing terrour" —a clear anticipation of Johnson's lifelong recognition of "poetical terrour" as a legitimate, if somewhat perilous, poetical quality —and in Imlac's "character" of the poet the "awfully vast" becomes a source of poetic imagery of equal importance with the "elegantly little." Like Imlac's, Johnson's "sphere of attention" was magnified to include mountain and desert, the crags of the rock, and "whatever is dreadful." In the cavern, which Coleridge made measureless to man, Johnson has placed a "stream, which entered a dark cleft of the mountain," which "fell with a dreadful noise," and which had its own secret passages. The sea ("boundless and immense"), the pyramids, the awesome solitude, the catacombs, and God ("the being whom I fear to name") — such are the invocations of sublimity in *Rasselas*.[22]

It would be tedious to cite all the evidence available for the presence of this type of sublimity in Johnson. We turn rather to the *Life of Milton* for his most important use of the sublime as a critical concept.[23] In so applying the idea, he was, of course, following what had become by the time he wrote on Milton almost an established critical practice. Milton had become the most sublime of the English poets. But Johnson's application of the concept was not merely a gesture to a critical fashion. He is using a concept about which he knew a great deal in his own emotional life, about which he could not be indifferent, and with which he had been preoccupied both in life and literature for many years.

It is characteristic of Johnson that in connection with Milton he should concern himself with those two important and insistent contrasts: the sublime and the beautiful, the sublime and the pathetic. He seldom discovered one of the traits present in a work of literature without feeling called upon to consider the other two. So it is with the beautiful in Milton, which Johnson relegates to a subordinate position: "The characteristick quality of his poem is sublimity. He sometimes descends to the elegant, but his element is the great. He can occasionally invest himself with grace; but his natural port is gigantick loftiness. He can please, when pleasure is required; but it is his peculiar power to astonish." [24] In direct contrast to Pope, there is here occasional beauty but pervasive and controlling sublimity. Similarly Johnson felt the need of introducing the pathetic into his evaluation of Milton, if only to comment that there is in *Paradise Lost* but little opportunity to express it. The critic was determined to keep his categories distinct. In assessing the sublimity of Milton's epic, he goes out of his way to exclude as irrelevant both the beautiful and the pathetic.

What kind of sublimity prevails in Milton — the rhetorically elevated or the emotional sublimity of awe and grandeur? The evidence points to the presence of both. In *Paradise Lost* Johnson discovers a "sublimity variously modified, sometimes descriptive, sometimes argumentative." These adjectives seem to be rhetorical terms, referring respectively to style and subject matter, to manner and theme. In the passage from Addison that Johnson had quoted to illustrate his definition of the *sublime*, Addison had found that the "perfect sublime" included the following: "nobleness of thoughts" (the *argumentative* sublimity of Johnson, the sublimity of theme and design, of epic plot and structure); and "the magnificence of the words, or the harmonious and lively turn of the phrase" (Johnson's *descriptive* sublimity).

But in addition to these conventional rhetorical categories there is the other sublime — the sublime of greatness in man and nature, of terror and astonishment, of the awful and the forbidding. It is aroused by the "wide realms of possibility" in which Milton's gigantic imagination loved to sport. One finds in reading this *Life* that the great, the vast, the awful, the gloomy, the dreadful often astonish the intellect, crowd the imagination, strike and fill the mind. And all these are, in their way, the evocations of psychological and emotional sublimity. Indeed the "poetical terrour" is at times so intense that "we recede with reverence" or "shrink with horrour" from those "awful scenes."

That gesture of admitting poetic terror as a genuine source of poetry only to recede from it in fear when it appears brings us directly to those serious limitations upon the sublime which Johnson's religion and rationality both made almost inevitable. His religion was darkened by fear and the sense of danger; because of those very qualities it became at times almost intolerable. Again and again he denied the artistic validity of religious poetry not from a lack of the requisite sensibility but from too much sensibility. The theme was too terrible, too overpowering, too sublime for the "wings of wit." Poetic devices were all too often inappropriate to it. This powerful religious sensibility lies behind the passage on Milton, which reveals Johnson at once attracted to and repelled by the poetic representation of solemn religious themes. Having discussed the fall and expulsion of Adam and Eve, he says:

"Of the ideas suggested by these awful scenes, from some we recede with reverence, except when stated hours require their association; and from others we shrink with horrour, or admit them only as salutary inflictions, as counterpoises to our interests and passions. Such images rather obstruct the career of fancy than incite it.

"Pleasure and terrour are indeed the genuine sources of poetry; but poetical pleasure must be such as human imagination can at least conceive, and poetical terrour such as human strength and fortitude may combat. The good and evil of Eternity are too ponderous for the wings of wit; the mind sinks under them in passive helplessness, content with calm belief and humble adoration." [25]

The paradox is that Johnson was too deeply religious to enjoy or even tolerate religious poetry. Themes of the highest and most solemnizing dignity, as he knew all too well, aroused disquieting emotions. When "strong devotion to the skies aspires," Johnson was apparently not in the mood for the enjoyment of verse. And this deep and disturbing sensibility of his gave him solemn pause in contemplating the sublimity of Milton.

The rationalist in Johnson also tended to limit the flight of the imagination toward sublimity, which might became a "dangerous prevalence of imagination." Reason and the terrible-sublime could not be expected to prevail together. Johnson, as a man of broad humanistic learning, must also have had serious doubts about the value of cultivating the emotions of wonder and astonishment, almost always conceived of as the concomitants of the sublime.

"That wonder is the effect of ignorance, has been often observed. The awful stillness of attention, with which the mind is overspread at the first view of an unexpected effect, ceases when we have leisure to disentangle complications and investigate causes. Wonder is a pause of reason, a sudden cessation of the mental progress, which lasts only while the understanding is fixed upon some single idea, and is at an end when it recovers force enough to divide the object into its parts, or mark the intermediate gradations from the first agent to the last consequence."

Johnson's comment on Yalden, who had the misfortune to pen the line, "Awhile th' Almighty wond'ring stood," is an extension of the concept and provides a quotable definition of *wonder*: "He ought to have remembered that infinite knowledge can never wonder. All wonder is the effect of novelty upon ignorance." God, so often considered the cause of the sublime emotion in men, is himself incapable of the sublime. And man is likest God when he is fully aware that too strong a taste for the sublime is a confession of human weakness and ignorance.[26]

Such, then, is the teasing paradox that emerges from a consideration of Samuel Johnson and the sublime. He alternately spurs and reins the steed of fancy. Although frequently tempted to higher flight, he dares not remain too long upon the wing. Those two motions of attraction and repulsion appear again and again in his own creative work, when the sublime in any form is present. In the first chapter of *Rasselas* there are, as I have indicated, many imaginative effects that suggest sublimity: the cavern with its "massy" iron gate, the stream which entered "a dark cleft of the mountain . . . and fell, with dreadful noise, from precipice to precipice, till it was heard no more." But Johnson soon cries "Enough!" and these qualities remain only a kind of somber undertone to the normal details of human life and society. In a passage in *London* he works briefly but unmistakably with the sublime:

> Has heaven reserv'd, in pity to the poor,
> No pathless waste, or undiscover'd shore;
> No secret island in the boundless main?

Generalized though these images are (and it should not be forgotten that Johnson found grandeur in generality), they create a mood of solemnity which is evaporated by the witty flash of political satire in the succeeding line: "No peaceful desart yet unclaim'd by Spain?" But what is implicit in the foregoing passages is obvious in *A Journey to the Western Islands*; the writer feels in himself and tries to express the lonely and dismal grandeur of the Buller of Buchan only to experience, by his own statement, a recoil of the mind when the terror had ceased to please:

"When we came down to the sea, we saw some boats, and rowers, and resolved to explore the Buller at the bottom. We entered the arch, which the water had made, and found ourselves in a place, which, though we could not think ourselves in danger, we could scarcely survey without some recoil of the mind. The basin in which we floated was nearly circular, perhaps thirty yards in diameter. We were inclosed by a natural wall, rising steep on every side to a height which produced the idea of insurmountable confinement. The interception of all lateral light caused a dismal gloom. Round us was a perpendicular rock, above us the distant sky, and below an unknown profundity of water. If I had any malice against a walking spirit, instead of laying him in the Red-sea, I would condemn him to reside in the Buller of Buchan.

"But terrour without danger is only one of the sports of fancy, a voluntary agitation of the mind that is permitted no longer than it pleases."

Johnson therewith turns to a minute examination of the place as a niche for smugglers and pirates.

The same double motion of his mind complicates the critical

evaluation of *Paradise Lost*. He was powerfully attracted to Milton's epic, which, "considered with respect to design, may claim the first place, and with respect to performance the second, among the productions of the human mind." And the critic felt awe before the grandeur and sublimity of the poem. The poet, a man of the most exalted genius, revealed the "power of displaying the vast, illuminating the splendid, enforcing the awful, darkening the gloomy, and aggravating the dreadful" — all clearly and unmistakably qualities of the sublime. He raised "wonder by the sublimity of his mind" as well as by the sublimity of his theme and manner. He "never fails to fill the imagination." But now comes the inevitable recoil of mind: "Such images rather obstruct the career of fancy than incite it. . . . Poetical terrour [must be] such as human strength and fortitude may combat." [27]

Emotions of sublimity frequently agitated the breast of Samuel Johnson, but madness and melancholy were too high a price to pay for their indulgence. This important psychological fact about the man accounts, I think, for his acquiescence in the separation of the sublime from the beautiful in accord with much contemporary criticism, and for his insistence upon the separation of the sublime from the pathetic, in stout resistance to the newer currents of taste in his age. His inability to contemplate the sublime without serious disturbance of spirit, so unlike the equanimity with which he faced the beautiful and the pathetic, helps to explain the contradictions in the *Life of Milton* perhaps as much as does the conflict between his high regard for Milton's epic verse and his low esteem of Milton the man and politician. But if the confusion of emphasis is annoying, the treatment of the sublime is everywhere instinct with the author's rich humanity.

CHAPTER VIII

True Wit

IN AN influential essay that prophesied one of the most important literary trends of this century, T. E. Hulme wrote: "I want to maintain that after a hundred years of romanticism, we are in for a classical revival, and that the particular weapon of this new classical spirit . . . will be fancy" — the necessary instrument of that "cheerful, dry and sophisticated" verse which the critic desired.[1] Hulme might well have used the word *wit*, a term which in contemporary criticism has once again become important and in some contexts crucial. Mr. Eliot understands it to be a combination of thought and sensuousness, in which seriousness is intensified by the levity with which it is allied. It is "a quality of sophisticated literature"; it possesses "bright, hard precision"; it fuses those Coleridgean and Johnsonian opposites, the familiar and the strange; and it is produced only by solid intellect and long tradition.[2]

Mr. Eliot does not only pursue the implications of what is for him its basic meaning, "a tough reasonableness beneath the slight lyric grace." He also attempts to determine a "line of wit"[3] which would exemplify historically the qualities of the new definition. That line was drawn to exclude the Victorians, the Romantics, and Milton and to lead directly back to Donne, Marvell, and the metaphysical poets. In such criticism, both in its semantic and historical aspects, Mr. Eliot and his followers, however original their conclusions, have actually proceeded along fundamentally traditional paths. From his own day to the present, Donne's most characteristic quality has been described as *wit*, and it is inevitable that the twentieth century in its sponsorship, no less than the eighteenth in its rejection, of the metaphysical school should have been concerned with the meaning of this term. Moreover, almost every poet and critic who has used the term has sooner or later felt the necessity of defining it anew and has also felt that in so doing he was getting at the very essence of poetry.

Samuel Johnson was likewise interested in the basic meaning of *wit*. After using the term now in one and now in another of its conventional meanings, he finally came to redefine it in his famous evaluation of the school of Donne — a passage to which much attention has necessarily been paid in our own day as perhaps the most trenchant critical opposition to what has been currently recommended as guide and model. In that definition, and more especially in its application, he has given us one of his subtlest interpretations of literary pleasure.

I

Johnson apparently felt that some kind of definition was necessary because of the semantic confusions that attended the word. "It was about the time of Cowley that *Wit*, which had been till then used for *Intellection* in contradistinction to *Will*, took the meaning whatever it be which it now bears." Johnson had distinguished the following meanings in his Dictionary: "1. The powers of the mind; the mental faculties; the intellects. This is the original signification. 2. Imagination; quickness of fancy. . . . 3. Sentiments produced by quickness of fancy. . . . 4. A man of fancy. . . . 5. A man of genius. . . . 6. Sense; judgment . . ."

It is noteworthy that none of the definitions clearly suggests what is for us perhaps the primary meaning of the word, whether it refers to the person or the quality he possesses: "a person [in the words of the Oxford English Dictionary] of lively fancy, who has the faculty of saying smart or brilliant things, now always so as to amuse." But Johnson was surely aware of some such meaning as this, for his use of the word in connection with the comedies of Congreve suggests conversational celerity and brilliance. Congreve's characters are "intellectual gladiators" whose "every sentence is to ward or strike" and whose "wit is a meteor playing to and fro with alternate coruscations." But such wit as this Johnson did not find particularly comic, urbane, or social; it was closer to the surprise and admiration produced by tragedy than to merriment and levity. This suggests that like almost every critic since Hobbes he conceived wit to be virtually synonymous with the combining and associative power of the imagination: the rapid and vehement ability to achieve the *discordia concors,* the perception of similitude in dissimilars. Wit in this sense, however much abused by the metaphysical poets, was intellectual power of the highest order, absolutely indispensable in literary achievement.[4]

But it is with what Johnson called a "more noble and more adequate conception" of wit that we are here concerned. He apparently believed with Joseph Trapp that *wit* should be given as "positive and adequate a Definition" as possible and be rescued from "that vulgar and narrow Sense by which it denotes only Jokes and pointed Turns . . ."[5] He was also aware that almost every important critic since Dryden had attempted to define *wit* in its larger as well as in its narrower sense and that such broad definitions were actually attempts to isolate the distinguishing quality of all imaginative writing. The occasion that prompted the passage about to be cited was clearly an important one, and one would therefore expect that to it the critic would devote the very highest analytical powers of which he was capable.

"Those however who deny [the metaphysicals] to be poets allow them to be wits. Dryden confesses of himself and his contemporaries that they fall below Donne in wit, but maintains that they surpass him in poetry.

"If Wit be well described by Pope as being 'that which has been often thought, but was never before so well expressed,' they certainly never attained nor ever sought it, for they endeavoured to be singular in their thoughts, and were careless of their diction. But Pope's account of wit is undoubtedly erroneous; he depresses it below its natural dignity, and reduces it from strength of thought to happiness of language.

"If by a more noble and more adequate conception that be considered as Wit which is at once natural and new, that which though not obvious is, upon its first production, acknowledged to be just; if it be that, which he that never found it, wonders how he missed; to wit of this kind the metaphysical poets have seldom risen." [6]

Wit, then, is a combination of the familiar and the unfamiliar, the natural and the new, the obvious and the original. It unites contradictory qualities, each of which is highly unsatisfactory when separated from the other. Novelty and naturalness had each in its turn been the subject now of Johnson's highest praise and now of his severest censure. Curiosity, for example, is "one of the permanent and certain characteristicks of a vigorous intellect," "the thirst of the soul," a distinctive mark of that restless being man, whom Providence has made "always impatient for novelty." "The highest praise of genius is original invention." "No man ever yet became great by imitation. . . . That which hopes to resist the blast of malignity, and stand firm against the attacks of time, must contain in itself some original principle of growth." But the critic who expressed such sentiments as these could on other occasions find the taste for novelty puerile if not vicious, a "pause of reason," and at times even futile since the themes of literature are being continually exhausted and fame daily becoming more difficult: "Every truth brought newly to light impoverishes the mine, from which succeeding intellects are to dig their treasures." When considering either novelty or familiarity in isolation, Johnson blows both hot and cold. The reason lies in their separation. Each alone is like one of the sundered bodies in Plato's *Symposium*, restlessly and fretfully searching for the divided half which can make it whole. Neither one found rest until it met its opposite in wit.[7]

The originality of Johnson's theory does not fully appear until we examine its most important application, which is made in his comment upon the *Rape of the Lock*. Although the word *wit* is not once used, the whole passage is devoted to the familiar and un-familiar and to the way in which they are united in literary art. Curiously enough, what Pope had failed to define he had been able to exemplify, and it is to him and not to Cowley and Donne that Johnson turns for the embodiment of his "more noble and more adequate conception" of wit.

"To the praises which have been accumulated on *The Rape of the Lock* by readers of every class, from the critick to the waiting-maid, it is difficult to make any addition. Of that which is universally allowed to be the most attractive of all ludicrous compositions, let it rather be now enquired from what sources the power of pleasing is derived.

"Dr. Warburton, who excelled in critical perspicacity, has remarked that the preternatural agents are very happily adapted to the purposes of the poem. . . . Pope brought into view a new race of Beings, with powers and passions proportionate to their operation. The sylphs and gnomes act at the toilet and the tea-table, what more terrifick and more powerful phantoms perform on the stormy ocean or the field of battle; they give their proper help and do their proper mischief.

"Pope is said by an objector not to have been the inventer of this petty nation; a charge which might with more justice have been brought against the author of the *Iliad*, who doubtless adopted the religious system of his country; for what is there but the names of his agents which Pope has not invented? Has he not assigned them characters and operations never heard of before? Has he not, at least, given them their first poetical exist-ence? If this is not sufficient to denominate his work original, nothing original ever can be written.

"In this work are exhibited in a very high degree the two most engaging powers of an author: new things are made familiar, and familiar things are made new. A race of aerial people never heard of before is presented to us in a manner so clear and easy, that the reader seeks for no further information, but immediately mingles with his new acquaintance, adopts their interests, and attends their pursuits, loves a sylph and detests a gnome.

"That familiar things are made new every paragraph will prove. The subject of the poem is an event below the common incidents of common life; nothing real is introduced that is not seen so often as to be no longer regarded, yet the whole detail of a female-day is here brought before us invested with so much art of decoration that, though nothing is disguised, every thing is striking, and we feel all the appetite of curiosity for that from which we have a thousand times turned fastidiously away."

To this analysis Johnson brought his sharpest critical acumen. He considered Pope's poem "the most airy, the most ingenious, and the most delightful of all his compositions," and he fully acquiesced in the poet's fortunate rejection of Addison's counsel not to add the celestial machinery. The new version "exhibited boundless fertility of invention," and Pope "could never afterwards produce any thing of such unexampled excellence." These critical paragraphs are vastly more than a general encomium. Enough of such praise had already been heaped upon the poem. They are presented as an analysis of literary pleasure: "Let it . . . be now enquired from what sources the power of pleasing is derived." [8]

II

Johnson's conception of literature as an expression of both the familiar and the unfamiliar had been in his mind from the very beginning of his career as a critic. He had early recognized its importance. The letter on Du Halde's *History of China*, which appeared in the *Gentleman's Magazine* in 1738, provides the first statement of the notion.

"As the satisfaction found in reading descriptions of distant countries arises from a comparison which every reader naturally makes, between the ideas which he receives from the relation, and those which were familiar to him before; . . . so it varies according to the likeness or dissimilitude of the manners of the two nations. Any custom or law, unheard and unthought of before, strikes us with that surprise which is the effect of novelty; but a practice conformable to our own pleases us, because it flatters our self-love, by showing us that our opinions are approved by the general concurrence of mankind. Of these two pleasures, the first is more violent, the other more lasting; the first seems to partake more of instinct than reason, and is not easily to be explained, or defined; the latter has its foundation in good sense and reflection, and evidently depends on the same principles with most human passions.

"An attentive reader will frequently feel each of these agreeable emotions in the perusal of Du Halde . . ." [9]

Even clearer is Johnson's statement of the idea in a volume which appeared in 1739, entitled *A Commentary on Mr. Pope's Principles of Morality, or Essay on Man. By Mons. Crousaz . . .* Crousaz's translator and annotator was Samuel Johnson, who also provided notes to the translation of Du Resnel's Preface to his French translation of Pope's *Essay*. In a paragraph in which Du Resnel contrasts the fire and imaginative vigor of the Italians with the more solid and commonsensical qualities of the English appears this sentence: "The Ideas of the *Italians* have indeed the Grace of Novelty, but then they generally appear such as might have been easily struck out." What Du Resnel states casually Johnson, in his note upon the sentence just quoted, erects into a principle which expresses "the highest Perfection of Writing." The statement is relevant here because it is a clear expression of those very qualities which Johnson found, many years later, to be present in the "more noble and more adequate conception of wit": "The *Abbe*, in this Comparison, whether by Design or not, ascribes to the *Italians*, perhaps the highest Perfection of Writing; such Thoughts as are at once new and easy, which, tho' the Reader confesses that they never occurred to him before, he yet imagines must have cost but little Labour. This is not the Character which other Critics give of those Authors."

Johnson's denial that the Italians had achieved such perfection does not interest us here. But the fact that in 1739 he used language that is very close to his crucial definition of wit in the *Life of Cowley* is of the highest significance. It is also significant that he thus early finds this simultaneous expression of the "new and easy" to be "perhaps the highest Perfection of Writing." [10]

To this important principle, stated so early in his critical career, Johnson returns often.[11] It was not, however, given full exemplification until he wrote his comment on the *Rape of the Lock*, which I have quoted in full. Nowhere else has he explored with such penetration the subtle relations that exist between those indispensable but antithetical qualities, novelty and familiarity.

That Johnson was right about Pope's poem should easily be granted; but it is unfortunate that in his criticism of Shakespeare, great though it is, he did not find opportunity to apply and illustrate his principle. In connection with Shakespeare, Johnson is chiefly concerned with only one side of the process: the ability to make the unfamiliar familiar. Shakespeare "approximates the remote, and familiarizes the wonderful." In the notes on the *Tempest* — surely an occasion for discovering that double power so fully displayed in Pope's poem — Johnson attempts to rationalize the "System of Enchantment" on historical grounds. In the discussion of Caliban — that prime example for eighteenth-century criticism of the creative power of the imagination — he merely comments upon the diction, which he finds entirely consistent with the thought and temperament of the speaker. In other notes the conception of literary pleasure as a fusion of these opposites is perhaps perceptible, but only fleetingly. Prince Hal's character is "great, *original*, and *just*." The metaphor in *Henry V* in which the French are urged to rush upon the English "as doth melted snow upon the vallies" he finds to be "at once *vehement* and *proper*." Of the death of Cardinal Beaufort in *2 Henry VI* he says the beauties of the scene are such that "the superficial reader cannot miss them, the profound can image nothing beyond them." [12]

III

How is Johnson's conception, in its fullest and latest articulation, related to those of his predecessors? And with what other ideas of his own should it be linked?

1. One of its most obvious affiliations is with the learning process itself. The very words *familiar* and *unfamiliar* suggest this relation. As Aristotle had perceived,[13] every word which teaches us something is pleasant, and metaphors are delightful because they unite words that are strange with words that are already familiar. Aquinas believed wonder to be a cause of pleasure, not because of the emotional agitations it produced but

because it "is a kind of desire for knowledge. . . . Consequently wonder is a cause of pleasure, in so far as it includes a hope of getting the knowledge which one desires to have." [14] Hobbes also had stated very clearly the pleasurable effects of knowledge:

"That which giveth a Poem the true and natural Colour consisteth in two things, which are, *To know well* . . . and *To know much*. A signe of the first is perspicuity, property, and decency, which delight all sorts of men, either by instructing the ignorant or soothing the learned in their knowledge. A signe of the latter is novelty of expression, and pleaseth by excitation of the minde; for novelty causeth admiration, and admiration curiosity, which is a delightful appetite of knowledge. . . . From *Knowing much*, proceedeth the admirable variety and novelty of Metaphors and Similitudes, which are not possible to be lighted on in the compass of a narrow knowledge." [15]

In a manner somewhat reminiscent of all these, Johnson finds that Pope in the *Rape of the Lock* at once satisfies knowledge and arouses curiosity. His sylphs and gnomes he has "presented to us in a manner so clear and easy, that the reader seeks for no further *information*." And at the same time he makes us feel the "*appetite of curiosity* for that from which we have a thousand times turned fastidiously away."

2. Neoclassical critics commonly believed that the familiar lay in the idea or the sentiment, which should express the common sense of mankind and thus could not be expected to be original, and that the unfamiliar lay in linguistic decoration of one kind or another, in agreeable turns of phrase, in illustration, in metaphor and simile, in versification. From this critical dogma Johnson could never fully liberate himself. He finds, for example, that *Lycidas* is deficient because "there is no nature, for there is no truth; there is no art, for there is nothing new." [16]

But in the definition of wit which we are now considering this notion is vigorously rejected. Of Pope's famous expression of it,

> True wit is Nature to advantage dress'd,
> What oft was thought, but ne'er so well express'd,

Johnson says: "But Pope's account of wit is undoubtedly erroneous; he depresses it below its natural dignity, and reduces it from strength of thought to happiness of language." Elsewhere, if Fanny Burney's account can be trusted, his attack is even stronger. He calls the couplet "a definition both false and foolish. Let wit be dressed how it will, it will equally be wit, and neither the more nor the less for any advantage dress can give it. . . . 'What oft was thought,' is all the worse for being often thought, because to be wit, it ought to be newly thought. . . . How can the expression make it new? It may make it clear, or may make it elegant; but how new?" [17]

All this may seem to be little short of revolutionary, for Johnson has heaped scorn upon an important article in the neoclassical creed. But it should not for a moment be thought that he has eliminated from the formula of literary pleasure the function of decorated language. Such language, functionally used, possesses the power of making the familiar unfamiliar. Thus the all too common details of domestic life produce pleasure in Pope's poem because they appear "invested with so much art of decoration that, though nothing is disguised, every thing is striking." Similar powers of language appear in the passage on death in Congreve's *Mourning Bride*, which Johnson called the "most poetical paragraph" in the "whole mass of English poetry": "He who reads these lines enjoys for a moment the powers of a poet: he feels what he remembers to have felt before, but he feels it with great increase of sensibility; he recognizes a familiar image, but meets it again amplified and expanded, embellished with beauty, and enlarged with majesty." [18]

How, then, is Johnson's different from the traditional view? The difference lies in the fact that he refused to confine wit to language alone or to merely one function of language. Verbal embellishment operates only on one side of the antithesis and assists in making the familiar new, but even then its function is interpreted psychologically. It is valuable because it can provide "great increase of sensibility."

3. Johnson's antithesis between the familiar and the unfamiliar suggests still another traditional problem of criticism: that of

reconciling the probable and the improbable. By accepting too literally the doctrine of *natural* and *historical* probability he had stumbled again and again in confronting the supernatural in literature. He usually tried to explain it away on historical or religious grounds.[19] But for Pope's poem, neither expedient would do: the poem was a product of the Enlightenment, not of the Dark Ages, and the Rosicrucian beings possessed the sanction of neither religious truth nor historical belief. Besides, Johnson is not interested in explaining them away or justifying them on any grounds other than aesthetic. By virtue of their presence the poem has become as truly original as any literary work can possibly be. How, then, have these unheard-of aerial beings become so familiar that the reader "loves a sylph and detests a gnome"? In part through the *aesthetic* probability of Aristotle, who had found that the incidents of a plot were most affecting "when they occur unexpectedly and at the same time in consequence of one another; there is more of the marvellous in them then than if they happen of themselves or by mere chance. Even matters of chance seem most marvellous if there is an appearance of design; . . . for incidents like that we think not to be without a meaning."[20] This profound insight guides Johnson even when he evaluates a poem vastly different from the tragic drama discussed in the *Poetics*: the preternatural agents of the *Rape of the Lock* are "very happily adapted to the purposes of the poem . . . they give their proper help, and do their proper mischief."[21]

4. Probability was closely associated in neoclassical criticism with propriety, and Dryden had defined wit, in its largest signification, as "a propriety of thoughts and words; or, in other terms, thoughts and words elegantly adapted to the subject."[22] This definition, which, as Dryden said, arose from contemplating the great example of Vergil, must have been more satisfactory to Johnson than Pope's, since it did not confine wit to an effect of language alone but located it in both diction and thought. Yet he could not have found it fully satisfactory. Addison had said that if Dryden is right, "I am apt to think that *Euclid* was the greatest Wit that ever set Pen to Paper."[23] This is essentially the

real objection, if not to Dryden, at least to much neoclassic and rationalistic criticism — that it provided no adequate basis for distinguishing geometry from belles-lettres. Johnson's definition, as we shall presently see, does make such provision. It is concerned chiefly with the production of pleasure. It does not make propriety normative. It equates familiarity and novelty and does not tip the scales in either direction.

These are the important antecedents of Johnson's conception of wit. To all of them it is in some way related, and it is certainly rich and complex enough to include many strains of thought and to return many echoes. But in its totality, his is exactly similar to none of his predecessors'. It represents, more perhaps than any other of his critical perceptions, as radical a departure from traditional neoclassical dogma as his loyalty to some of its values would permit.

IV

If Johnson's meaning is not exhausted by these antecedent parallels and if much remains that is only vaguely or generally implied by his predecessors, it becomes necessary to examine more closely what was distinctive in his conception. Wit consists of two elements that are genuinely antithetical. It therefore differs from many other composite ideas which merely bring together divergent qualities possessing a greater or less degree of similarity or contrast. The familiar and unfamiliar are direct opposites; the same thing cannot logically be both familiar and unfamiliar at the same time. They thus differ from such common juxtapositions as the reason and the imagination, the wit and the judgment, instruction and pleasure, and many other pairs that appeared in eighteenth-century thought. A true antithesis could, of course, be a mechanical and static opposition of irreconcilable qualities, and one might intend only to say that one element of the poem (the fable, for example) is novel and another element (the language) is familiar. But Johnson attempts a kind of reconciliation that involves change, transposition of terms, and a considerable degree of transvaluation. What was familiar in life (the details of personal and social life) becomes unfamiliar in the poem; what was unfamiliar in life (the celestial machinery) becomes familiar in the poem. At the same time the reader does not forget the natural situation that preceded the artificial.

Let us consider the process for each side of the antithesis, and begin with what was originally unfamiliar. Pope's aerial beings are completely unknown to one's experience of reality, but in their poetical existence they have become so familiar that the reader "immediately mingles with his new acquaintance, adopts their interests, and attends their pursuits." At the same time, even after they have been thus domesticated, he remembers that they exist only in poetry and that they retain qualities that arise from their original unreality. He is therefore impelled to praise the poet for his inventiveness. His pleasure is enhanced by the fact that the sylphs and gnomes possess this somewhat paradoxical quality of natural artificiality or, if one prefers, of artificial naturalness. The antithetical process, which takes place at the same time, is directly parallel. Those domestic and social details, which in their real state are overfamiliar and perhaps even disgusting, are so freshened and enlivened with novelty that they become in the poem the object of newly aroused curiosity. But here too the reader remembers them as they had been and wonders at the poet's ability to utilize and transform such intractable materials. A sylph becomes a friend without one's ever forgetting that it is a sylph; a lap dog becomes something new and strange, about to perish with earth, air, and sea in universal chaos, without one's ever forgetting that it is a lap dog still.

Such a process as this may indeed be peculiarly characteristic of mock epic, with its bathetic alternations of the elevated and the low, but I think it true to say that something like it takes place in dramatic representation and indeed in all mimetic art. To Johnson "a play read, affects the mind like a play acted." Drama is "credited with all the credit due to a drama. It is credited, whenever it moves, as a just picture of a real original. . . . The delight of tragedy proceeds from our consciousness of fiction; if we thought murders and treasons real, they would please no more. Imitations produce pain or pleasure, not because they are mistaken for realities, but because they bring realities to mind." [24] Johnson's conception of imitation, then, differs both from the French school of delusion, in which the action of a play was intended to represent with exact literalness both temporal and spatial reality, and from the illusion of Coleridge's dramatic criticism, in which the mind suspends disbelief and attains a state of full imaginative acceptance. Johnson's spectator is always in his senses.

Under no other system could the reconciliation of the familiar and the unfamiliar take place in quite the same way. One responds to the *Rape of the Lock* not only because it is fictional but *because one is conscious that it is fictional*. If one submitted completely to a work of literature as reality, one would cease to remember that the gnome one now detests is still a gnome or that the box from which all Arabia now breathes is still a part of the lady's morning toilet. These two planes of reality are always present and must always be reckoned with. The mind moves back and forth from one to the other. Only thus does the familiar become the unfamiliar, or the unfamiliar the familiar, without ceasing to be what it once was. One contemplates art and remembers nature; simultaneously but inversely one remembers nature and contemplates art. That to Johnson seems to have been the most satisfactory theoretical conception of a literary pleasure which was imaginative without divorce from reality, and intense without disturbance of rational sanity and of emotional equilibrium.

v

This discussion of the reconcilement of such opposites as the familiar and the unfamiliar leads directly to Johnson's theory of antithesis. The commonest type of antithetical expression in eighteenth-century thought and creation presented opposing qualities for the purpose either (1) of setting one off against the other to achieve clarity of meaning or force and memorableness of expression or (2) of indicating the desirable mean that lay between them. In either case each member remained essentially what it had been when it existed by itself. Even in the antitheses of imaginative literature the marriage of opposites is not a sacrament in which both become one flesh, but rather a *mariage de convenance*, in which each party pursues its own interest while at the same time performing some kind of function in the new union.

1. The principle of contrast and opposition, so often reiterated in the eighteenth century, was both rhetorical and aesthetic. Joseph Trapp [25] has summarized its most important aims. "Among the many Embellishments of Writing, few are attended with greater Beauty than *Antitheta*. The Reason is obvious, because Contraries illustrate, and recommend each other by Comparison. . . . When the Thoughts are thus set against each other, they appear with Energy, and strike the Mind with redoubled Force." Such reasons as these may fully explain the preponderance of *antitheta* in Johnson's own style and also that persistent critical habit of his to view a work of literary art as a balance of opposing qualities which can be easily upset if each is not given sufficient weight and emphasis.

Consider, in addition to the many that have already appeared in these pages, only one example. Johnson required that dramatic characters be general and at the same time individual, and found that on the whole Shakespeare satisfied this exacting rule: "Characters thus ample and general were not easily discriminated and preserved, yet perhaps no poet ever kept his personages more distinct from each other." But in *Macbeth* Shakespeare had not fully accomplished what he was usually capable of: "This play is deservedly celebrated for the propriety of its fictions, and the solemnity, grandeur, and variety of its action; but it has no nice discriminations of character, the events are too great to admit the influence of particular dispositions, and the course of the action necessarily determines the conduct of the agents." This statement is as typical as any. It shows that one set of qualities pulls too strongly in one direction and therefore requires a set of opposing qualities to restore the balance. The solemnity and grandeur of

Macbeth tend toward generality and elevation, to which Shakespeare had not satisfactorily opposed the antithetical and therefore moderating qualities of particular and minute discrimination.[26]

2. Opposites are introduced for a variety of philosophical and semantic reasons. An author who wishes to enforce the claims of Christianity — at least that aspect of it, prominent in St. Paul and St. Augustine, which Charles Williams has called the way of rejection — would find himself preoccupied with sets of irreconcilable opposites like flesh and spirit, pride and humility, godliness and worldliness. His purpose would be best served by the absolute opposition of the good to the bad, in which the emphasis is unmistakably placed on one side: "Walk not after the flesh but after the spirit." Although such a purpose appears prominently in Johnson and should never be underestimated, his commonest antitheses do not, I think, normally arise from that kind of dualism, but rather from the Aristotelian and stoical opposition of qualities which perceives value to lie in the mean between them.

The Aristotelian mean could be either absolute or relative. But in all such constructions the relation between opposing qualities is far more complicated than in the Pauline exhortation, and the area of value is not delimited in so clear-cut a way. Johnson's criticism of life was as much stoical as it was Christian, and he was often guided by a firm conviction of the value of the golden mean. "Among many parallels which men of imagination have drawn between the natural and moral state of the world, it has been observed that happiness, as well as virtue, consists in mediocrity; that to avoid every extreme is necessary . . . and that the middle path is the road of security . . ." The context is moral, but Johnson finds the principle applicable to all areas of human endeavor: "Thus the maxim of Cleobulus the Lindian, μέτρον ἄριστον, *Mediocrity is best*, has been long considered as an universal principle, extended through the whole compass of life and nature." Each virtue is, by a kind of universal fate, always prone to become evil by excess and must be pulled back to normality and safety by an opposing quality. And this is as true of the "grace of art" as of the "gift of nature."

Fate wings with ev'ry wish th' afflictive dart,
Each gift of nature, and each grace of art,
With fatal heat impetuous courage glows,
With fatal sweetness elocution flows.[27]

In the conception of true wit with which this chapter is concerned, however, Johnson has unmistakably transcended this view
of the nature of antithesis. His abstract definition of wit as that
"which is at once natural and new, that which though not obvious
is, upon its first production, acknowledged to be just" is doubtless
a reflection of Addison's Horatian comment that the incidents of
the eighth book of *Paradise Lost* unite "the Graces of Nature"
with "the Beauties of Novelty" and consist of sentiments which
are natural without being obvious — "the true character of all fine
Writing." [28]

But compare Johnson's extension of this precept into the complicated doctrine of the fusion of the familiar and unfamiliar with
the interpretation of Hume, who also followed Addison and said
of his maxim that "there cannot be a juster and more concise definition of fine writing." Hume then proceeds to interpret the
natural and the original in terms of simplicity and refinement and
finds the ideal to be "a just mixture" of both. That in itself constitutes an important difference between his and Johnson's conceptions, but the chief difference lies in the fact that Hume discovers
value in these antithetical qualities only because of the mean that
lies between them. "First, I observe, That though excesses of both
kinds are to be avoided, and though a proper medium ought to
be studied in all productions, yet this medium lies not in a point,
but admits of a considerable latitude." He then continues that it
is impossible verbally to explain exactly where that just medium
lies, but that one should be more on guard against the excess of
refinement than of simplicity, since "the endeavour to please by
novelty leads men wide of simplicity and nature, and fills their
writings with affectation and conceit." [29]

How much more dynamic and subtle is Johnson's conception
of the relations of novelty and familiarity! In Hume there is no
awareness of the differences between the appearance of each,

in nature first and then in art; of the translation of each quality into its opposite by the effectual operation of the poem itself; or of the fact that each element even after its transformation retains something of its old nature. In Johnson — at least in connection with the *Rape of the Lock* — there is no concern with finding a mean between the two qualities, no warning that one may become an excess without the other, and no attempt to favor one over the other. Johnson's formula retains both extremes. He inverts their positions but does not attempt to reduce them to a mean.

It is indubitable that in his important criticism of the *Rape of the Lock* Johnson had arrived at a conception of literary art that viewed it as a new ordering of human experience in which the relations found in nature are transposed and "revalued." It may therefore be fruitfully compared with the conceptions of certain later critics which it clearly anticipates. Coleridge, who more than any other critic saw art as a reconciler of opposites, included among the discordant qualities which it must fuse "a sense of novelty and freshness with old or customary objects." But while Johnson's view is confined to novelty and familiarity, Coleridge sought fusion everywhere: heat and cold, the common terror of small insects and huge mammoths, the excess of both humanity and disinterestedness in polite society, darkness and light, passion and intellect, the naked savage and the "gymnosophist," "nothingness and the intensest absolute being." "O the depth of the proverb, 'Extremes meet'!" he exclaimed. No such metaphysical enthusiasm ever characterized Johnson.

Both critics saw that there must be a translation of one quality into the terms of its opposite and that aesthetic imitation was both like and unlike reality. In Coleridge, however, the difference was more important; in Johnson, the similarity. Coleridge stressed the difference because to him an imaginative work was a new creation in which the original reality had not merely been re-ordered but had first been destroyed and then remade. The imitation therefore possessed a new organic life of its own, to which the laws of reality were always somewhat irrelevant. Johnson stressed the similarity, because one never can forget reality and because one enjoys the artistic transposition only because one remembers the original condition. The mind remains always in touch with reality, always judging, always comparing. Johnson said: "When the imagination is recreated by a painted landscape, the trees are not supposed capable to give us shade, or the fountains coolness; but we consider, how we should be pleased with such fountains playing beside us, and such woods waving over us." Coleridge said: "[Dramatic illusion] consists — not in the mind's judging it to be a forest, but, in its remission of the judgment that it is not a forest." The mind voluntarily breaks its connections with reality and submits to a new set of imaginative data. It willingly suspends its disbelief and enters a world of imaginative illusion in which a new set of beliefs becomes valid.[30]

Mr. Eliot has said in prose that the "auditory imagination . . . fuses the old and obliterated and the trite, the current, and the new and surprising, the most ancient and the most civilized mentality," [31] and in verse that

> . . . every phrase
> And sentence that is right (where every
>   word is at home,
> Taking its place to support the others,
> The word neither diffident nor ostentatious,
> An easy commerce of the old and the new,
> The common word exact without vulgarity,
> The formal word precise but not pedantic,
> The complete consort dancing together)
> Every phrase and every sentence is an end
>   and a beginning . . .*

"An easy commerce of the old and the new": Johnson would have understood that. And he would have been pleased with the awareness of the mean and the extremes that many of Mr. Eliot's phrases, like so many of his own, express. But Mr. Eliot (in his prose essay) makes the fusion of the old and the new an effort largely of the auditory imagination. The invigoration comes from

* "Little Gidding," V, from *Four Quartets* (quoted by permission of the publisher, Harcourt, Brace and Company, Inc.).

far below the "conscious levels of thought and feeling," and the mind must sink "to the most primitive and forgotten, returning to the origin, and bringing something back . . ." Such exploration of the individual and racial subconscious is a search for syllable and rhythm, and it is the word that is invigorated. Johnson's criticism, quite apart from complete unawareness of the pulsations of primitive and uncivilized speech and from what would have been the strongest kind of aversion had he been aware of them, was never in any context so exclusively auditory and verbal. Nevertheless, his enthusiastic appreciation of the *Rape of the Lock* reveals that he responded to a commerce between the old and the new that brought a sylph to an eighteenth-century lady of quality and raised a bodkin to the dignity of Agamemnon's scepter. The poem did not, of course, unite "the most ancient and the most civilized mentality." But, as Johnson perceived with full clarity, the wit of Pope did bring fairyland to Hampton Court.

CHAPTER IX

Conclusion

A CONSIDERATION of Johnson's conception of *wit* as a union of familiarity and novelty has brought us to the very core of his theory of literary pleasure. His demand that literature express both the familiar and the unfamiliar is perhaps his most basic aesthetic requirement.[1] A work of art is valid only when it arouses and retains the attention by its expression of available and experienced truth and by its originality. Truth and familiarity, universal and verifiable positions, arise from fidelity to nature. Originality may be achieved in several ways: through language — its rhythms and rhymes, its mimetic powers, its capacity for metaphor and simile; through form or structure that keeps the reader interested and propels him forward; through the representation of objects in nature which are beautiful and sublime and which by their very presence evoke delight or wonder; through the moving of tenderness and pathos, joy and laughter, by presentations of human action. It is only by accommodating itself to both members of Johnson's antithesis — novelty and familiarity — that art becomes valid.

This requirement is, of course, empirical; literary art begins in the experience of the author and ends finally in the experience of the reader. Hence, it is relevant for the critic to consider not only the specific means of evoking pleasure which have been employed in the literary work but also the author himself: what he knew and was capable of expressing; the cast of his particular genius; the fund of experience from which he drew. Nor can a critic, writing from such empirical principles as these, ignore the reader and his endowment. The common reader, so often despised by men of one-tenth Johnson's learning and sophistication, he often makes his ally. "In the character of [Gray's] *Elegy* I rejoice to concur with the common reader; for by the common sense of readers uncorrupted with literary prejudices, after all the refinements of subtilty and the dogmatism of learning, must be finally decided all claim to poetical honours." [2] It could not be otherwise in any criticism which views literature as the representation of the available and universal experience of life.

Such a view of literary art is admittedly that of the layman, who can only with the greatest difficulty ever be persuaded that "A poem should not mean / But be." Johnson was in no respect more unmistakably like a literary layman than in his refusal to consider a poem valuable for its own sake; it could never provide a completely unique kind of experience to which only aesthetic criteria are relevant. No one, I suppose, has ever identified Dr. Johnson with those who lovingly caress the poem as a beautiful and unchanging object that teases us out of thought as doth eternity. But, although a professional man of letters himself, he was really no more in sympathy with those who consider poetry a craft and the poem a kind of artifact: "A Poeme . . . is the worke of the Poet, the end and fruit of his labour and studye. *Poesy* is his skill or Crafte of making; the very Fiction it selfe, the reason or forme of the worke." Those are the words of Ben Jonson,[3] not of Samuel Johnson, who was no more a "classical" than he was a "romantic" aesthete. *Imitation* is an important term in Johnson's criticism chiefly because it points beyond itself to what is imitated. Though fully aware of the limits of each of the arts, though fully cognizant of important implications that arise from the fact that the peculiar medium of poetry is language, and though frequently indebted to Aristotle for specific insights into the nature of literary pleasure, Johnson is never exclusively concerned with exploring the ways in which the art of poetry presents problems peculiar to itself nor with the Aristotelian view that literary imitation is a presentation of life in matter and form other than its own natural matter and form and is governed by laws other than its own natural laws.

If, as has been suggested,[4] our age is indeed "The Era of Purity" in its conception of poetry, and if the current ideal is one that would eliminate from verse the practical, prosaic, and scientific use of language, Johnson today dwells in the antipodes. Not only did he refuse to conceive of poetical excellence as purely imaginative and as desirably free of the dross of prosaic meaning, but he did not seem to believe that even the poetical excellence of which he approved could exist for very long in a condition of unmixed purity. He seems rather to have felt that poetry, like human nature itself, was in a kind of middle state where vice balanced virtue and mediocrity excellence, and where critical justice could be done only after the most careful discrimination. On no play of Shakespeare and on no poem of Pope, however excellent he may have considered it, did he bestow unqualified, unmitigated praise. Even the realm of literature could not escape the taint of some kind of Original Sin; and Parnassians, like everyone else, have all sinned and come short of the glory of God. Johnson was as much of a realist about poetical nature as he was about human nature. Those who looked upon any human production as the pure essence of poetry or who sought an elixir that could transmute all the metals of life into pure poetic gold are as surely chasing chimeras as the seeker of sublunary happiness. Of a poem which he called "the noblest ode that our language ever has produced," Dryden's *Anne Killigrew*, he said: "The first part flows with a torrent of enthusiasm. . . . All the stanzas indeed are not equal. An imperial crown cannot be one continued diamond; the gems must be held together by some less valuable matter."[5]

It should never be forgotten that Johnson's frequent demand that literature both instruct and please is essentially only one requirement, not only because it is inconceivable that excellence could exist when only one quality is present but also because in a very real sense one value rescues the other and makes it more excellent than it could otherwise be. Literature of course must engage and hold the attention, else the reader lays the book down or casts it into the fire. But pleasure is never fully and finally pleasurable when it is purely or solely imaginative and private, but only when it is historically or experientially authentic. In comparing Dryden's and Pope's odes for St. Cecilia's Day, Johnson praises Dryden's, which introduces such real personages as Alexander on his imperial throne, the lovely Thais at his side, and Timotheus seated above him playing on his tuneful lyre, and which reconstructs a vivid and historically imaginable scene; he thought less of Pope's ode, which vaguely and generally, though with lovely melody and exquisite meter, praises the power of music in a succession of allegorical and mythological scenes. "Dryden's plan is better chosen; history will always take stronger hold of the attention than fable: the passions excited by Dryden are the pleasures and pains of real life, the scene of Pope is laid in imaginary existence. Pope is read with calm acquiescence, Dryden with turbulent delight; Pope hangs upon the ear, and Dryden finds the passes of the mind." [6]

To find the passes of the mind: that is the requisite of all literary art. It is an appeal to nothing less than the whole man and all his faculties. Reading is itself an experience within the larger experience of all of life, and art is therefore to be judged, as all experience must finally be judged, by the canons of morality, truth, and empirical validity. How could it be otherwise? One does not, to paraphrase George Bernard Shaw, check one's values along with one's hat at the door of the theater. Can characters one despises in life enlist one's sympathy upon the stage? "I cannot reconcile my heart to *Bertram*," [7] said Johnson in his final note to *All's Well That Ends Well*, and his dilemma — if dilemma it be — is that of all those who cannot be one person in life and quite another when approaching literature. This, again, is the layman's point of view, but any one who writes to please many and please long cannot ignore that stubborn tendency of man to carry over into literature, even when he wishes to escape from life, the values by which he lives. Morality, Johnson would seem to tell us, is in some form inescapable; and that literature which does not choose to illustrate and enforce it will in one way or another have to reckon with it. Literary pleasure and literary passion; pity, fear, and wonder; dramatic approval or disapproval; and sympathetic or antipathetic curiosity — all these are ultimately impossible without moral value. No critic, not even Matthew Arnold, has so forcefully maintained that the twin requirements of pleasure and morality cannot be separated without irreparable violence being done to both. That which is pleasurable without morality is a monstrosity; that which is moral without pleasure will accumulate the dust of neglect.

The very force of Johnson's convictions and of their expression has made him seem outrageously dogmatical to many, who have been able to tolerate him only as an interesting eccentric or as the last example of the completely outmoded system of neo-classical criticism, which for over a century had foisted upon the native English richness the arid pomp of Nature, Reason, and the Rules. But any one who looks upon Johnson's criticism as a series of judicial pontifications has seriously misconstrued its nature and purpose and has failed completely to understand the tentative and skeptical cast of the mind that produced it. Like any other empirical system that wishes to escape anarchy, Johnson's does indeed assume the ultimate possibility of disclosing general law and principle. But he did not believe that criticism had attained the stability and permanence of an established intellectual discipline, and therefore the only course of action open to the critic was to increase the accumulation of specific data by considering individual works of art, by examining previously held positions, and by stating as clearly as possible the reasons for one's determinations.

His whole critical career is as notable for what it attacked as for what it attempted to establish. From its beginning to its end — both in the earlier topical essays on such matters as the pastorals, versification, exordial verses, romances, and letter-writing and in the later considerations of specific literary works one by one as they had appeared chronologically in the production of an author's lifetime — he waged relentless war upon authority, prescription, imitation, and outworn tradition. He attempted to cut away the overlaying and obscuring growth of pseudo-statement and to substitute only such determinations as were capable of verification by firsthand experience. Johnson's reader is never asked to believe that a general law has been operative from Homer to Blackmore or from Vergil to Pomfret. He is asked instead only to accept whatever general principle seems to arise from an inductive and empirical process of specific examination, sometimes line by line and stanza by stanza, and sometimes work by work through the entire career of an author.

Often the treatment is too brief and summary, and the steps of the reasoning are lost in a sudden conclusion. But more often than not such evaluations are intended as vigorous challenges to the reader to make an examination for himself. As Professor Tinker has said, the opinions of Johnson "pique our pride, make us review the evidence, restate the case, and criticize the critic. They certainly do not terminate the discussion but initiate a critical inquiry in us, the readers." [8] I am persuaded that Johnson would not have wished it otherwise. For the truest view of his criticism is that which looks upon it as experience moving gradually toward principle, and what is presented as experience can be tested only by experience, by more experience, and by still more experience. The highest praise of his critical endeavors is that they are empirically lively in themselves and the cause of that empirical liveliness that is in others.

Johnson once praised the "unimitated, unimitable" Falstaff for speaking like "a veteran in life." [9] The phrase is applicable to the critic himself, whose mastery is nowhere surer and nowhere more endearing than when he investigates what he called the "parallel circumstances and kindred images" [10] that ought to exist between literature and life. Consider his comment on those lines of Shakespeare which Mr. Eliot used as the epigraph of *Gerontion* and which appear in that speech on the vanity of human wishes which the disguised Duke of *Measure for Measure* delivers to Claudio, who lies in prison under the sentence of death:

> Thou hast nor youth, nor age:
> But as it were an after dinner's sleep,
> Dreaming on both.

Before these lines, themselves a part of a larger apostrophe to life, Johnson pauses, impressed with their great beauty.

"This is exquisitely imagined. When we are young we busy ourselves in forming schemes for succeeding time, and miss the gratifications that are before us; when we are old we amuse the languour of age with the recollection of youthful pleasures or performances; so that our life, of which no part is filled with the business of the present time, resembles our dreams after dinner, when the events of the morning are mingled with the designs of the evening." [11]

For Johnson, Shakespeare's lines represent a reading of life. They penetrate to a universal and verifiable experience and lay bare the inescapable human tragedy of frustrated hope. But the critic has also revealed their aesthetic integrity, for there is no image which remains unaccounted for. He has drawn from the "after dinner's sleep" the images of morning and evening and made them symbols of youth and age; and he has sensed that the single word "dreaming" spreads the mists of illusion and inaction back to youth and forward to age, engulfing all our life, "of which no part is filled with the business of the present time."

For some the verses may possess incantatory ritual power which transports the reader to the realm of the imagination, and for such the prose paraphrase may evaporate the charm. But Johnson finds the lines both "exquisitely imagined" and paraphrasable and is led by them back into life and experience. Anything more than that and anything other than that, poetry cannot legitimately be expected to accomplish.

Notes

The following abbreviations have been used in the annotations.

Life . . . *Boswell's Life of Johnson,* ed. George Birkbeck Hill and L. F. Powell. 6 vols. Oxford, 1934–1950.

Poets. . . *Lives of the English Poets,* by Samuel Johnson, ed. George Birkbeck Hill. 3 vols. Oxford, 1905.

Raleigh. . *Johnson on Shakespeare,* ed. Walter Raleigh. Fifth impression. Oxford, 1925.

Works . . *The Works of Samuel Johnson.* 9 vols. Oxford, 1825.

Brief notes have been combined wherever clarity and convenience would permit. In such cases the references appear in the order in which they were quoted or alluded to in the text. Citations from the Dictionary come from the first edition of 1755, unless otherwise indicated. Reference is not made to the Dictionary in the notes, except when clarity requires it.

CHAPTER I. EXPERIENCE AND REASON

[1] *Idler* no. 24 (*Works,* IV, 220); *Rambler* no. 41 (*Works,* II, 200).

[2] *Idler* no. 44 (*Works,* IV, 279). Compare *Rambler* no. 41, in which Johnson seems to consider the memory, and not the reason, the distinguishing human faculty: "Of memory, which makes so large a part of the excellence of the human soul, and which has so much influence upon all its other powers, but a small portion has been allotted to the animal world. . . . Memory is the purveyor of reason. . . . It is, indeed, the faculty of remembrance, which may be said to place us in the class of moral agents" (*Works,* II, 200–201). This shift of emphasis from reason to memory is, I think, the product of Johnson's empirical psychology.

[3] Aristotle, in *Metaphysics* i.1 (980b–981a), likewise associates memory and experience, making them basic to science and art: "Now from memory experience is produced in men; for the several memories of the same thing produce finally the capacity for a single experience. And experience seems pretty much like science and art, but really science and art come to men

through experience; for 'experience made art,' as Polus says, 'but inexperience luck.' "

⁴ *Empirical* is defined: "1. Versed in experiments. . . . 2. Known only by experience; practiced only by rote, without rational grounds." *Empirically*: "1. Experimentally; according to experience. . . . 2. Without rational grounds; charlatanically; in the manner of quacks." The first definition in each case indicates that Johnson did admit a usage that was not pejorative.

⁵ *Life of Pope* (*Poets*, III, 94); *Life of Butler* (*Poets*, I, 212); *Boswell's Journal of a Tour to the Hebrides*, ed. F. A. Pottle and C. H. Bennett (1936), p. 189.

⁶ *An Essay concerning Human Understanding*, II, i, 24.

⁷ *Table Talk* (London, 1835), I, 183 (July 2, 1830). "With Plato ideas are constitutive in themselves" (*ibid.*, p. 182).

⁸ *The Friend*, in *Complete Works* (New York, 1858), II, 144–145. Coleridge is here talking about that exalted faculty, the reason, and not about the judgment, which for him operated upon empirical reality much in the Lockean manner but as a power vastly inferior to the reason. "Until you have mastered the fundamental difference, in kind, between the reason and the understanding as faculties of the human mind, you cannot escape a thousand difficulties in philosophy. It is preeminently the *Gradus ad Philosophiam*" (*Table Talk*, I, 130; May 14, 1830). Johnson, of course, knew of no such distinction.

⁹ *Idler* no. 24 (*Works*, IV, 219).

¹⁰ *Rambler* no. 7 (*Works*, II, 33).

¹¹ *Rasselas*, Chap. XLVIII (*Works*, I, 306–307). See Locke, *Essay*, IV, iii, 6, and Bolingbroke, *Works* (Philadelphia, 1841), III, 205 and *passim*.

¹² *Life*, I, 367; I, 466. See *Life*, IV, 252–253, for an interesting defense of the senses and factual observation in connection with the Ossianic controversy.

¹³ "Dr. Johnson's Refutation of Berkeley," *Mind*, LVI (April 1947), 132–147. See especially pp. 132, 136–139, 144–145.

¹⁴ *Some Turns of Thought in Modern Philosophy* (1933), p. 10.

¹⁵ "An Empirical Survey of Empiricisms," *Studies in the History of Ideas*, III (1935), 13–14.

¹⁶ *Works*, VI, 281. The *Life of Boerhaave* was published in the *Gentleman's Magazine* in 1739, when Johnson was thirty years of age.

¹⁷ *Rambler* no. 137 (*Works*, III, 149).

¹⁸ *Rambler* no. 19 (*Works*, II, 97); *Rambler* no. 24 (*Works*, II, 119–120); *Rambler* no. 179 (*Works*, III, 339–341); *Adventurer* no. 99 (*Works*, IV, 87); *Life of Boerhaave* (*Works*, VI, 278).

¹⁹ *Life*, I, 454; *Rambler* no. 154 (*Works*, III, 230).

²⁰ *Rambler* no. 154 (*Works*, III, 230); *Life*, II, 361; *Life of Milton* (*Poets*, I, 178); *Preface to Shakespeare* (Raleigh, p. 39).

²¹ *Life of Watts* (*Poets*, III, 309). Johnson also says of Watts's book that it is "in the highest degree useful and pleasing," and that its "radical principles" may be found in Locke (*Poets*, III, 309).

²² Isaac Watts, *The Improvement of the Mind* (Boston, 1833), pp. 37–38, 40.

²³ *Life of Cowley* (*Poets*, I, 59).

²⁴ (a) See topic "Truth," in Joseph E. Brown, *The Critical Opinions of*

Samuel Johnson (1926), pp. 250–253, for a list of passages that illustrate this function of reason even when the word itself is not used. (b) See entire *Rambler* no. 137, a discussion of the function of reason (*Works*, III, 147–151). (c) *Rambler* no. 151 (*Works*, III, 217); *Rambler* no. 158 (*Works*, III, 249–250); *Rambler* no. 139 (*Works*, III, 157–162); *Adventurer* no. 95 (*Works*, IV, 81). (d) *Rambler* no. 38 (*Works*, II, 185–186); *Rambler* no. 129 (*Works*, III, 113); the *Fountains* (*Works*, IX, 181, 183, 190); Definition no. 11 under *Reason* in Dictionary. (e) *Rambler* no. 208 (*Works*, III, 462); *Idler* no. 59 (*Works*, IV, 324).

[25] Gibbon, *Autobiography* (Everyman's Library), pp. 65, 72.

[26] Preface to Dodsley's *Preceptor*, in Allen T. Hazen, *Johnson's Prefaces & Dedications* (1937), p. 185. See *Life of Pope* (*Poets*, III, 164–165).

[27] *A New Treatise on the Art of Thinking* (London, 1724), I, 46, 48–49.

[28] Cited in A. W. Evans, *Warburton and the Warburtonians* (1932), p. 34.

[29] *Rambler* no. 23 (*Works*, II, 113) (italics added); *Life*, III, 291.

[30] *Logick*, 2d ed. (London, 1726), p. 179 (II, ii, 9). Johnson said of this work that it "has been received into the universities, and therefore wants no private recommendation" (*Life of Watts* [*Poets*, III, 308]).

[31] *Preface to Shakespeare* (Raleigh, p. 59).

[32] *Preface to Dictionary* (*Works*, V, 34) (italics added).

[33] *Posterior Analytics*, I, i (71a).

[34] *Philosophical Works*, tr. Haldane and Ross (1911), I, 7 (italics added).

[35] These words come from a sentence of John Wilkins, added by Johnson to illustrate the first definition of *reason* in the fourth edition of the Dictionary. The citation is not made in the first three editions.

[36] "A New Life of the Author," *Works of Bacon* (London, 1711), I, li.

The extent to which the empiricism studied in this chapter is valid for Johnson's literary criticism will appear subsequently. The point of view expressed here receives support, I think, from W. K. Wimsatt's thorough study of what he calls the "physico-philosophical core" of Johnson's style in the *Rambler* (*Philosophic Words* [1948], p. xiii). He finds not only that Johnson's habit of using scientific words and images is "among the most permanent attachments of his mind" (p. 69) but that "the work of Locke alone would have been enough to insure a thorough immersion of Johnson's mind in empirical epistemology" (p. 95). He says that Johnson quotes Watts's *Improvement* "more than 150 times in the first volume of the Dictionary" (p. 71). For additional evidence of the use of Watts, see pp. 72, 96, and 159; for the use of Locke, pp. 94–99 and pp. 154–155; for the use of Bacon, *passim* but especially pp. 148–149. For additional evidence of Locke's influence upon Johnson, see Kenneth MacLean, *John Locke and English Literature of the Eighteenth Century* (1936).

I have noticed that Johnson almost always turns to Locke for illustrations in defining such words as *nominal, sign, idea, inherent, cause, effect* — except, however, *innate*, where one surely would have expected it. Johnson does remind one of Locke in saying that pity and virtue are not natural (*Life*, I, 437, 443). Nevertheless, he seems to have shared Watts's hesitation (*Logick*, pp. 28–29 [I, iii, 1]) in accepting fully Locke's denial of innate ideas (see note 30 to this chapter). In one crucial matter, however, Johnson decided against Watts and agreed with Locke, Bolingbroke, and Voltaire, none of whom he mentions: that the mind does *not* always think (*Idler* no. 24 [*Works*, IV, 220–221]).

¹ The quotations come from a review of the first four volumes of Johnson's *Lives of the Poets* in the *Annual Register* for 1779, 2d ed. (London, 1786), pp. 179–180 (2d series of pages).

² D. Nichol Smith, ed., *Eighteenth Century Essays on Shakespeare* (Glasgow, 1903), Introduction, p. xxxi; *Preface to Shakespeare* (Raleigh, pp. 44–45).

³ *Life of Swift* (*Poets*, III, 11).

⁴ *Life of Dryden* (*Poets*, I, 411). Johnson's notes on the witchcraft in *Macbeth* provide an excellent example of his historical criticism (Raleigh, pp. 167–170, 173–176).

⁵ *The Rise of English Literary History*, pp. 140–141. Wellek supplies many examples of this type of historical summary in Johnson.

⁶ The quoted phrase comes from *Adventurer* no. 133 (Feb. 12, 1754), written by Joseph Warton and devoted to the relations between literature and society. Wellek's section on the eighteenth century in his *English Literary History* discusses fully the tendencies referred to in this paragraph.

⁷ *Adventurer* no. 58 (*Works*, IV, 32). The Horatian ode Johnson refers to is the third of Book III. Even so philosophical and generic a critic as Joseph Trapp, who found it "more suitable to my Nature (such as it is) to search into Things than Facts," found that at times "I could not come at the *Nature* of the Subject . . . without enquiring into the *History* of it" (*Lectures on Poetry . . . Translated from the Latin* [London, 1742], p. vi).

⁸ *Life of Dryden* (*Poets*, I, 410, 413, 418).

⁹ *Rambler* no. 3 (*Works*, II, 13); *Idler* no. 60 (*Works*, IV, 325).

¹⁰ *An Essay on Criticism*, I, 13–14; *A Tale of a Tub*, "A Digression concerning Critics."

¹¹ *Rambler* no. 92 (*Works*, II, 432). The metaphor of the critical microscope and telescope appears in *Rambler* no. 176 (*Works*, III, 328–329).

¹² *Rambler* no. 208 (*Works*, III, 464); *Rambler* no. 156 (*Works*, III, 239–240); T. S. Eliot, *The Sacred Wood* (London, 1920), pp. 3, 7.

¹³ *Critical Works of John Dennis*, ed. E. N. Hooker (1943), II, 392; Alexander Gerard, *An Essay on Taste*, II, ii (London, 1759, p. 90). For general discussions, see Hooker's Introduction (*Dennis*, II, lxxviii), and J. E. Spingarn's Introduction (I, lxxxviii–cvi) to *Critical Essays of the Seventeenth Century* (1908). I do not wish to suggest that the divergent emphases delineated here should be considered rigidly as schools, nor do I refer to the later critical debates about taste discussed by E. N. Hooker in "The Discussion of Taste, from 1750 to 1770 . . . ," *PMLA*, XLIX (June 1934), 577–592. This article is relevant to what is discussed later (*post*, pp. 35–37), Johnson's interest in the aesthetics of psychological effects.

¹⁴ *Life*, II, 191; *Life of Addison* (*Poets*, II, 145–146).

¹⁵ *Monsieur Bossu's Treatise of the Epick Poem*: . . . *Made* English *from the* French . . . , by W. F., 2d ed. (2 vols., London, 1719), I, 1–2.

¹⁶ "Of the Standard of Taste," in *Essays* (The New Universal Library; London, n.d.), pp. 170, 177–178, 168, 174.

¹⁷ *Preface to Shakespeare* (Raleigh, pp. 9–10) (italics added). Johnson says of Dryden as critic: "As he had studied with great diligence the art

of poetry, and enlarged or rectified his notions by *experience perpetually increasing*, he had his mind stored with principles and *observations . . .*" (*Life of Dryden* [*Poets*, I, 413]) (italics added). See *ante*, pp. 5–14.

[18] *Idler* no. 36 (*Works*, IV, 255).

[19] *Rambler* no. 156 (*Works*, III, 239, 240, 242). For the later discussion of the unities, see *Preface to Shakespeare* (Raleigh, pp. 24–30), in which, although it is a longer discussion and although it makes the same point, Johnson does not use such words as *nature* and *reason*, prominent in the earlier discussion in *Rambler* no. 156.

[20] "Review of a Free Enquiry into the Nature and Origin of Evil" (*Works*, VI, 52).

[21] *Science and the Modern World* (1925), p. 35.

[22] *Rhetoric*, i.1 (1356a). For a comprehensive and yet closely analytical survey of eighteenth-century criticism, in which these categories are used, see R. S. Crane's "Neo-Classical Criticism," under "English Criticism," in *Dictionary of World Literature*, ed. Joseph T. Shipley (1943).

[23] *Life of Congreve* (*Poets*, II, 216–217).

[24] Aristotle (*Poetics* iii) distinguishes between matters *related* (ἀπαγγέλλοντα) as in the epic and persons *doing* and *acting* (πράττοντας and ἐνεργοῦντας) as in the drama. See Dictionary under *drama, epic, satire, lampoon; Life*, II, 95; III, 283; *Life of Denham* (*Poets*, I, 77–78); *Life of Gay* (*Poets*, II, 283); *Idler* no. 77 (*Works*, IV, 376–377); *An Essay on Epitaphs* (*Works*, V, 259–266); *Rambler* no. 158 (*Works*, III, 250–252); *Rambler* nos. 36, 37, 152 (entire); Raleigh, p. 81; *Life of Milton* (*Poets*, I, 170–180); *Joseph Andrews*, Bk. III, Chap. 2.

[25] *Works*, V, 260; *Life of Milton* (*Poets*, I, 176).

[26] *Life*, III, 38; *Rambler* no. 125 (*Works*, III, 93).

[27] *Rambler* no. 125 (*Works*, III, 93–94). Johnson refers scornfully to "mechanical criticism" in *Rambler* no. 156 (*Works*, III, 241).

[28] *Rambler* no. 92 (*Works*, II, 432); *Rasselas*, Chap. X (*Works*, I, 220–221); *Life of Dryden* (*Poets*, I, 413); *Rambler* no. 156 (*Works*, III, 240) (italics added). For the psychological nature of Hobbes's criticism, see C. D. Thorpe, *The Aesthetic Theory of Thomas Hobbes* (1940), especially Chap. IV.

[29] *Life*, II, 90.

[30] Preface to *Sublime and Beautiful* (*Works* [Bohn's British Classics; London, 1876], I, 50) and Introduction (I, 54). Both the Preface and the Introduction constitute a defense of the experimental rather than the *a priori* method in aesthetic investigations. It was undoubtedly this which Johnson praised when he commended Burke's treatise.

[31] *Essays: On Poetry and Music*, 3d ed. (London, 1779), p. 4.

[32] *Rasselas*, Chap. X (*Works*, I, 221); *Preface to Shakespeare* (Raleigh, p. 16); *Idler* no. 97 (*Works*, IV, 433); *Life of Milton* (*Poets*, I, 170).

CHAPTER III. LITERATURE AND THE AUTHOR

[1] *Life of Dryden* (*Poets*, I, 412).

[2] "A New Life of the Author," *Works of Bacon*, ed. David Mallet (London, 1711), I, i.

[3] *Works of Pope* (London, 1806), I, cxix–cxxxi (the "moral" character); X, 363–380 (the "poetical" character).

⁴ "Dedicatory Epistle of Volpone" (1607), in *Critical Essays of the Seventeenth Century*, ed. J. E. Spingarn, I, 12.

⁵ *Life*, II, 63; *Life of Akenside* (*Poets*, III, 417).

⁶ Historical and literary characters are so much alike that D. Nichol Smith's description of the historical may be applied to the literary with some illumination of its purpose and function: "The truth is that a life and a character have different objects and methods and do not readily combine. It is only a small admixture of biography that a character will endure. And with the steady development of biography the character declined. A character must be short; and it must be entire, the complete expression of a clear judgment" (*Characters of the Seventeenth Century* [1918], p. li).

⁷ Thomas Lodge, "Defence of Poetry" (1579), in *Elizabethan Critical Essays* (1904), ed. G. G. Smith, I, 75. These quasi-medieval sentiments, which appear everywhere in sixteenth-century criticism, are not entirely absent from Imlac's description of the poet in *Rasselas*, Chap. X (*Works*, I, 220–223).

⁸ Pope's *An Essay on Criticism*, I, 119–124. The several characters of critics in Part III of this poem certainly stand in the tradition, as do all the satirical portraits of Dryden and Pope. Dryden is Johnson's great exemplar in the drawing of the brief character in criticism. It was Dryden's consistent purpose thus to isolate the distinguishing excellence of his literary predecessors. In addition to the characters in *Dramatic Poesy*, see the brilliantly phrased character of Lucretius in the *Preface to Sylvæ* (*Essays of Dryden*, ed. W. P. Ker [1900], I, 258–261). Sometimes Dryden's characters were presented antithetically — for example, Horace and Juvenal, Homer and Vergil, Chaucer and Ovid — a method which Johnson took over and used nowhere more brilliantly than in his antithetical portraits of Dryden and Pope. Dryden's frequent use of the portrait of the artist reflects a seventeenth-century critical development. "For, as the seventeenth century progressed, critics began to consider, in addition to the rules for the formation of the epic, the mental qualifications of the poet himself. . . . The critic considers the poem in connection with the poet" (Donald M. Foerster, *Homer in English Criticism* [1947], p. 2).

⁹ *Rambler* no. 156 (*Works*, III, 241–242). Johnson's objections to drawing rules merely from precedents that are famous and thus by example giving support to critical authority appear even more clearly in the opening paragraphs of an ensuing essay, *Rambler* no. 158 (*Works*, III, 248–250).

¹⁰ *Preface to Shakespeare* (Raleigh, pp. 30–31). The entire *Preface* is a kind of character of the poet. Its primary purpose is to summarize the general excellence of Shakespeare's literary character and to give him the position of a classic. To this task of total and general evaluation Johnson devotes all his powers, a striking contrast to the casual way in which he presents his judicial criticism of individual plays: "The poetical beauties and defects I have not been very diligent to observe. Some plays have more, and some fewer judicial observations, not in proportion to their difference of merit, but because I gave this part of my design to chance and to caprice" (Raleigh, pp. 53–54).

¹¹ *Life of Milton* (*Poets*, I, 194).

¹² *Life of Milton* (*Poets*, I, 170) and Hill's note 2, which demonstrates that Johnson's opinion is far from original; *Life*, III, 193–194. See *ibid.*, p.

193, n. 3, where Boswell refers to a literary contest in which Johnson defended Homer and Burke Vergil – an occasion which unfortunately took place years before the biographer had met his hero.

[13] *Life of Cowley* (*Poets*, I, 6); *Life of Prior* (*Poets*, II, 202); *Life of Milton* (*Poets*, I, 163); *Life of Hammond* (*Poets*, II, 315).

[14] *Tom Jones*, Bk. IX, Chap. 1 (see Horace *Ars Poetica*, lines 102–103); *Critical Works of Dennis*, ed. E. N. Hooker, I, 2. See also the editor's notes, which cite antecedents and parallels (I, 424). Hume, "Of Simplicity and Refinement in Writing," *Essays* (The New Universal Library), p. 142. The notes to the pages in Hill's edition of Johnson's *Poets*, cited in note 12 above, provide many additional parallels.

[15] Tolstoy, *What is Art*, especially Chap. V; Richards, *Practical Criticism* (1929), pp. 279–291; Eliot, "Tradition and the Individual Talent," in *The Sacred Wood* (London, 1920), pp. 47–53, and his reply to Richards in *The Use of Poetry and the Use of Criticism* (1933), pp. 121–127 and p. 124, n. 1.

[16] *Life of Pope* (*Poets*, III, 101).

[17] *Life of Thomson* (*Poets*, III, 297–298).

[18] Boswell's *Tour to the Hebrides*, ed. Pottle and Bennett (1936), pp. 19–20.

[19] *Life of Cowley* (*Poets*, I, 2). "But to the particular species of excellence, men are directed not by an ascendant planet or predominating humour, but by the first book which they read, some early conversation which they heard, or some accident which excited ardour and emulation" (*Life of Pope* [*Poets*, III, 174]). Although he is here denying Pope's theory of the ruling passions, Johnson's own view seems somewhat deterministic, even though the process he defends is casual and accidental. See Gibbon's denial of this notion, which he attributes to both Johnson and Reynolds (*Autobiography* [Everyman's Library], pp. 107–108).

[20] *Life of Roscommon* (*Poets*, I, 235); *Idler* no. 60 (*Works*, IV, 326); *Life of Pope* (*Poets*, III, 247). See *post*, pp. 89–96 for a more extensive discussion of Johnson's conception of the imagination.

[21] References illustrating the acceptance of faculty psychology by neoclassical criticism are too numerous to cite here, but see *Essays of Seventeenth Century*, I, x–xi, 4–5, 43–45, and Dennis's *Works*, II, xcviii, 507–508. Of the newer and antithetical view, the comment of Edward Young, in his *Conjectures on Original Composition*, is closely parallel to what Johnson has Dick Minim express, that "to neglect of learning, genius sometimes owes its greater glory" (*Works* [London, 1767], V, 130). Johnson's point of view seems to recall Dennis's that poetry provides "for the Satisfaction of all the Faculties, . . . of the whole Man together" (Dennis, *Works*, I, 263, and editor's note on p. 489) and to parallel Alexander Gerard's that "the powers of the human mind, however distinct in themselves, are generally complicated in their energies. Scarce any of them can be exerted in perfection without the assistance of many others" (*An Essay on Genius* [London, 1774], p. 5). Compare Coleridge in *Anima Poetae* (Nonesuch ed., 1933, p. 160): "Great injury has resulted from the supposed incompatibility of one talent with another, judgment with imagination and taste, good sense with strong feeling, &c."

[22] *Life of Pope* (*Poets*, III, 222).

[23] *Rambler* no. 145 (*Works*, III, 190); *Life of Addison* (*Poets*, II, 127, 145); *Life of Pope* (*Poets*, III, 247); *Adventurer* no. 99 (*Works*, IV, 87).

[24] Aristotle *Rhetoric* III. xi. 2 (1411b); Quintilian *Institutio* VIII. iii. 88–89. I have attempted no comprehensive survey of this term, a study which might prove interesting and useful.

[25] Scaliger, *Poetices*, III, xxvii; Puttenham, *Arte of English Poesie* (1589), III, iii, in *Elizabethan Critical Essays*, II, 148. The word ἐνέργεια should not be confused with ἐνάργεια, which Puttenham used to describe that quality of language which could "satisfie & delight th' eare onely by a goodly outward shew set upon the matter with words and speaches smothly and tunably running" (*Eng. Poesie*, III, iii, x, in *Eliz. Critical Essays*, II, 148, 166–167). The meaning of the latter term for the ancients may perhaps be best exemplified by Quintilian, who followed Cicero in explaining it as *illuminatio* and *evidentia* (*Institutio* IV. ii. 63; VI. ii. 32, 36; VIII. iii. 61–62). It referred to the orator's ability to exhibit the actual scene in language, and may be translated by such words as *clarity, distinctness, vividness, palpability*. It is used most appropriately in connection with imagery. Burke may well have had ἐνάργεια and not ἐνέργεια in mind when he used the word *energy* in the *Sublime and Beautiful* (V, v). He rejected the classical point of view that linguistic "energy" lay in clear, visual images, which, he thought, were often aesthetically undesirable. "Energy" lay rather in the mind's response to various types of phenomena.

[26] *Life of Denham* (*Poets*, I, 79).

[27] *Life*, II, 360.

[28] *Life of Pope* (*Poets*, III, 217).

[29] *Ante*, pp. 5–14, 28–29; *Life of Dryden* (*Poets*, I, 457); *Life*, II, 196; Raleigh, p. 176; *Rambler* no. 137 (*Works*, III, 149).

[30] Compare *Rasselas*, Chap. X (*Works*, I, 220–223), with Ben Jonson's description of the poet in *Essays of Seventeenth Century*, I, 52–57.

[31] *Preface to Shakespeare* (Raleigh, p. 37).

[32] *Eighteenth Century Essays on Shakespeare*, ed. D. Nichol Smith (1903), pp. xxvi–xxvii, 213.

[33] See note 21 to this chapter.

CHAPTER IV. NATURE

[1] *Preface to Shakespeare* (Raleigh, p. 11); *Rambler* no. 4 (*Works*, II, 18).

[2] *Life of Pope* (*Poets*, III, 255). This sentence comes from the criticism of Pope's epitaphs, first printed in *The Universal Visiter* [*sic*] in May 1756, and appended to the *Life of Pope*.

[3] *Letters on Chivalry and Romance*, ed. Edith J. Morley (London, 1911), p. 138 (Letter X).

[4] *Johnsonian Miscellanies*, ed. G. B. Hill (Oxford, 1897), I, 241; *Rasselas*, Chap. XLIV; *Idler* no. 20 (*Works*, IV, 206); *Life*, II, 90; III, 229–230.

[5] *Elizabethan Critical Essays*, ed. G. G. Smith, II, 201.

[6] Johnson everywhere tries to rationalize and naturalize the supernatural in Shakespeare (Raleigh, pp. 64–65, 68, 159–160, 164). He accepts the witchcraft of *Macbeth* on historical grounds (Raleigh, pp. 167–170, 173–176) and the supernaturalism of *Paradise Lost* on religious grounds, since in Christianity "the probable . . . is marvellous, and the marvellous is probable" (*Life of Milton* [*Poets*, I, 174]).

[7] *Life of Butler* (*Poets*, I, 216); Raleigh, pp. 185, 196; *Life of Gay* (*Poets*, II, 284). The phrase *dignus vindice nodus* comes from Horace *Ars Poetica*,

lines 191–192. Johnson was fully aware that a close following of history could have deleterious aesthetic effects. Although Dryden had no choice in *Absalom and Achitophel*, Johnson saw that devotion to historical truth adversely affected aesthetic probability: "As an approach to historical truth was necessary the action and catastrophe were not in the poet's power; there is therefore an unpleasing disproportion between the beginning and the end" (*Life of Dryden* [*Poets*, I, 437]).

⁸ *Life of Pope* (*Poets*, III, 224); *Life of Rowe* (*Poets*, II, 76).

⁹ *Life of Collins* (*Poets*, III, 337).

¹⁰ Note on *King John* III.i.70–71 (Raleigh, pp. 104–105).

¹¹ Raleigh, pp. 108, 111, 142.

¹² Raleigh, p. 108 (italics added).

¹³ Essay Supplementary to Preface (1815) in *Wordsworth's Literary Criticism*, ed. Nowell C. Smith (London, 1905), p. 185.

¹⁴ *Life of Thomson* (*Poets*, III, 298–299); *Preface to Shakespeare* (Raleigh, p. 39); *Life of Milton* (*Poets*, I, 178). I suggest that Johnson's conception of *liveliness* is related to three traditions: (1) classical ἐνάργεια, or vividness (see *ante*, pp. 50–51); (2) the Horatian *ut pictura poesis* (*Ars Poetica*, line 361), given new impetus by impulses from painting and a desire to achieve the *picturesque* in verse; (3) Lockean empiricism, which stressed *clear, distinct, real, adequate,* and *true* ideas — their "first freshness" and their "original exactness" (Locke's *Essay*, II, xxix–xxxii). All three are intimately related to a conception of art as a representation of particular nature.

¹⁵ *An Essay of Dramatic Poesy*, in *Essays*, ed. Ker, I, 36.

¹⁶ Raleigh, pp. 85, 142, 117–118.

¹⁷ Raleigh, p. 131.

¹⁸ *Life*, II, 262; *Prayers and Meditations*, no. 103 (*Miscellanies*, ed. Hill, I, 67). The date of the scene in Boswell is May 10, 1773; Johnson in his diary is describing the period between Easter and Whitsuntide of that same year.

¹⁹ R. G. Collingwood, "Plato's Philosophy of Art," *Mind*, XXXIV (April 1925), 154. The sentence quoted is the author's summary of a typical misunderstanding of Plato.

²⁰ *Life*, II, 195.

²¹ *Rambler* no. 37 (*Works*, II, 185); John Hawkins, *Life of Johnson*, 2d ed. (London, 1787), p. 253.

²² *Rasselas*, Chap. XXII (*Works*, I, 249). Although Johnson admired the learning of Clarke, calling him "the most complete literary character that England ever produced" (*Miscellanies*, ed. Hill, II, 305), Johnson was too antispeculative and empirical to have approved fully of a thinker whom Leslie Stephen properly called "the great English representative of the *a priori* method of constructing a system of theology" — one who more fitly than Tindal should be called a "Christian Deist" (*Hist. of Eng. Thought in the 18th Cent.*, 3d ed. [Reprinted, New York, 1949] I, 119, 129). Johnson refused to quote Clarke in the Dictionary because of his heretical views on the Trinity (*Life*, I, 189 and n. 1).

²³ Review of Soame Jenyns's *Free Enquiry* (*Works*, VI, 51–53); *Life of Boerhaave* (*Works*, VI, 273, 281–282); Hawkins's *Life*, 2d ed. (1787), p. 543.

²⁴ *Works*, VI, 19; *Rambler* no. 184 (*Works*, III, 361–362). The quotations from Ray and Blackmore under *fortuitous* in the Dictionary, the only ones used to illustrate that word, make the same point rather vigorously.

[25] *Life of Milton* (*Poets*, I, 182).

[26] Sermon IV (*Works*, IX, 319); Sermon XIV (IX, 419); Sermon X (IX, 377).

[27] Sermon I (*Works*, IX, 289).

[28] *Rasselas*, Chaps. XI and XLVIII (*Works*, I, 224, 308). Johnson praised Boerhaave because "he worshipped God as he is in himself, without attempting to inquire into his nature. He desired only to think of God, what God knows of himself. There he stopped, lest, by indulging his own ideas, he should form a deity from his own imagination, and sin by falling down before him" (*Life of Boerhaave* [*Works*, VI, 290–291]).

[29] *Life of Milton* (*Poets*, I, 182). See *post*, p. 149.

[30] *Speculations*, 2d ed. (Reprinted, 1949), p. 118. The date of the first edition is 1924.

[31] *Life of Milton* (*Poets*, I, 183).

[32] *The Christian's Magazine, or a Treasury of Divine Knowledge*, I (London, 1760), p. 8. Johnson's definition of *Deism* in the Dictionary is as follows: "The opinion of those that only acknowledge one God, without the reception of any revealed religion."

[33] *Rasselas*, Chap. XI (*Works*, I, 226); Preface to translation of Father Lobo's *Voyage to Abyssinia* (*Works*, V, 256); *Rambler* no. 4 (*Works*, II, 19–20); *Adventurer* no. 137 (*Works*, IV, 140–141).

[34] *Preface to Shakespeare* (Raleigh, p. 16). For other phrases in which Johnson refers to rational and moral universals, see *ante*, p. 14.

[35] *Preface to Shakespeare* (Raleigh, pp. 11, 15, 12, 105, 108) (italics added); *Life of Butler* (*Poets*, I, 214).

[36] Raleigh, p. 198.

[37] *Life*, II, 367; *Life of Gay* (*Poets*, II, 278); *Life of Addison* (*Poets*, II, 135).

[38] *Life*, III, 317; I, 398 and n. 2, 454–455; *Rasselas*, Chap. X (*Works*, I, 221–223).

CHAPTER V. PLEASURE

[1] *Preface to Shakespeare* (Raleigh, p. 16); *Life of Milton* (*Poets*, I, 170).

[2] *Life of Dryden* (*Poets*, I, 454).

[3] *Life*, II, 351–352. In the parallel but somewhat shorter comment in Boswell's *Journal* (*Boswell Papers*, ed. Scott and Pottle, X, 203–204), Johnson is represented as using the word *excellent*, not *exquisite*, as in the *Life*. Johnson was obviously irritated on this occasion (he was "not much in the humour of talking"), and Boswell's point of view, against which he was arguing, that poetry should "have different gradations of excellence," is in part Johnson's own (see *post*, pp. 79–80).

[4] *Life of Cowley* (*Poets*, I, 59).

[5] *Nicomachean Ethics* X. iii (1173b); X. iv (1174a). Here Aristotle says that "pleasure is not a movement," but in the *Rhetoric* (I. xi [1370a]) he argues that "pleasure is a movement, a movement by which the soul as a whole is consciously brought into its normal state of being . . ."

[6] *Life of Waller* (*Poets*, I, 284); Raleigh, p. 179.

[7] *Life of Addison* (*Poets*, II, 127).

[8] *Life of Dryden* (*Poets*, I, 439). The Latin phrase Johnson quotes comes from Horace *Odes* IV. ii. 7.

[9] *Johnsonian Miscellanies*, ed. Hill, I, 284–285.

[10] *Life,* III, 38; II, 453–455. While denying that either didactic or witty and satirical verse was poetry apparently because it lacked elevation, Johnson was careful to distinguish two kinds of "towering above the common mark": it had to be something that "men in general cannot do if they would" and not something that "every man may do if he would." In the latter category he placed the fopperies and depradations of the noted highwayman "Sixteen-String Jack," and also the verses of Gray, which he said elsewhere had a kind of "strutting dignity" (*Life,* III, 38).

[11] *Preface to Shakespeare* (Raleigh, p. 30) (italics added).

[12] *The History of Romances,* tr. Stephen Lewis (London, 1715), pp. 4–5.

[13] See Johnson's comments, quoted and summarized, under "Biography," "Autobiography," "Diaries," "Memoirs," and "History," in Joseph E. Brown, *Critical Opinions* (1926).

[14] *Rhetoric* I.xi.21–24 (1371b). See *Poetics* iv (1448b).

[15] Raleigh, pp. 173–176.

[16] *Life,* IV, 48–49.

[17] *Rambler* no. 92 (*Works,* II, 431–432).

[18] I have attempted to distinguish Johnson's theory of generality from anything resembling Platonism because Professor Bredvold has found that "Neo-Classical esthetics, being fundamentally ideal in principle, developed under the authority of Aristotle's doctrine of imitation and the Stoic conception of Nature, to the point where it came very much to resemble Platonism" ("The Tendency toward Platonism in Neo-Classical Esthetics," *ELH,* I [Sept. 1934], 101–102). He considers Dryden's quotation of and comment on the Platonist Bellori "food for thought," since the English critic finds "the Platonic conception of beauty both pertinent and appealing" (p. 105). He says of Reynolds and others: "Had they been metaphysicians, they would have been Platonists" (p. 117).

From such ideas, Johnson's must be sharply distinguished, however much he may seem at times to reflect them, especially when he discusses morality and general nature. Even in Dryden and Reynolds, I am somewhat more impressed with the basic divergencies from any kind of Platonism than is Professor Bredvold. Having quoted Bellori's highly Platonic passage on divine ideas and the "amendment" of nature through art, Dryden says of it: "In these pompous expressions . . . the Italian has given you his Idea of a Painter; and though I cannot much commend the style, I must needs say, there is somewhat in the matter" ("A Parallel of Poetry and Painting," *Essays,* ed. Ker, II, 123). He then quotes a passage from Philostratus the Younger, which he calls "somewhat plainer" (p. 123) but which is notable because there is virtually no Platonism in it and because it is a kind of Aristotelian and even empirical plea for the study of particular nature, of human anatomy, and of the achievement of generality by means that seem predominantly inductive. But after considerable hesitation and even embarrassment Dryden does finally accept "an idea of perfect nature," in accordance with which the artist corrects Nature "from what she is in individuals, to what she ought to be . . ." (p. 125) — an idea which, when applied to literature, he finds regulative only of epic poetry (p. 127). Reynolds in his Third Discourse says that the "idea of the perfect state of nature, which the artist calls the ideal beauty, is the great leading principle by which works of genius are conducted" (Oxford, World's Classics, p. 27). More rhetorically in the closing peroration of the Ninth Discourse, he refers to the idea of "general and intellectual" beauty which the artist "dies at last without imparting" (p. 144). But he makes it clear in the Third Discourse that what the Platonists call divine is "not to be sought in the heavens, but upon the earth" (p. 26) and that its acquisition is anything but a Plotinian ascent but arises instead from "a reiterated experience, and a close comparison of the objects in nature" (p. 27). Nevertheless both Dryden and Reynolds seem to accept a natural aesthetic ideal. Johnson does not.

See Hoyt Trowbridge, "Platonism and Sir Joshua Reynolds," *English Studies*, XXI (Feb. 1939), 1–7. Trowbridge argues that "the true philosophical affinity of Reynolds's classicism is not Plato but John Locke" (p. 1).

[19] *Rambler* no. 208 (*Works*, III, 462).

[20] "Conciliation with America," *Works* (Bohn's British Classics), I, 456, 464, 461.

[21] *Life of Pope* (*Poets*, III, 114). "The course of eighteenth-century poetry suggests that the maximum intensity of satisfaction in generalization was reached somewhere about the middle of the century" (Bertrand H. Bronson, "Personification Reconsidered," *ELH*, XIV [Sept. 1947], 173). "The personified abstraction . . . was rich in poetic values. It was considered the product of strong, sublime emotions and a more than usually active imagination . . .; it represented the height of creativity. . . . Far from being a mere abstraction, it is a means of vivid and detailed particularization and materialization" (Earl R. Wasserman, "The Inherent Values of 18th Century Personification," *PMLA*, LXV [June 1950], 460).

[22] *Life of Pope* (*Poets*, III, 114). See *ante*, pp. 71–72.

[23] *Life of Cowley* (*Poets*, I, 45). See *ante*, pp. 71–72, and *post*, pp. 145–146.

[24] Raleigh, pp. 158–159.

[25] *Logick*, 2d ed. (London, 1726), p. 31 (I, iii, 1).

[26] *Rasselas*, Chap. X (*Works*, I, 222). The entire context of Imlac's discourse on description is empirical. The discussion of the tulip is a response to the prince's comment: "In so wide a *survey*, you must surely have left much *unobserved*" (*ibid.*) (italics added).

[27] Trapp, *Lectures on Poetry* (London, 1742), p. 46; Gray's *Essays and Criticisms*, ed. C. S. Northrup (1911), p. 93; *Rambler* no. 92 (*Works*, II, 432); *Life of Pope* (*Poets*, III, 247); *Letters of Johnson*, ed. G. B. Hill (Oxford, 1892), II, 440 (italics added). For further discussions of generality in Johnson, see W. K. Wimsatt, *The Prose Style of Samuel Johnson* (1941), pp. 50–59; the discussions by Friedman and Wimsatt in *Philol. Quar.*, XXI (April 1942), 211–213, and XXII (Jan. 1943), 71–76; Scott Elledge, "Theories of Generality and Particularity," *PMLA*, LXII (March 1947), pp. 147–182.

[28] *Enquiry concerning Human Understanding*, Sect. II ("Of the Origin of Ideas"). R. D. Havens, in "Johnson's Distrust of the Imagination," *ELH*, X (Sept. 1943), 243–255, has helpfully brought together a number of passages from Johnson on the imagination. I fully agree with his conclusion that Johnson had no notion of the "esemplastic" power of imagination, but, as this and ensuing chapters attempt to show, I do not find that Johnson's concessions to that faculty in such matters as novelty and originality are for the most part granted reluctantly. I find Johnson's attitude toward imagination a combination of fascination and fear.

[29] *Essay on Truth*, I, ii, 4, in *Essays* (Edinburgh, 1776), p. 61n.

[30] *Rambler* no. 89 (*Works*, II, 418).

[31] *Rasselas*, Chaps. XLII and XLIV (*Works*, I, 290, 293).

[32] "It was the turbulence and power of his imagination which put him so much on guard against it" (W. B. C. Watkins, *Perilous Balance* [1939], p. 89). "Examples could be multiplied without end in illustration of the ferment and tumult of Johnson's nature" (Bertrand H. Bronson, *Johnson Agonistes* [Cambridge, Eng., 1946], p. 6). The essays of Mr. Watkins and Mr. Bronson fully demonstrate the point cited and should completely dispose of the nineteenth-century notion, still somewhat prevalent, that Johnson was by nature insensitive and obtuse.

[33] See Arnold's conception of "the imaginative reason," discussed by F. E. Faverty in *Matthew Arnold the Ethnologist* (1951), pp. 176-179.

[34] Preface to *Annus Mirabilis* (*Essays*, ed. Ker, I, 14-15) (italics added). The point I make is the same as that of T. S. Eliot (*The Use of Poetry . . . and Criticism* [1933], pp. 47-50), who cites Dryden's passage in full, analyzes it closely, and says that "we must remark that 'invention' is the first moment in a process only the *whole* of which Dryden calls 'imagination' . . ." (p. 48).

[35] *Life of Milton* (*Poets*, I, 194, 177); *Life*, II, 239 (italics added). See *ante*, pp. 49-50.

[36] *Ante*, p. 52; Shelley, *A Defence of Poetry*, in *Prose Works*, ed. Richard H. Shepherd (London, 1912), II, 32; Eliot, *Use of Poetry and . . . Criticism*, p. 49; *Life of Gray* (*Poets*, III, 433); *Life of Milton* (*Poets*, I, 139); *Life of Pope* (*Poets*, III, 219); J. E. Brown, *Critical Opinions*, under topic "Composition."

[37] *Life*, III, 198, 199; II, 168.

CHAPTER VI. LANGUAGE AND FORM

[1] W. K. Wimsatt, *The Prose Style of Samuel Johnson* (1941), supersedes all previous studies.

[2] *Life*, III, 280; I, 100; *Autobiography of Gibbon* (Everyman's Library), p. 141; *Life of Dryden* (*Poets*, I, 422); *Life*, II, 191-192 and 191, n. 3 (for reference to Hume).

[3] *Rambler* no. 122 (*Works*, III, 83).

[4] *Rambler* no. 208 (*Works*, III, 464); *Life*, I, 439; *Life of Pope* (*Poets*, III, 250); *Life of Milton* (*Poets*, I, 190); *Life of Addison* (*Poets*, II, 149). For a contemporary opinion of Milton's style closely comparable to Johnson's, see F. R. Leavis, *Revaluation* (1949), pp. 52-53. This work was first published in 1936.

[5] Dr. Chapman has pointed out to me that Johnson deprecated the use of *nervous* in the physiological sense (see *Letters*, ed. Hill, II, 359). See *ante*, pp. 50-51, 53; F. W. Bateson, *English Poetry and the English Language* (1934), p. 58. For additional evidence of Johnson's praise of the forcible and the concise and his censure of the wordy, see *Life*, I, 204; II, 227; III, 37, 173, 258; IV, 5, 24. Johnson does not seem to have been as aware as Gibbon that the concise could easily become excessively abrupt and therefore obscure, owing to "the desire of expressing perhaps a common idea with sententious and oracular brevity . . ." (*Autobiography*, pp. 97-98).

[6] *Idler* no. 70 (*Works*, IV, 356); *Life of Cowley* (*Poets*, I, 35-36); *Adventurer* no. 58 (*Works*, IV, 30). "Ultimately therefore 'perspicuity'

was a duty to society. It was not so much a doctrine of style as a philosophy of conduct. . . . To the Augustans language was primarily a social instrument and the test was intelligibility" (Bateson, p. 56).

[7] *Poets*, I, 420.

[8] Bateson, pp. 67–68; *Life of Pope* (*Poets*, III, 238, 250).

[9] Locke's *Essay*, III, ii, 1, 2; *The Plan of an English Dictionary* (*Works*, V, 11); *Preface to the English Dictionary* (*Works*, V, 27); *Rambler* no. 168 (*Works*, III, 292). Johnson alludes to Quintilian's statement in the *Institutio* (I. vi. 16): "Non enim, cum primum fingerentur homines, analogia demissa caelo formam loquendi dedit, sed inventa est postquam loquebantur, et notatum in sermone quid quomodo caderet."

[10] *Life of Cowley* (*Poets*, I, 47). Johnson here censures the irregularity of the Pindaric ode in English.

[11] *Life of Butler* (*Poets*, I, 212). The Latin quoted comes from Horace *Epis*. II. i. 212. Johnson is here speaking of literary work in its totality, but the principle applies to versification alone: "We are soon wearied with the perpetual recurrence of the same cadence" (*Rambler* no. 86 [*Works*, II, 405]). Johnson, in connection with versification only, seems to have admitted the principle of variety a bit grudgingly. It was necessary psychologically, but "it always injures the harmony of the line, considered by itself . . ." (*Works*, II, 405).

[12] *Life of Milton* (*Poets*, I, 169–170); *Rambler* no. 121 (*Works*, III, 79). The eighteenth century was notoriously innocent about the sonnet, even perhaps to the extent of not always distinguishing between the Spenserian and Shakespearean forms. See Raymond D. Havens, *The Influence of Milton on English Poetry* (1922), Chap. XIX, especially pp. 481, 486–487, 488–489, 494, 523. It may be that Johnson's censure of the sonnet is confined to the Petrarchan form since it was the best known and most widely used until about 1790. See Havens, p. 523. Earl R. Wasserman (*Eliz. Poetry in the Eighteenth Century* [1947], pp. 151–152) says: "The eighteenth-century sonnet, when it is at all derivative, is usually Miltonic. Shakespeare's sonnets continued to be neglected as unworthy of him, and Spenser's . . . probably owed their slight reputation to . . . the *Faerie Queene*. However, unlike most other Elizabethan sonnets except Drummond's, Spenser's were known and read."

[13] Dryden's *Essays*, ed. Ker, I, 8; *Life of Roscommon* (*Poets*, I, 237); Addison's *Remarks on Italy* (1705), in *Misc. Works*, ed. A. C. Guthkelch (London, 1914), II, 60; *Life*, II, 124; *Life of Milton* (*Poets*, I, 192–193) (italics added). In spite of the strictures against blank verse referred to in this paragraph (and there are many other instances to be found in Johnson), his practice was more liberal than his theory: "But whatever be the advantage of rhyme I cannot prevail on myself to wish that Milton had been a rhymer, for I cannot wish his work to be other than it is . . ." (*Poets*, I, 194). He also found the use of blank verse appropriate in Thomson's *Seasons* and Young's *Night Thoughts* (*Poets*, III, 299, 395).

[14] *Life of Dryden* (*Poets*, I, 468).

[15] *Life of Pope* (*Poets*, III, 251). Johnson admits that "new sentiments and new images others may produce . . ."

[16] *Rambler* nos. 86, 88, 92 (*Works*, II, 402–407, 412–416, 421–426); Wallace C. Brown, *The Triumph of Form* (1948), p. 74; *Notes on the English Divines*, in the Nonesuch ed. of Coleridge (1933), p. 406. Johnson's metrical

system was essentially that of Edward Bysshe. See the important article by A. Dwight Culler, "Edward Bysshe and the Poet's Handbook," *PMLA*, LXIII (Sept. 1948), 858–885, especially pp. 872–878, 881, which describes the system of syllabic versification, traces its influence, and summarizes Johnson's relations to it.

In the matter of rhythmic substitutions, Johnson is most conservative. Substitutions in the first pair of syllables, he says, "may be considered as arbitrary," but "a poet who, not having the invention or knowledge of Milton, has more need to allure his audience by musical cadences, should seldom suffer more than one aberration from the rule in any single verse." He frowned upon trochaic substitutions, except, of course, in the first foot of a line. The ancients considered the iambus and trochee as opposite in effect: "to confound them, therefore, . . . is to deviate from established practice." Besides, such metrical inversions he found inharmonious to the ear. *Rambler* no. 86 (*Works*, II, 406, 407).

Although I have not studied the matter thoroughly, my impression is that Johnson's own practice followed his theory. In an analysis of about 80 lines of his poetry, I found an occasional lightening of the accent, in what we should call a pyrrhic substitution, and an occasional spondee. But I found no trochees outside the first two syllables, and in those syllables only the following: *London* (lines 1–20), in line 8; *Vanity* (lines 1–20), in line 12; *Drury Lane Prologue* (lines 1–20), none; *Irene* (lines 1–20), in lines 2, 16, 18.

[17] *Rambler* no. 88 (*Works*, II, 413); *Rambler* no. 90 (*Works*, II, 425); *Life of Pope* (*Poets*, III, 248); *Rambler* no. 86 (*Works*, II, 407); Campion's *Observations on . . . Eng. Poesie*, in *Elizabethan Critical Essays*, ed. G. G. Smith, II, 330; *Spectator* no. 29; *Life of Prior* (*Poets*, II, 210); *Life of Pope* (*Poets*, III, 248). Johnson occasionally revealed the fear that language that had reached such elegance in his own day might "too soon pass to affectation" (*Idler* no. 63 [*Works*, IV, 337]).

[18] *Literary Remains*, in the Nonesuch *Coleridge* (1933), p. 315. Coleridge resurrected the word *sensuous* to refer to "passive" and "recipient" perception; it was thus distinguished from the creating imagination (*Biographia Literaria*, Chap. X [Nonesuch, p. 235]). Though useful in the campaign against generality and the mean (*Anima Poetae* [Nonesuch, p. 173]), *sensuous* was certainly not one of Coleridge's most important critical terms. He makes it clear that sensation is not beauty but a single component in beauty; it must not distract attention from the organic *forma informans*, which tends to swallow it up (Nonesuch, pp. 312–313).

[19] Under *sensuous*, H. J. Todd in his revision of Johnson's Dictionary (2d ed., 1827) disagrees with Johnson's interpretation of Milton's meaning: "The sense seems to be simply that of *sensual*, as affecting the senses."

[20] *Rambler* no. 92 (*Works*, II, 432); *Rambler* no. 94 (*Works*, II, 442–443, 445); Trapp, *Lectures on Poetry* (London, 1742), p. 66; Pope's note no. xv to the *Iliad*, Book IV, line 176.

[21] *Idler* no. 60 (*Works*, IV, 328–329); *Life of Pope* (*Poets*, III, 230–232); *Rambler* no. 94 (*Works*, II, 442–448); *Life of Cowley* (*Poets*, I, 62).

[22] *Essay*, III, ii, 1.

[23] *Idler* no. 34 (*Works*, IV, 249); *Life of Cowley* (*Poets*, I, 51); *Life of Dryden* (*Poets*, I, 431); *Idler* no. 45 (*Works*, IV, 283); Raleigh, p. 73; *ante*, pp. 62–63. For a discussion of various attempts to represent Achilles' shield,

see Lessing's *Laokoön*, Chap. XIX. Johnson's concern with the aesthetics of painting is a far deeper one than is usually realized. For a discussion of Johnson's surprisingly extensive use of Dryden's *Du Fresnoy* in his Dictionary and its implications, see W. K. Wimsatt, "Samuel Johnson and Dryden's *Du Fresnoy*," *Studies in Philol.*, XLVIII (Jan. 1951), 26–39.

[24] For a brief but illuminating discussion of whether imagery "is basically sensuous or basically comparative" and of other related matters, see Josephine Miles, "The Problem of Imagery," *Sewanee Rev.*, LVIII (Summer 1950), 522–526, a review of R. H. Fogle, *The Imagery of Keats and Shelley*.

[25] *Life*, I, 403; *Life of Milton* (*Poets*, I, 167); letter to Bennet Langton, June 16, 1781 (*Life*, IV, 132); *ante*, pp. 62–63.

[26] *The Plan of an English Dictionary* (*Works*, V, 15).

[27] For examples of Johnson's censure of "broken" metaphors, see *Lives of Addison, Pope*, and *Gray* (*Poets*, II, 128–129; III, 265, 436).

[28] "*Longinus* proves . . . that, when the Passions are violent, and rage like a Torrent, the Elocution may have manifold Metaphors" (Edward Manwaring, *Institutes of Learning* [London, 1737], p. 8).

[29] *Life of Pope* (*Poets*, III, 229–230). Johnson here remembered his Dictionary definition of 1755, in which he had described a simile as "a comparison by which anything is illustrated or aggrandized" (*ante*, p. 115).

[30] *Life of Cowley* (*Poets*, I, 20); *Life of Addison* (*Poets*, II, 129–130, 131; *Life of Dryden* (*Poets*, I, 441); *Life of Pope* (*Poets*, III, 230).

[31] *Life of Pope* (*Poets*, III, 228); *Life of Dryden* (*Poets*, I, 457); *Life of Cowley* (*Poets*, I, 41); *Life of Pope* (*Poets*, III, 229–230); *Life of Denham* (*Poets*, I, 78–79).

Mr. Allen Tate has cited Denham's lines and Johnson's comment, which he finds understandable only if one conceives his real objection to be that Denham's words cannot be translated into a "high degree of abstraction" ("Johnson on the Metaphysicals," *Kenyon Rev.*, XI [Summer 1949], p. 381). I do not find this interpretation fully accurate. Although Johnson liked the abstract, the antithesis involved is not between the abstract and the concrete, but between the literal (or the real) and the metaphorical (or the ambiguous, the untrue, the fabulous, the remote, the incomprehensible). Here it is the real versus the ambiguous, and the ambiguity lies in the referent, not the analogue. The "nonsense" here does not come "from the vehicle" but the "tenor." But I agree with Mr. Tate that according to Johnson the idea being illustrated "ought to be detachable from the literal image of the flowing river."

For further evidence of Johnson's dislike of the comparison compounded of the literally true and the metaphorically untrue (or vague), consider his discussion of the implications of the metaphor "the *body* politic," in *Idler* no. 34: "Other parallels are fortuitous and fanciful, yet these have sometimes been extended to many particulars of resemblance by a lucky concurrence of diligence and chance. The animal body is composed of many members, united under the direction of one mind: any number of individuals, connected for some common purpose, is therefore called a body. From this participation of the same appellation arose the comparison of the body natural and body politick, of which, how far soever it has been deduced, no end has hitherto been found.

"In these imaginary similitudes, the same word is used at once in its primitive and metaphorical sense. Thus health, ascribed to the body natural, is opposed to sickness; but attributed to the body politick stands as contrary to adversity. These parallels therefore have more of genius, but less of truth; they often please, but they never convince" (*Works*, IV, 249–250).

[32] *Life of Thomson* (*Poets*, III, 299–300); *Life of Pope* (*Poets*, III, 225); *Life of Pope* (*Poets*, III, 99).

[33] Geoffrey Tillotson, "The Manner of Proceeding in Certain Eighteenth- and Early Nineteenth-Century Poems," *Warton Lecture on English Poetry* (British Academy, 1948), p. 24. Tillotson says, "But Johnson did not see that the difference between the designs of these mainly descriptive poems [the *Seasons* and *Windsor Forest*] and the designs of *The Vanity of Human Wishes* and the *Imitations of Horace* was not great" (pp. 24–25). My opinion is that he *did* (see his comment, cited above, on the order of the *Essay on Criticism*) but looked to that kind of didactic poetry for other excellences than the formal and structural.

[34] *English Poetry and the English Language*, pp. 59–64.

[35] *Rambler* no. 158 (*Works*, III, 249–250).

[36] *Ante*, p. 122 and n. 32; *Life of Pope* (*Poets*, III, 99); *Parrhasiana: or, Thoughts upon Several Subjects . . . by Monsieur Le Clerc . . . Done into English by* **** (London, 1700), p. 69. The "*Search after Truth*" is the English title of Malebranche's best-known work. Critics seem to have applied this type of logic most frequently in attacking "the Pindaric madness." For a brief discussion of English opinion of Pindaric form, see *Works of Dennis*, ed. E. N. Hooker, I, 510–511. It was apparently the digressiveness of Pindar and the obscurity of transition in the odes that were most frequently censured. Horace Walpole, on May 22, 1753, complained to Montagu that "your transitions are so Pindaric that without notes we don't understand them . . ." (*Correspondence with Geo. Montagu*, ed. W. S. Lewis and R. S. Brown [1941], I, 146).

[37] Preface to the *Preceptor* (Hazen, *Prefaces & Dedications*, pp. 184–185). Johnson recommends Le Clerc among others. He called logic "the Art of arranging and connecting Ideas, of forming and examining Arguments . . ."

[38] *Rambler* no. 139 (*Works*, III, 157–158).

[39] *Letters on Chivalry and Romance*, ed. Edith J. Morley (1911), pp. 121–122 (Letter VIII).

[40] *Rambler* no. 139 (*Works*, III, 157–162); *Life of Milton* (*Poets*, I, 189).

[41] See *ante*, pp. 30, 36, 90.

[42] Preface to Shakespeare (Raleigh, pp. 32–33).

CHAPTER VII. THE BEAUTIFUL, THE PATHETIC, AND THE SUBLIME

[1] *Ante*, pp. 83–84.

[2] *Rambler* nos. 86, 88, 90, 92, 94.

[3] Compare this definition from the first edition with that of the fourth (1773), revised by Johnson himself: "Elegance. Elegancy. . . . 1. Beauty rather soothing than striking; beauty without grandeur; the beauty of propriety not of greatness. 2. Any thing that pleases by its nicety." Clearly the division between sublime beauty and elegant beauty is sharper here. Notice that there are two definitions instead of one, that the last phrase in the first revised definition is an addition, and that the phrase "of art" is dropped after the word "beauty" in the first phrase. Having found the "elegantly

little in nature" (see Imlac's speech, quoted and discussed in my next paragraph) and having used *elegance* as a synonym for beauty either of nature or art, Johnson could not in 1773 restrict the use of *elegance* to art as he had originally done in 1755.

⁴ *Life of Thomson* (*Poets*, III, 299); *Life of Collins* (*Poets*, III, 338); *Life of Milton* (*Poets*, I, 182); *Life of Addison* (*Poets*, II, 127); *Life of Waller* (*Poets*, I, 291). Johnson did not always write with this distinction in mind. In his general comment on *Othello* (Raleigh, p. 200), he uses the phrase "the beauties of this play" to refer to all kinds of general excellencies. But it is more typical to associate beauty with the poetical, the smooth, the just, and the exquisite (Raleigh, pp. 104, 127, 138). Samuel H. Monk (*The Sublime* [1935], p. 100, n. 47) has suggested that in writing Imlac's speech, which separates the "awfully vast" and the "elegantly little," Johnson was thinking of Burke's *Sublime and Beautiful*. The extent of my indebtedness to Monk's indispensable study throughout this chapter will be apparent.

⁵ *Letters of Johnson*, ed. G. B. Hill (Oxford, 1892), I, 224, 226, 253 (italics added).

⁶ Henry Home, Lord Kames, *Elements of Criticism*, 7th ed. (Edinburgh, 1788), I, 196.

⁷ *Life of Pope* (*Poets*, III, 247, 225–226, 228, 229, 232, 235, 246, 242. This type of beauty includes Pope's versification (see *ante*, pp. 103–108).

⁸ *Life of Pope* (*Poets*, III, 239–240). See Joseph Warton, *Essay on the Genius and Writings of Pope*, 2d ed., corrected (1762), I, iv–v, x. Beattie found Pope pathetic in *Eloisa* and the *Unfortunate Lady* and sublime in the *Essay on Man* and the *Messiah* (*Essays on Poetry and Music* [London, 1779], p. 18n.); and Bowles, who says that Warton "seems particularly to have been misunderstood by Johnson," finds Pope pre-eminent in the pathetic but not in the sublime (*Works of Pope*, ed. Bowles [London, 1806], X, 362, 369–370).

⁹ *Life of Pope* (*Poets*, III, 242, 243–244).

¹⁰ *Life of Prior* (*Poets*, II, 206). The phrase from Johnson with which I conclude this section on beauty (*Life of Pope* [*Poets*, III, 223]) concludes his famous comparison of Dryden and Pope, which is similar to the contrasts between Homer and Vergil, Shakespeare and Jonson, the English drama and the French, nature and art, that appear in Dryden, Pope, Addison, Johnson himself, and many others. But it also suggests the contrast between the sublime and the beautiful. The adjectives used of Pope are those associated with beauty and constitute a good summary of this section. The fact that Johnson ranks Dryden slightly above Pope, Shakespeare above the French classical dramatists, and Homer above Vergil should always be kept in mind. Johnson fully enjoyed literary beauty, but he did not consider it the very highest of literary qualities. A "wren was not an eagle" (*Life*, II, 125).

¹¹ *The Sublime*, p. 14.

¹² *Life of Waller* (*Poets*, I, 294); *Life of Cowley* (*Poets*, I, 20, 55–56, 32); *Life of Milton* (*Poets*, I, 180). Johnson's separation of the sublime and the pathetic is roughly comparable to the first two members of Addison's division of Milton's "beautiful" passages into the "Sublime," the "Soft," and the "Natural" (*Spectator* no. 369); to Dennis's separation of the passions into the "Vulgar" and the "Enthusiastick" (*Grounds of Criticism*, Chap. IV [*Works*, ed. Hooker, I, 338–339]); and to Horace's (*Ars Poetica*, lines 99–100) *pulchra* and *dulcia*. See Hooker's note in Dennis, *Works*, I, 516.

[13] Preface to the *Preceptor* (1748), in Hazen, *Prefaces & Dedications*, p. 180; *Rasselas*, Chap. X (*Works*, I, 220–221, 222); *Life of Prior* (*Poets*, 202) (italics added).

[14] *Life of Dryden* (*Poets*, I, 457–458).

[15] *Preface to Shakespeare* (Raleigh, pp. 16, 18, 19) (italics added).

[16] Raleigh, pp. 150–152, 165; *Life of Otway* (*Poets*, I, 245); *Life of Rowe* (*Poets*, II, 69 and n. 6); *Johnsonian Miscellanies*, ed. Hill, I, 283–284; II, 196–197. "What is nearest touches us most," he wrote to Mrs. Thrale on July 11, 1770. "The passions rise higher at domestic than at imperial tragedies" (*Letters*, ed. Hill, I, 162).

[17] *Preface to Shakespeare* (Raleigh, pp. 28, 23). Johnson often censured Shakespeare for evaporating pathos by a conceit or pun (Raleigh, pp. 23–24, 180, 188–189, 199), but he felt that it was difficult to continue the pathetic too long (Raleigh, p. 107, 111).

[18] Raleigh, p. 172; *Works of Virgil*, ed. Jos. Warton (London, 1753), Postscript, IV, 447; *Boswell's London Journal* (1950), ed. F. A. Pottle, p. 182; *Essays*, ed. Ker, I, 212; *Spectator* no. 419; *Works of Dennis*, ed. Hooker, II, 4, 425; Theobald's Preface (1733), in D. N. Smith, ed., *Eighteenth Century Essays on Shakespeare*, pp. 63–64; Morgann, *Essay on Falstaff* (1777), *ibid.*, p. 249.

The word *sentimental* does not occur in Johnson's Dictionary. He understood *sentiment* to mean "Thought; notion; opinion" or "The sense considered distinctly from the language or things; a striking sentence in a composition." Thus *sentiment* is for him, theoretically at least, divorced from feeling. The word *pathetic*, as he used it, would make *sentimental* unnecessary. The student of the period must never blur the distinction between sentiment as feeling and sentiment as moral sentence. Sterne is, of course, the great exemplar of the former, but Johnson denied that his writing was truly pathetic (*Life*, IV, 109). Richardson's was, but only because it expressed sentiment as truth, not as feeling for its own sake (*Life*, II, 48–49, 174–175). Fielding's Blifil and Sheridan's Joseph Surface are men of sentiment not because they are men of feeling (both are cold villains) but because they hypocritically mouth morality. Fielding and Sheridan were satirizing that kind of moral sentiment which, without feeling, became hypocritical and vicious. It cannot be too much emphasized that for Johnson the pathetic, in order to be acceptable, must be controlled by nature, reason, and morality. He praised Richardson for having "taught the passions to move at the command of virtue" (*Rambler* no. 97 [*Works*, II, 458]).

[19] *A Commentary, with notes, on the Four Evangelists and the Acts of the Apostles* (1777), I, x. Hazen (*Johnson's Prefaces & Dedications*, pp. 154–157), who says "there can be no doubt that the *Life* is by Johnson," gives a full bibliographical description. For a summary and discussion of Longinian echoes in Johnson, see Percy H. Houston, *Dr. Johnson* (1923), pp. 44ff.

[20] *Life of Cowley* (*Poets*, I, 21).

[21] *Life*, V, 433–434. For Johnson's religion, see *ante*, pp. 65–71.

[22] *Rasselas*, Chaps. I, IX, X, XXXI, XLVIII (*Works*, I, 200–201, 218, 221, 266, 308). See also *Rambler* no. 80 (esp. *Works*, II, 376), a kind of prose poem on the seasons, influenced by Thomson's *Seasons* and by Milton's *Il Penseroso*. The fact that this essay was written in 1750, some seven years

before Burke published the *Sublime and Beautiful*, shows that he did not contribute to Johnson's imagination a taste for sublimity but merely sharpened his distinction between the sublime and the beautiful.

[23] It may be asked at this point why Dryden, who could not achieve the pathetic, did not exemplify the sublime for Johnson. Milton was, of course, much more sublime, but there is another reason. In Dryden's representations (in the *Conquest of Granada*) of "illustrious depravity and majestick madness," "the ridiculous is mingled with the astonishing" (*Life of Dryden* [*Poets*, I, 349]). See also *ibid.*, p. 460. Nor could Johnson accept the sublimity of Gray and allied writers; he found in their odes "a kind of strutting dignity" (*Life of Gray* [*Poets*, III, 440]).

[24] *Life of Milton* (*Poets*, I, 177). Johnson was neither the first nor last to consider sublimity the characteristic quality of Milton: Dryden, Addison, Dennis, Coleridge, and many others have so treated Milton. Ever since Minturno had made *admiration* one of the ends of poetry, that quality had been considered the peculiar province of the epic and, in English criticism, of Milton. But Johnson adhered to this conception of the nature of Milton's genius as firmly as any of them. When Hannah More wondered that the author of *Paradise Lost* should write such poor sonnets, Johnson replied, "Milton, Madam, was a genius that could cut a Colossus from a rock; but could not carve heads upon cherry-stones" (*Life*, IV, 305).

[25] *Life of Milton* (*Poets*, I, 182). For Johnson's objection to religious poetry, see *Lives of Cowley, Waller, Denham* (*Poets*, I, 49–50, 291–292, 75) and *ante*, p. 68.

[26] *Rambler* no. 137 (*Works*, III, 147); *Life of Yalden* (*Poets*, II, 302–303).

[27] *London*, lines 170–174; *Journey to the Western Islands*, ed. R. W. Chapman (1924), pp. 17–18; *Life of Milton* (*Poets*, I, 170, 177, 178, 182). Compare Johnson's comment on the view of the sea from Slanes Castle: "From the windows the eye wanders over the sea that separates Scotland from Norway, and when the winds beat with violence must enjoy all *the terrifick grandeur of the tempestuous ocean. I would not for my amusement wish for a storm; but as storms, whether wished or not, will sometimes happen, I may say, without violation of humanity, that I should willingly look out upon them from Slanes Castle*" (*Western Islands*, ed. Chapman, pp. 16–17) (italics added).

CHAPTER VIII. TRUE WIT

[1] "Romanticism and Classicism," *Speculations*, 2d ed. (Reprinted, London, 1949), pp. 113, 137. The date of the first edition is 1924.

[2] "Andrew Marvell," *Homage to John Dryden* (1924), pp. 34–46.

[3] The phrase is Mr. Leavis's, whose chapter so entitled in *Revaluation* (London, 1949 [first pub., 1936], pp. 10–41) accepts Mr. Eliot's definition and also attempts to determine a historical succession. It excludes the songs of *Comus* as being gracious without intellectual implication; the coarse and insensitive wit of Cowley; the limited and inferior refinement of Waller; the somewhat powerful but monotonous public and social quality of Dryden; the delicate triviality of Herrick. It finds acceptable, because the balance between tough reasonableness and lyric grace is satisfactorily maintained, the lyrical verse of Jonson (vital and urbane), of Carew (light and strong), of Marvell (metaphysical and elegant), and of Pope (witty and solemn and subtly varied in the last *Dunciad*).

For a discussion of the many complex meanings of the term in connection with an interpretation of Pope's use of it, see William Empson, "Wit in the Essay on Criticism," *Hudson Rev.*, II (Winter 1950), 559–577.

[4] *Life of Cowley* (*Poets*, I, 36, 20); Oxford Dict. under *wit* (definition no. 10); *Life of Congreve* (*Poets*, II, 228). I wish to emphasize that this chapter is not concerned with *wit* in the senses given in this paragraph. For a discussion of those meanings, see the discussions of the imagination and the metaphor, *ante*, pp. 89–94, 115, 117–119. The best study of wit in connection with the epigram and the conceit and of the revolt against the metaphysicals is W. Lee Ustick and Hoyt H. Hudson, "Wit, 'Mixt Wit,' and the Bee in Amber," *Huntington Library Bull.*, No. 8 (Oct. 1935), pp. 103–130. See also W. B. C. Watkins, "Dr. Johnson on the Imagination: A Note," *Rev. Eng. Studies*, XXII (April 1946), 131–134, for a discussion of wit as *discordia concors*.

In the *Life of Cowley*, Johnson discriminates three conceptions of *wit*: (1) *wit* as "happiness of language" — Pope's definition which Johnson calls "erroneous"; (2) "a more noble and more adequate conception" of *wit* as a combination of novelty and familiarity, of which the metaphysicals were incapable; (3) *wit* as the *discordia concors*, of which the metaphysicals had "more than enough." This last definition I have discussed earlier (*ante*, pp. 117–119); I quote it here for the sake of completeness: "But Wit, abstracted from its effects upon the hearer, may be more rigorously and philosophically considered as a kind of *discordia concors*; a combination of dissimilar images, or discovery of occult resemblances in things apparently unlike" (*Poets*, I, 20).

The third definition I have separated from the others because it seems to me to be a definition of metaphor, simile, and conceit, and ought therefore to be discussed in those connections. It is certainly not Johnson's most basic or most adequate definition, involving total literary effect. Those honors belong to the second definition. When he considers the third definition, he is limiting the subject to the conceit and to imagery. He separates this definition from "its effects upon the hearer," and that for Johnson is to neglect, for the moment, what he considered most important (see *ante*, pp. 35–36). His third definition is presented "more rigorously and philosophically," that is, more scientifically, technically, and exactly, but not more profoundly or adequately. The third definition is a brilliant one. Johnson uses it elsewhere. But it is limited, and I have therefore felt that it may satisfactorily be separated from the second, which is the subject of this chapter and which illuminates the very essence of poetical pleasure.

For a discussion of the three definitions of *wit*, considered together, see W. R. Keast's able article "Johnson's Criticism of the Metaphysical Poets," *ELH*, XVII (March 1950), 59–70, especially p. 65.

[5] *Lectures on Poetry* (London, 1742), p. 102.

[6] *Life of Cowley* (*Poets*, I, 19–20). Compare Horace *Ars Poetica*, lines 240–243:

> ex noto fictum carmen sequar, ut sibi quivis
> speret idem, sudet multum frustraque laboret
> ausus idem: tantum series iuncturaque pollet,
> tantum de medio sumptis accedit honoris.

"My aim shall be poetry, so moulded from the familiar that anybody may hope for the same success, may sweat much and yet toil in vain when attempting the same: such is the power of order and connexion, such the beauty that may crown the commonplace" (tr. by H. R. Fairclough). See *post*, p. 169.

[7] *Rambler* no. 103 (*Works*, II, 486, 487); *Rambler* no. 80 (*Works*, II, 375); *Life of Milton* (*Poets*, I, 194); *Rambler* no. 154 (*Works*, III, 233); *Rambler* no. 137 (*Works*, III, 147); *Idler* no. 3 (*Works*, IV, 158). See also *Rambler* nos. 121, 143; *Idler* nos. 44, 66, 84; *Adventurer* no. 95.

[8] *Life of Pope* (*Poets*, III, 232–234, 101, 103, 104).

[9] *Works*, VI, 1–2. Boswell ascribed this letter to Johnson (*Life*, I, 157), but Dr. Powell says that it "may have been touched by Johnson, but is not, I think, wholly his" (Appendix B, *Life*, II, 483). The style of the passage I have quoted is certainly not distinguished, but the idea is Johnsonian. See *Idler* no. 97, devoted to travel literature, in which Johnson says that a writer of travels must, like all other authors, instruct and please: "He that instructs must offer to the mind something to be imitated, or something to be avoided; he that pleases must offer new images to his reader, and enable him to form a tacit comparison of his own state with that of others" (*Works*, IV, 433).

[10] I quote from p. 312 of the rare Yale copy of the 1739 issue of the *Commentary*, which bears the imprint of A. Dodd. The attribution of the translation of Crousaz and of the annotations to Johnson was made by Dr. Powell (*Life*, IV, 494–496). A. T. Hazen announced the discovery of the Dodd issue of 1739 in the London *Times Lit. Supp.*, Nov. 2, 1935, p. 704, and said that Cave's edition of 1742 was "merely a reissue of the unused sheets of the earlier edition." See also *Yale Univ. Library Gazette*, X (Jan. 1936), 48–49, and Dr. Chapman's note, *Rev. Eng. Studies*, N.S., I (Jan. 1950), 57.

[11] *Rambler* no. 36 (*Works*, II, 179); *Adventurer* no. 95 (*Works*, IV, 82–83). I am indebted to Professor W. R. Keast for calling my attention to the relevance of these passages.

[12] *Preface to Shakespeare* (Raleigh, pp. 14, 64–65, 66, 124, 129–130, 138) (italics added).

[13] *Rhetoric* III.x. 2–3.

[14] *Summa Theologica*, Part II, First Part, First Number, Qu. 32, Art. 8.

[15] "Answer to Davenant" (1650), in *Critical Essays of the Seventeenth Century*, ed. Spingarn, II, 63, 65.

[16] *Life of Milton* (*Poets*, I, 163).

[17] Cited by Joseph E. Brown, *Critical Opinions of Johnson*, p. 433. As W. B. C. Watkins (*Rev. Eng. Studies*, XXII [April 1946], 131), points out, Johnson may have been unfair to Pope in not quoting the second half of the famous passage:

> Something, whose truth convinc'd at sight we find,
> That gives us back the image of our mind.

For a comprehensive discussion of Pope's conception of wit, see Hooker, "Pope on Wit . . . ," in R. F. Jones, *The Seventeenth Century* (1951), pp. 225–246. Of Pope's full meaning (as Hooker explains it) Johnson was ignorant.

[18] *Life of Congreve* (*Poets*, II, 229, 230).

[19] See *ante*, pp. 59–60.

[20] *Poetics* ix (1452a). Johnson had undoubtedly thought long about this

principle of Aristotle. He once referred to "the difficulty of making variety consistent, or uniting probability with surprise . . ." (*Rambler* no. 122 [*Works*, III, 82]).

²¹ Johnson had qualified this somewhat by accepting, earlier in the *Life of Pope*, Dennis's criticism that "by all the bustle of preternatural operation the main event is neither hastened nor retarded . . . but what are such faults to so much excellence!" (*Poets*, III, 235). It is clear that Johnson does not consider the question of probability crucial to his evaluation.

²² "The Author's Apology for Heroic Poetry," *Essays*, ed. Ker, I, 190. See *ibid.*, I, 256, 270; II, 9.

²³ *Spectator* no. 62.

²⁴ *Preface to Shakespeare* (Raleigh, p. 28).

²⁵ *Lectures*, pp. 129–130.

²⁶ *Preface to Shakespeare* (Raleigh, p. 13); *Notes to Shakespeare* (Raleigh, p. 177). For a discussion of Johnson's stylistic antitheses, in which several types are discriminated, see Wimsatt, *Prose Style of Johnson*, pp. 38–49.

²⁷ *Rambler* no. 38 (*Works*, II, 185, 185–186); *Vanity of Human Wishes*, lines 15–18. For other discussions of the golden mean in Johnson, see *Rambler* nos. 25 and 129 and the *Fountains* (*Works*, II, 122; III, 113; IX, 181, 183, 190).

²⁸ *Spectator* no. 345. See *ante*, pp. 155–156.

²⁹ "Of Simplicity and Refinement in Writing," *Essays* (The New Universal Library), pp. 140, 141, 143.

³⁰ The references to Coleridge come from the Nonesuch edition (1933), pp. 316, 164–165, 180, and from Alice D. Snyder, *The Critical Principle of the Reconciliation of Opposites as Employed by Coleridge* (1918), p. 50. I have found Professor Snyder's study most helpful in the consideration of the antithesis in criticism. The references to Johnson come from the *Preface to Shakespeare* (Raleigh, p. 28).

³¹ "Matthew Arnold," in *The Use of Poetry and . . . Criticism* (1933), p. 111.

CHAPTER IX. CONCLUSION

¹ I am indebted to Professor W. R. Keast for making clearer than it had been, both in personal conversation and in the article referred to above (note 4 to Chap. VIII), the fundamental nature of this concept.

² *Life of Gray* (*Poets*, III, 441).

³ *Critical Essays of the Seventeenth Century*, ed. Spingarn, I, 51. "Elizabethan poetry and Elizabethan criticism were expressions of essentially the same impulse. The poetry was a kind of criticism. They were applications, one practical, one theoretical, of a single attitude to literature — that of the craftsman" (F. W. Bateson, *English Poetry and the English Language*, p. 27).

⁴ F. A. Pottle, "Pure Poetry in Theory and Practice," *The Idiom of Poetry* (1941), pp. 80–100, especially p. 81.

⁵ *Life of Dryden* (*Poets*, I, 439).

⁶ *Life of Pope* (*Poets*, III, 227).

⁷ Raleigh, p. 103.

⁸ C. B. Tinker, *Essays in Retrospect* (1948), p. 29.

⁹ Raleigh, pp. 125, 121.

¹⁰ *Rambler* no. 60 (*Works*, II, 286).

¹¹ Raleigh, p. 78.

Index

INDEX

Decay, 74: law of, 69
Decoration, linguistic, 15, 16, 134, 136, 162. *See also* Art
Definition, literary, 34
Deism, 20, 28, 69, 188: defined, 189
Delight, 37, 91: rational, 24; literary, 90. *See also* Tragedy
Demonstration, mathematical, 11
Denham, Sir John, 101, 105, 121, 122, 195
Dennis, John, 27, 46, 54, 73, 144, 186, 196–199, 202
Depravity, total, 69
Descartes, René, 16, 19, 20, 66, 125
Description, 86, 88, 115, 158: in poetry, 113
Descriptive, 114, 122: verse, 132; sublimity, 148
Dewey, John, 10
Diaries, 46
Diction, 80, 85, 156, 160, 163: ambiguity, 86; pure, 98; primary meaning, 99; poetic, 100–102; negative theory of, 101. *See also* Language
Didactic, 122: verse, 190
Didacticism, 76. *See also* Morality
Dignity: naked, 85; natural, 162
Dilettantism, 37
Disbelief, willing suspension of, 166, 171
Discordia concors, 155, 200
Dissimilars, 118, 155, 200
Diversion, defined, 79
Domestick tragedy, 142
Donne, John, 106, 107, 153, 155, 157: school of, 154
Doublets, 129, 131, 137
Drama, 30, 33, 81, 127, 165, 184, 197: sentimental, 141; tragic, 163
Dreadful. *See* Sublime, Terror
Dreamer, portrait of, 91
Drummond, William, 193
Dryden, 24, 27, 34–35, 53–54, 63, 93–94, 99, 101–102, 105–106, 108, 112, 118, 121, 144, 155, 163–164, 188, 190–191, 195, 199: as critic, 25; *Essay of Dramatic Poesy*, 38, 40; praised, 38–39; *Anne Killigrew*, 81, 175; energy of, 90; *Annus Mirabilis*, 113; *St. Cecilia's Day*, 119, 176; pathetic in, 139–140; characters of, 185

Du Bos, l'abbé Jean Baptiste, 36
Du Fresnoy, Charles Alphonse, 62, 195
Du Halde, Jean Baptiste, 158, 159
Du Resnel, Jean François, 159
Durham Cathedral, 131
Dyer, John, 81

Earle, John, 40
Elegance, 129, 131, 133, 134, 135–136, 138, 148, 153, 194, 196–197: defined, 130. *See also* Beauty
Elegy, pastoral, 44
Elevation, 144, 168, 190: of style, 99. *See also* Sublime
Eliot, T. S., 26, 47, 77, 94, 153–154, 171, 178, 183, 186, 192, 199
Elizabethan, 193, 202
Embellishment, 15, 134, 136, 161, 162
Emotion, 92, 109, 130, 132, 137, 141, 146, 149: communication of, by artist, 44–47; religious, 67–68. *See also* Pathetic, Sentiment, Sublime
Empiric, defined, 5
Empirical, 16, 27, 29, 52, 53–54, 55, 75, 83, 85, 87–89, 116, 173–174, 176, 177–178, 180, 188, 190–191: criticism, 28; investigation, 29; reality, 37; epistemology, 58; defined, 181. *See also* Reality
Empiricism, 6, 8, 9, 93, 182, 188: defined, 5; of Locke, 13
Energy, 62, 68, 167, 187: defined, 49–51; mental, 52–53; in style, 99
Enlightenment, 163: French, 33
Epic, 33, 44, 81, 93, 117, 145, 184, 190
Epigram, 200
Epistemology, 6, 182
Epitaphs, 33, 34, 187
Erskine, Andrew, 143
Euclid, 163
Evil, 71, 90
Excellence, 93, 186: achieved, 49; higher, 84; poetic, 86, 175, 189
Excess, 15, 168–169
Experience, 3ff, 28–29, 42, 51, 53, 55, 57, 59, 62–63, 83, 89–90, 103, 173–174, 178–181, 184, 191: defined, 5, 8–14. *See also* Empirical
Experimental method, 10, 11, 12, 17, 184. *See also* Science